September 11:
West Coast Writers Approach Ground Zero
Edited by Jeff Meyers

HAWTHORNE BOOKS & LITERARY ARTS | *Portland, Oregon*

Hawthorne Books
& Literary Arts
P.O. Box 579
Portland, OR 97207
hawthornebooks.com

9
8
7
6
5
4
3
2
1

Library of Congress
Cataloging-in-Publication
Data

September 11: West
Coast writers approach
ground zero / edited by
Jeff Meyers.
    p. cm.
    ISBN 0-9716915-0-9
    1. Terrorism—United
States—Psychological
aspects.
2. September 11 Terrorist
Attacks, 2001—Psycho-
logical aspects.
3. Terrorism.
I. Meyers, Jeff, 1965— .
II. Title: West Coast
writers approach ground
zero.

HV6432.S4513 2002
973.931–dc21

2002006849

Certain of the essays
and poems in *September
11: West Coast Writers
Approach Ground Zero*
appeared originally in
other publications; a
list of those pieces and
publications, as well as
individual copyright
information, is pro-
vided opposite the table
of contents.

Acknowledgments

THE EDITOR WOULD LIKE TO THANK HIS WIFE, ARDEN, FOR her support, patience, and love, as well as Gary Cole, Brian Hamilton, and Stephen Weeks for their keen eyes and honest opinions.

The publisher would like to thank: Jeff Meyers for his patience and tenacity in bringing this collection to publication; Adam McIsaac for providing support and enthusiasm above and beyond excellent book design; Michelle Piranio, for her tireless effort; all the contributors who agreed to participate in this anthology; City Arts and Lectures, San Francisco; Literary Arts, Inc., Portland; and Seattle Arts and Lectures for helping us contact authors and giving us excellent ideas throughout the process; and all the readers of this book, who enable us to continue publishing.

Contents

SEPTEMBER 11: *West Coast Writers Approach Ground Zero*

Introduction
Jeff Meyers

I can be expected to look for truth, but not to find it.

—Denis Diderot | *Pensées philosophiques*

I HAVE ALWAYS LOVED BLACK-AND-WHITE PHOTOGRAPHY and cinema. There is a simplicity, a bloodless clarity that appeals to me on a very primal level. It is very easy to believe that the truth stands revealed and unadorned, uncomplicated by the violence of a red or the calm of a blue. In a way, I do not trust colors. They confuse and obscure important moments, distract me from what should be right before my eyes.

I think this is why I read and why I write. I am hoping that between the scratches of black on white the truth will announce itself, that the words will pinpoint an emotion or ignite an intellectual epiphany, define the world in ways that I can understand with some sense of certainty.

Since September 11 I have been reading a lot.

About a week after the tragedy...attack...or whatever word works for you (I am still unable to find the correct vocabulary), I became aware of a type of "samizdat" literature proliferating via the Web. E-mailed essays and photocopied articles circulated amongst my friends and family. We all became eager links in an Internet daisy chain of opinion, criticism, and rumination that went beyond the messages fed to us by mass media. Magazine articles from eight years ago seemed liked foolishly ignored warnings. Quotations from Shakespeare and statements by Hermann Göring became remarkably poignant or prescient. W. H. Auden enjoyed a newfound popularity after his poem "September 1, 1939" was quoted frequently in the aftermath of September 11 (a fact that would, undoubtedly, disturb him, since he stated that the poem was dishonest and demanded that it not be published again in his lifetime). We were reading and reading, and then reading more. Every essay, article, and quote—from Greek philosophers to WWII politicians to civil rights leaders—became another colorful piece in the jigsaw puzzle we hoped to solve: How should we feel about the events of September 11?

We were looking for guidance, explanations, new points of view, or maybe just the reassurance that pain and sorrow and grief have always been a part of history and that, ultimately, life goes on.

When Hawthorne Books asked me to edit this anthology, it seemed like a natural evolution in that quest for answers. Whatever the reason or rationale those around me had for turning to the written word, the importance of writers was indisputable. And so I believed, perhaps naïvely, that by gathering these poets, authors, and essayists together to share their thoughts and emotions about 9/11, some sort of truth might be found.

When first approached for contributions, many of the writers replied that they didn't know what to say, had nothing to say, or weren't ready to say anything about September 11.

On the one hand, I was baffled. It seemed I couldn't walk ten feet without someone somewhere offering his or her take on the subject. There appeared to be no end to the certainty with which so many people spoke of September 11. The remarks varied from being self-righteous to sorrowful, self-important to introspective, bitterly cynical to gently hopeful. There was no shortage of color in the comments and opinions of people around me. Surely these writers had something to say.

On the other hand, I was asking them to do something I myself could not: find something definitive to say. I understood their inability to articulate this moment. Far too often I have stared at a blank sheet of paper for hours, day after day, unable to find anything to write. There are times when words seem inadequate or indulgent. Modesty tugs at your sleeve and asks that you keep your mouth shut, if just this one time. I did not begrudge them their reluctance.

My hope, however, went beyond the contrivance of collecting the voices and views of West Coast writers. My hope was that this anthology would not only provide something for the readers of today but, more importantly, for those who might stumble across it tomorrow.

This May my wife will be giving birth to our first child. I can't help but wonder about the world that will greet him. I know my sentiment is hardly unique or profound. But in clichés we often find the truth. (There's that word again.) The events of this past fall have been an angry reminder of how small we all are in the face of history. I imagine the day, sometime in the future, when an event will prompt my son to read what the writers of today had to say about September 11. I believe he, like so many of my friends and family, and like me, will look to the writers of yesterday for a connection to the past, for reassurance that we are not alone in our experiences. I believe that, ultimately, this was the sentiment that attracted more than a few of the contributors.

This collection is, in a way, an experiment. Most of the writing will probably fade into history as a snapshot of a specific time and place. While it may give immediate comfort or intellectual provocation to those reading it today, it will, undoubtedly, become overshadowed by the next great tragedy or historical event.

Most times, I think that when we read we tend to make a looking glass of the words. I think we seek validation of our thoughts and feelings, reassurance that the world is just the way it appears to us. No one essay or story or poem is that mirror, but rather each is a fragment of reflection that approximates the truth but ultimately shows us only small pieces of ourselves.

The best writing pushes us past those reassurances, forces us to reevaluate what we see, and reconsider our worldview. The mirror takes on a funhouse quality, and the image becomes less certain. The colors twist and contort, challenge what we thought was truth.

I believe that the pieces in this collection rise to that level. I am certain that something here will reemerge for those readers in the future. What may appear to be obvious or outlandish or indulgent today may very well seem like profound wisdom fifty years from now. Whether it is the gentle epiphanies in Amy Gerstler's "Dark and Light," the passionate fury in Harlan Ellison's "Terrorists," or the quiet empathy of Tom Clark's poem "The Pilots," I have no way of knowing. I only know that the written word has the power to reach through time and offer the reader solace, insight, and on rare occasions, enlightenment.

To the writers, I thank you for your generosity. I am grateful for your participation and humbled by your dedication. This is a difficult moment in our modern history and your attempts to address it are appreciated more than you will ever know.

As for myself, every day brings a new opinion or emotion. My affection for black-and-white images is far less certain today, and it is impossible for me to find one emotion, one thought, one truth. I am sure I am not alone. Ultimately, I suspect that the truth is a chameleon and that, perhaps, the trouble isn't with color; the trouble is that black-and-white doesn't really exist.

History of the Airplane
Lawrence Ferlinghetti

And the Wright brothers said that they had invented
something that could make peace on earth when their wonderful
flying machine took off at Kitty Hawk into the kingdom of birds
but the parliament of birds was freaked out by this man-made bird
and fled to heaven

And then the famous *Spirit of Saint Louis* took off eastward and
flew across the Big Pond with Lindy at the controls in his leather
helmet and goggles hoping to sight the doves of peace but he did not
even though he circled Versailles

And then the famous Flying Clipper took off in the opposite
direction and flew across the terrific Pacific but the pacific doves
were frightened by this strange amphibious bird and hid in the orient sky

And then the famous Flying Fortress took off bristling with guns
and testosterone to make the world safe for peace and capitalism
but the birds of peace were nowhere to be found before or after Hiroshima

And so then clever men built bigger and faster flying machines and
these great man-made birds with jet plumage flew higher than any
real birds and seemed about to fly into the sun and melt their wings
and like Icarus crash to earth

And the Wright brothers were long forgotten in the high-flying
bombers that now began to visit their blessings on various Third
Worlds all the while claiming they were searching for doves of peace

And they kept flying and flying until they flew right into the 21st
century and then one fine day a Third World struck back and stormed
the great planes and flew them straight into the beating heart of
Skyscraper America where there were no aviaries and no parliaments
of doves and in a blinding flash America became a part of
the scorched earth of the world

And a wind of ashes blows across the land
And for one long moment in eternity
There is chaos and despair

And buried loves and voices
Cries and whispers
Fill the air
Everywhere

When a whole nation is roaring Patriotism at the top of its voice,
I am fain to explore the cleanness of its hands and purity of its heart.

RALPH WALDO EMERSON

Terrorists
Harlan Ellison

Sir, if a man has experienced the inexpressible, he is under no obligation to
attempt to express it.   —Samuel Johnson

IT IS WICKEDLY DIFFICULT ATTEMPTING TO GENERATE
a sense of gravitas when you have convinced yourself that you
have nothing to say that anyone should properly need to hear.

Let me try this:

Why can't I get that portion of the human race to which I have
access to understand that it has been systematically gulled, hood-
winked if you will, had enough smoke blown up its kilt to refloat
the *Lusitania*, by disingenuous egalitarian bunkum, into believing
"Everyone is Entitled to His or Her Opinion" when, in truth, everyone is only entitled to his or her *informed* opinion; and all the witless
upchuck devoid of fact or common ratiocination is merely the chit-

tering of intellectually-arid hominids swathed in Old Navy *schmatahs*. No, I can't launch into it that way. Sounds too Elitist. Don't even *dare* to suggest that some folks are smarter than some other folks. That ain't The American Way. All opinions have the same weight: Herman Kahn, Debbie Reynolds, Miss Cleo, Colin Powell. Joyce Carol Oates. Adam Sandler.

Okay, let's go a different way. How about this:

In the dead of night, masked marauders should stalk and ensnare Jerry Falwell in his bed, his coiffed cap of majestic silver hair mussed as a haystack, drag him into the bayou, to an abandoned cray fisherman's shanty, hang him up with his arms handcuffed behind his back on a slaughterhouse hook screwed into the top half of a Dutch door, strip him to his gourmand gut, slick and pale as a planarian worm, and beat him across the belly with an aluminium ballbat till his piss runs red.

Oh, whoa! Can't do that either. Sounds—at *best*—stone vicious, meanspirited, sadistic. This is Moral Jerry, the voice of Gawd Above. Can't write such stuff, not The American Way. Jerry talks to the Lord, and the Lord gets right back to him. Only a card-carrying member of the ACLU would doubt that. So, um, let me see…would this work:

The phone rang. It was October 19th, 2001. Only thirty-eight days after the September 11 attacks on the World Trade Towers and the Pentagon. No one was talking about anything else, because nothing mattered as much; but the fabricators of *tchatchke* novelties were already casting the molds for the cute antimony ashtrays with the rubble stumps and American flags unfurled. And my phone rang.

It was Carole Chouinard, one of the "talent coordinators" for the ABC-TV talk show *Politically Incorrect with Bill Maher*.

They wanted me to come on the show as part of the usual disparate quartet of opinionated citizens, some of whom (like me) had a tenuous yet deathlike grip on the appellation "celebrity."

I'd done the show perhaps fifteen or twenty times over the years, all the way back to its original incarnation out of New York on Comedy Central cable. But I hadn't heard from them in more than a year, ever since the telecast in which I'd explained to Maher (with some difficulty of comprehension on his part) that I didn't fantasize about other women when my gorgeous and brilliant wife, Susan, and I were in bed, mostly because my dick had fallen off years ago in a particularly frigid high-wind-chill evening in Manhattan, outside the St. Moritz.

So I was glad to hear from them.

When you've been writing professionally for just abaft fifty years, it gets more and more strenuous trying to keep any sort of a commercially viable profile that permits you—if you're a freelancer—to continue earning a decent living without recourse to scripting a film that will star Pauly Shore, or doping racehorses, both of which will send you to the 8th and inner circle of Hell. (Only difference: with the former, you take the express.)

So doing *Politically Incorrect* didn't pay much; but in terms of keeping one's name and kisser in front of the fickle masses for an extra eyeblink or two, well, it was a halibut swimming in a beneficent sea.

So I said, sure I'll come on the show. When? And Carole said, we'll be taping as usual at CBS Television City after our hiatus, Tuesday, November 20th. I said that's peachykeen, and what will the topics be?

And Carole—quite correctly—reminded me that they don't finalize the discussion topics till the day of the telecast, in order to keep *current* with the savory flavors of the breaking news; but that I'd get my précis probably on Monday the 19th.

Ah, I thought, no more beaks and feet; my fifteen minutes has done rolled 'round again…

TV GUIDE CARRIED THE LISTING, AND I WAS THE ONLY name officially slotted in (I'm usually a last-minute replacement for Queen Latifah. Other than that I'm a short, white Ohio Jew, age 68, we could've been separated at birth, y'know what I'm sayin'?). In fact, in the fax I received from Assistant Talent Coordinator Stephanie Lynn on November 19th, the other three guest chairs were to be occupied by ex-*M*A*S*H* star and political activist Mike Farrell, a very smart cookie; actress Charlotte Ross, now on *NYPD Blue*; and ultraconservative Representative Dana Rohrbacher. Now, I have no idea of how deep and wide runs Ms. Ross's intellect or awareness of current events, but those other two guys are sharp and knowledgeable.

Thus it was, one day before the telecast, that I received advisement of my on-camera companions, along with the three topics that had been chosen by Maher and his staff for discussion.

And here are the topics, exactly as presented to me:

1. America has taken great pains to assemble a coalition of nations in its fight against terrorism. Is a coalition important?

2. President Bush says the noose is getting tighter around Osama bin Laden. When he is caught, what should we do to him? Should he be killed on sight? Should he be tried in court? Should Saddam Hussein be next?

3. Undoubtedly, the fight for increased homeland security could benefit from increased tax dollars. Are Americans more willing to sacrifice—financially and otherwise—than politicians admit?

I stared at that faxed page for a long time.

One spends a lifetime wondering if one's ethics are report card "A"—buttressed by courage sufficient to understand at every testpoint not only that you gotta *do* The Right Thing, but to *know* when it's time to do The Right Thing. We are a weasely little species, capable of alibi and obfuscation at a level of instant adroitness that would put a turkey vulture to shame. If you doubt it for a second, pick a television court show like *Judge Judy* and watch it for a week. Will make your gorge buoyant.

I stared at that faxed page for a long time.

Everybody wants to be on television. Everybody. At the scene of a fifty-car-smashup, bodies strewn everywhichway like bloody pick-up-sticks, there will invariably be some gobbet of human phlegm who, with slack jaw and extruded tongue, positions him- or herself behind the stringer with the mike, who waves to the world or to Mom while squishing an ejected large colon 'neath his/her Nikes. Pedestrians in malls, passersby in markets, patrons in moviehouses, all pant and drool as their progress is impeded by a total stranger with a hand-mike, seeking their oracular wisdom.

The late British Prime Minister Harold Macmillan once wrote, "I have never found, in a long experience of politics, that criticism is ever inhibited by ignorance."

And, hell, we *pay* politicians to have opinions.

Everybody wants to be a dancing bear on television, and every-body *deserves* to shoot off a big mouth on the tube because, as *everybody* knows…We Are All Entitled To Our Opinion.

Doesn't matter if we're dumb as a box of Hamburger Helper, as uninformed as a hemorrhoid, as surfeited with jingoism and urban myth as a foot-soldier in the White Aryan Army, by gosh we're entitled to express that bone-stick-stone opinion, endlessly, at the top of our lungs, ungrammatically, like uh *totally* and, gawd willin' and the crick don't rise, on *tele*muthuhfuggin*vision*!

I stared at that faxed page for a long time.

THEN I CALLED *POLITICALLY INCORRECT* AND TOLD NORA Burdenski or Carole or Marilyn Wilson or Stephanie or *some*one that I was going to have to do what I had never ever done before, in more than forty years of talk-show appearances. I was going to have to excuse myself from the panel. Tomorrow night.

When you tell someone who has booked a talk show slot cut and sewn to fit your shape only, that you are doing a bunk, there is—first—a moment of silence one encounters only in undefiled Pharaonic tombs. That moment, as they refer to it in Indonesia, is *djam karet*, the moment that stretches. A caesura gorged with billions of Roentgens of incipient hysterics.

Then they take that esteemed cortical-thalamic pause, for they know if they explode it will only serve to solidify your dastardly intention. The voice grows soft, cashmere, Reddi-Wip, plangent; soothing and as confidential as words whispered in the death cell at Dannemora.

"Oh my."

I say nothing.

"Well, this really is terribly short notice, Harlan. We even have the limo laid on to bring you to the studio."

"Yes, I know, Nora [or Marilyn, Carole, Stephanie], and you've worked with me enough times to perceive that this is an unusual circumstance, because...have I *ever* pulled this sort of thing on youse guys?"

"No, you haven't. Are you sick?"

"Not in the accepted, non-psychiatric sense of the word; no, I'm just fine, dear heart. But I cannot sit on that show with the topics Bill is planning to throw at us."

"Why, what's wrong with them?"

"Nothing's 'wrong' with them; I just don't have any intelligent opinions on them. I truly have nothing to say."

"But you're so *funny*; you *always* have something to say on *any-*thing! That's why we call on you so often."

"Yeah, you'd think I'd have something to shoot off my big bazoo about, wouldn't you? But, in truth, kiddo, I just *don't*."

"You have no opinions about 9/11?" Astonishment trembled in her voice. This was a concept she could not parse. A Flat Earth Theory for the 21st Century. In the word of the evil Sicilian, Vizzini, who kidnapped Buttercup, *Inconceivable!*

"I was three thousand miles away from ground zero when it happened," I said, beginning to get annoyed. "I saw it on teevee, for chrissakes! I wasn't *there*, though I know there are people who delude themselves that they 'saw' the Manson murders or the Lindbergh baby kidnapping or the assassination of JFK because they glommed a docudrama on the tube. It was a horror show, and I was watching live as the second plane dissolved through the wall of the second tower, and I spent days trying to reach friends of mine who lived in the area, or worked in the buildings, but..."

How the hell do you say what comes next?

"...but *I wasn't affected*. I didn't lose anyone close to me. I was a spectator. I'm enraged at the atrocity, just like everyone else, but what the hell does *my* opinion mean? It's just more hot air and posturing, expelled like all the hot air by the hundreds of wanna-bes who've been on the tube for the last month. I have nothing to say that anyone needs to hear!"

"But you'll be great on the show. You can say what you've just said to me."

"I can go drain valuable airtime on a coast-to-coast hookup, to say that I'm empty of opinion? That I know nothing more than what I read and see in the news, and there are actual people out there who've been through it, but I'm a bigmouth on the other end of the continent who should shut up and sit down? Is that my contribution to the advancement of Western Civilization on this particular topic?"

"But this is really inconvenient, it puts us in a hole."

"Don't you think I'm well aware of that? Don't you think I sat and stared long and hard at those topics trying to dredge up something meaningful that would validate my sticking my teeny opinions in the faces of three million viewers? And I don't delude myself that *Politically Incorrect* is news, kiddo: it's mere show biz, it's entertainment. Nonetheless, I am affronted when you put on guests who are as uninformed and as outright stupid as—" and I named half a dozen recent guests, "—so I'd rather not be a hypocrite and balm my own cheap need for exposure at the expense of three million people's patience. I grant you the show, and even the lowliest opinion by the dopiest standup comic pseudo-pundit, is better than the entirety of those Grand Guignols presided over by Letterman and Leno and Conan the Borebarian, but it ain't *Nightline* or the editorial page of the *New York Times*.

"I understand that jerking you around like this will likely mean I'm persona non grata at *Politically Incorrect*, but I find myself inexplicably troubled by the ethical considerations of pretending to know something in front of so many people, when I just don't have the vaguest opinion on these weighty topics. So…well, maybe you can get Queen Latifah to stand in for me. We were separated at birth, you know."

Well, there were a couple of cajoling calls an hour or so later, but by that time I'd firmed my resolve, though I knew such behavior would redound to my detriment profile-wise.

There was even a call from the new Producer who had taken over when Scott Carter left the show to produce Candice Bergen's short-lived chat-a-thon. He said he understood perfectly what my bizarre concern was, he assured me *he* felt sanguine about my coming to do *what I'd agreed to do*, and he further assured me that even if I screwed them over this summarily, it would IN NO WAY deter him from inviting me back, and soon. Very soon. Almost sooner than I could envision.

I thanked him for his understanding and compassion, and told him that as a lifelong blabbermouth of infinite hubris I found this spike of ethical constriction most unnerving. But I was, for better or worse, fixed in my decision.

He said he'd make sure I was invited back in December.

We parted amicably.

That was five months ago as I write this. Listen, *amigos*, do we hear the silence of Pharaonic tombs? The silence of petrogeny? The silence of Coventry? I'll be placing a small personal ad in the *Green Sheet* seeking the whereabouts of my lost fifteen minutes. Maybe on milk cartons.

I HAVE NEVER EXPRESSED A PUBLIC OPINION ON THE nightmare of 9/11. I've been asked by others, but I just shrug and mumble something to the effect that it isn't my *place* to have a public opinion. Even though I hold with Voltaire: "My trade is to say what I think," there are some things in this sad and painful world that are too large, too significant, too troubling for the squirrel chatter of the mook in the street. My pal Tony Isabella notes: "Hell hath no fury like that of the uninvolved." But, boy, did I catch the shit. On one of the websites "dedicated" to my comings and goings, a guy went on at sibilant length as to how "unpatriotic" I am, not man enough to let others know how I felt about the sudden vaporized disappearance of a few thousand innocents. I chose not to reply.

Then, something straight out of the *Manual of Synchronicity* went down, and I found to my chagrin that I did, indeed, have an opinion—if not about 9/11 directly, well, at least it was a strong opinion about terrorists.

You won't like it, and you may echo that gnat's e-post that I'm not a Good Amurrican, but I'll pass it along, anyhow. Do with it what you will.

(A pause. I am an American. Says so on my passport. I served in the U.S. Army for two years, I have paid loads of taxes for half a century, I marched for civil rights with Martin Luther King, Jr., worked with César Chavez on the grapefruit strike in the Coachella Valley, spoke for more than 1,100 actual hours in dozens of venues on behalf of the Equal Rights Amendment, and I once sued a large corporation for screwing its customers and won a rebate for them, not to mention a policy change. I am an American. My response to your cavil that I'm "unpatriotic" is a soft, sane, reasoned bleep you and the snake you slithered in on.)

On September 17th, less than a week after the suicide slaughters, when Bill Maher's show went back on the air for the first time after the 9/11 events, he made some comments about the turmoil, the roiling and chaos, the vast number of opinions by everyone from Jennifer Aniston to Geraldo Rivera, the intrepid war correspondent. Among his remarks was one that prompted White House Press Secretary Ari Fleischer to chide him, "This is not a time for remarks like that."

The remark. Maher suggested—and I concur with his proper use of terminology—that you could call those brutal skyjackers rabid, you could call them demented, or brainwashed, or merciless, amoral, devoid of kindness or compassion, the heartless dregs of a mad society...but you could not, rationally, call them "cowards." Cowards do not saddle up a flying coffin filled with something like 24,000 gallons of high-octane jet fuel and hurtle at full throttle into a World Trade Center spire, turning themselves into screaming flaming gelatine, their eyeballs melting, their rib cage exploding, their hair burning down through their brain. Assholes, maybe. Religious fanatics, damned skippy. But not cowards. Wrong word.

A bit of convenient jingoism used by the Ashcrofts and the Bushes to demonize what is already demonic. But not cowards. To an enormous segment of the world's population they are the equivalent of Audie Murphy, Sergeant York, Captain America, the kid who throws himself on the grenade to save his buddies, the old lady who pushes the toddler out of the way of the Peterbilt and gets turned into roadkill for her trouble. We call those people heroes.

See, I told you that you wouldn't like it, where I was going. But don't expend all your outrage just yet; I plan to take this a lot further.

Maher's remark loosed the Apocalypse upon him. Now, I am not a friend of his, nor do I agree with him most of the time, nor has he ever expressed so much as a fartwhistle of interest in getting to know Susan and me. When I do the show, he is always sedulous in making a green room appearance to thank his guests, but apart from exchanging passing courtesies, I know *you* better than I know Bill Maher. But I became incensed at the mindless, lockstep behavior of empty patriotism that the great manipulable wad of American slopebrows unleashed on him. Samuel Johnson had it screwed down tight when he observed that "Patriotism is the last refuge of a soundrel." I offer Timothy McVeigh and Richard Nixon as examples.

And while the *New York Times* was running a special section titled "A Nation Challenged"—a four-month-long project that included more than 1,800 "Portraits of Grief" remembering the victims of September 11th—and setting itself up to win seven Pulitzers, Maher was fighting to keep his sinecure. He became a pariah. For expressing a logical but not hysterical opinion.

Sure, here in our beloved republic you are "entitled to your opinion," just as long as you don't voice it when the lynch mob is raising the flag and the cross.

But, still, I didn't post my agreement publicly, because it wasn't necessary. Dozens of righteous (as opposed to *self*-righteous) commentators jumped to Maher's defense, including that blowhard bully Bill O'Reilly. "Censorship of anything, at any time, in any place, on whatever pretense, has always been and always will be the last resort of the boob and the bigot." Eugene O'Neill. Now dead, so no one can bust *his* chops.

But what happened next, almost simultaneously with Maher's oh-spare-me-the-imprudence-of-it-all, was the force that yanked the wooden stake out of me widdle vampire heart.

Jerry Falwell, the pimp of religious recidivism, went on Pat

Robertson's tube and blamed the World Trade Center Towers bombings on those who run abortion clinics, homosexuals, feminists, and the liberal scum who refuse to allow Christian fundamentalists to take over the schools more than they have already. (The fact that something like sixty-five per cent of all science teachers in high schools believe in the wacky creationist theory of the universe ought to scare the crap out of anyone but a bible-thumping true believer.) There he was, that smooth, slick planarian worm of a minister, telling everyone that it was the fags and the feminazis and the baby-killers who were to blame.

Now, just to remove the thorn from your paw, to deny you that disreputable forensic-debating rathole into which the Blind Faithful predictably scuttle—"Well, Dr. Jerry is bein' quoted outta contex"—I will now offer for your predilection vast windy sections of Pat Robertson's interview with Falwell from the 13 September 2001 edition of *The 700 Club*. Two days after the great death. Two days into the American heartache. (Please note, all pecksniffs: in the original manuscript of this essay, I reproduced the *totality*, every last word of this obstinately wearisome exchange. Just so no one could *possibly* suggest there had been any flummery. But the good barristers who vet this material pointed out that even though I'd taken this from *The 700 Club*'s own website, where it appears sans copyright; and even though it had been broadcast live over the public airwaves; and even though there was a surety that this was what is called "fair use," that the censorious carrion birds who serve the Messrs. Falwell & Roberson might, nonetheless, initiate a nuisance lawsuit if I was to republish the entirety of the TV duologue. So we cut it, this seriatum babble by Tweedledum and Tweedledumber. Here's the essence. If you think, in a last-straw grasp at paranoid justification for the monstrousness you are about to read, that I have misrepresented even by a scintilla, I urge you to go to the anointed website to fill in the blankety-blanks.) Clip and save:

Falwell in full flight, followed by the comments of Robertson on the same episode of *The 700 Club* prior to Falwell's appearance.

PAT ROBERTSON: Well after Tuesday's attacks, many Americans are struggling with grief, fear and unanswered questions. How should Christians respond to this crisis?

JERRY FALWELL: ...I've never sensed a togetherness, a burden, a broken heart as I do in the Church today, and just 48 hours, I gave away a booklet I wrote 10 years ago. I gave it away last night on the Biblical position on fasting and prayer because I do believe that that is what we've got to do now—fast and pray. And I agree totally with you that the Lord has protected us so wonderfully these 225 years. And since 1812, this is the first time that we've been attacked on our soil, first time, and by far the worst results. And I fear, as Donald Rumsfeld, the Secretary of Defense said yesterday, that this is only the beginning. And with biological warfare available to these monsters; the Husseins, the Bin Ladens, the Arafats, what we saw on Tuesday, as terrible as it is, could be miniscule if, in fact, if in fact God continues to lift the curtain and allow the enemies of America to give us probably what we deserve.

PAT ROBERTSON: Jerry, that's my feeling. I think we've just seen the antechamber to terror. We haven't even begun to see what they can do to the major population.

JERRY FALWELL: The ACLU's got to take a lot of blame for this.

PAT ROBERTSON: Well, yes.

JERRY FALWELL: And, I know that I'll hear from them for this. But, throwing God out successfully with the help of the federal court system, throwing God out of the public square, out of the schools. The abortionists have got to bear some burden for this because God will not be mocked. And when we destroy 40 million little innocent babies, we make God mad. I really believe that the pagans, and the abortionists, and the feminists, and the gays and the lesbians who are actively trying to make that an alternative lifestyle, the ACLU, People For the American Way, all of them who have tried to secularize America. I point the finger in their face and say "you helped this happen."

PAT ROBERTSON: Well, I totally concur, and the problem is we have adopted that agenda at the highest levels of our government. And so we're responsible as a free society for what the top people do. And, the top people, of course, is the court system.

JERRY FALWELL: Amen. Pat, did you notice yesterday? The ACLU, and all the Christ-haters, the People For the American Way, NOW, etc. were totally disregarded by the Democrats and the Republicans in both houses of Congress as they went out on the steps and called out on to God in prayer and sang "God

Bless America" and said "let the ACLU be hanged." In other words, when the nation is on its knees, the only normal and natural and spiritual thing to do is what we ought to be doing all the time—calling upon God.

Not counting the occasional "Amen!" used in place of their natural grunts (human speech not being their native tongue), this extended badinage was in no way percipient for our little town meeting here. It was mostly hype and hustle, disingenuous back-slapping and mutual greasing about what a powerful force for paleolithic thinking Jerry is, and how we'uns is all gonna get t'gethuh in Bedford on Sunday for an exploitative prayer memorial and pocket picking. I have excised these sections because they put my typewriter to sleep. I had to bitch-slap it to get it to continue. I am sedulous in trying to present the full indictment here, but when the self-serving palaver is about as appropriate as argyles on a turtle, well, you'll just have to take my word for it—untrustworthy though I may be—that between what you've just read and what is to follow, there was nothing, how shall I put it, exculpatory. Just boring. But now, let us surge forward.

Pat Robertson's Comments Preceding the Falwell Interview:

PAT ROBERTSON: And we have thought that we're invulnerable. And we have been so concerned about money. We have been so concerned about material things. The interests of people are on their health and their finances, and on their pleasures and on their sexuality, and while this is going on, while we're self-absorbed in the churches as well as in the population, we have allowed rampant pornography on the internet. We have allowed rampant secularism and occult, etc. to be broadcast on television. We have permitted somewhere in the neighborhood of 35 to 40 million unborn babies to be slaughtered in our society. We have a court that has essentially stuck its finger in God's eye and said we're going to legislate you out of the schools. We're going to take your commandments from off the courthouse steps in various states. We're not going to let little children read the commandments of God. We're not going to let the Bible be read, no prayer in our schools. We have insulted God at the highest levels of our government. And, then we say "why does this happen?"

Well, why it's happening is that God Almighty is lifting his protection from us. And once that protection is gone, we all are vulnerable because we're a free society, and we're vulnerable.

So get this straight: all you've been told by the left-wing liberal kneejerk commie-and-queer-dominated news media is *all wrong*. You now have the straight dope from the straightest dope in America. Jerry Falwell, who speaks to God, and God *speaks back to him*, has told you that it wasn't religious fanatics serving an all-powerful god who threw themselves into fiery hell, it was the ACLU, the American Civil Liberties Union, the ones who take up the cases of poor schnooks who've been fired for blowing the whistle on corporate polluters and subhuman sweatshop owners. The ACLU, that says the First Amendment is pretty much sacrosanct, even when it means defending scumbags like serial killers and members of the much-beloved American Nazi Party.

But the gargoyles of the ACLU couldn't have brought down the Towers alone. Hell no, they needed those godless self-involved sluts devoid of Family Values, those ferocious harridans who reject their rightful role as punching bags and soup makers for Manuel and Meyer Machismo. The heathen Feminists, damn their uplift bras! And, of course, the faggots and lesbos, those unmentionable corrupters of the young—unlike the good priests of the Catholic Church, princes all, who merely seek little princelets with whom they can share *Divino Afflante Spiritu*—who so upset the Falwells and Robertsons of the world that mere mention of them causes Righteous Televangelists to lubricate embarrassingly.

See, isn't that all clear now. Not the dedicated children of Islam, but home-grown nasties right here. And not even the stand-up American patriots who shoot physicians and bomb medical centers, who tie niggers and butt-fuckers to trailer hitches behind SUVs and drag 'em till they plow a decent furrow, who blow up half of downtown Oklahoma City in the name of God and the American Way… but people who pay dues to the ACLU and want to decide what happens to their lives and bodies themselves instead of having self-appointed little autarchs like Falwell and Robertson calling the shots.

I didn't have an opinion worth voicing on 9/11, till I read what that termite Falwell had to say on 9/13. Now I have an opinion; but not one I much think would go over well with the studio audience at *Politically Incorrect*.

But here it is.

Osama bin Laden and his crew of degenerate thugs, and Jerry Falwell and *his* cadre of sicko-pervo-freakos, with Pat playing the Gabby Hayes sidekick, all worship the same god. Not the gentle succoring Jesus, and not the kindly warmhearted Allah, but some third entity, some horned and astigmatic sulfur-breathing deity who battens on hatred and loathing and the spreading of Elitist snakeoil promising 73 virgins or the Pearly Gates, if only you will waste your lives in pointless denigration of everyone Pat and Osama and Jerry point to as enemies of the all-powerful God. It is hard to slam religion when there are so many decent Christians, Jews, Buddhists, Muslims, even Atheists. But if nobody notices that the same religious insanity that drives little girls to wear bustiers of C-4 is the one that Falwell and Robertson slather across our daily bread, then we become as one with the hypocrites who manifest astonishment that priests bugger choir boys. As though it hasn't been going on for five thousand years!

How many lives has Falwell ruined? How many walking zombies inculcated with religious lunacy has he set on the path to murder and arson and rape and madness? There is no difference at all, *in my opinion*—which I'm entitled to—between a terrorist egomaniac like bin Laden and his al Qaeda, and Falwell with his Moral Majority. No difference.

Neither of them serve a sane god; neither of them will go to heaven; neither of them belong in a world as sad and troubled as this one.

You want an opinion...try this:

Falwell and Robertson ought to be in chains, sharing a hut at Gitmo's Camp X-Ray, where the good terrorists are sent.

All over the globe, people are being slaughtered in the name of God, said Salim Muwakkil in the *Chicago Tribune* last April. It's been that way throughout history, but no one dares "take religion to task for the evil it has ushered into the world."

And don't give me any of that banana oil about all the wonderful things like the Renaissance and illuminated manuscripts that religion has proffered. That's what a man-made succoring faith is *supposed* to do! It's not, however, supposed to do all the *rotten* stuff it does. Like burning Giordano Bruno and turning Galileo into a craven wimp; like stoning witches to death and flinging people onto the *strappado* for the pleasure of the Inquisitions; like banning books and art and dance; like dynamiting gloriously beautiful ancient Buddhist statues; like telling the gullible and uneducated that they must empty their pockets of milk and medicine money even as they hate and hate and hate all those with lifestyles unlike the ones Jerry and Pat and Osama trumpet as Moral Values; lifestyles of honor they cannot live up to themselves.

I have no opinions on what happened on September 11th, 2001. None that need be voiced, because they're even less informed than yours, and frankly, if you're like me, you don't know actual jack…

But you asked, and you persisted in asking, and you pressed me to shoot off my big bazoo, so I give you the opinion to which, as a dumb-as-ditchwater average American, I am entitled.

Do with it what you will.

While I go in search of some gravitas, and my lost fifteen minutes of fame.

A Clamor of Symbols
Sallie Tisdale

THIS IS A GOOD TIME TO BE IN THE CANDLE BUSINESS.
Candles—especially many candles put together—are the new sec-
ular symbol of community. Cell phones have abruptly come to represent family togetherness. And firefighters' helmets are now our
most potent symbol of sacrifice. Human beings have always made
symbols; twenty-first-century culture has perfected the art of the
instant symbol. First there is one roadside shrine—a little white
cross, a candle, flowers—and then there are a thousand. Each
school shooting has drawn a wall of flowers and teddy bears within hours. Once absorbed, such symbols tend to stick around. The
misbegotten swastika is still undergoing rehabilitation, but the

peace sign may never die. Every rainbow now says gay pride. Pink is breast cancer. Yellow means separation.

You didn't know that about yellow? Sometime in the last century, the traditional green willow twig for absent lovers turned into a yellow ribbon. During the Iranian hostage crisis, absent lovers became prisoners. Today yellow ribbons are used to represent inmates, POWS, political prisoners, teen suicides, children with cancer, and—just to confuse the issue—Aussie endurance horseback riding and the "No Taxes on the Web" campaign.

All language is symbolism; each word we utter, a representation. The cultural symbols springing up now are a peculiar shorthand for ideas that otherwise require a lot of words—and which may not be so easily agreed upon if we were to discuss the issues.

We use symbols to communicate and create intimacy, but also to map territory, to define sides. We can't really do one without doing the other. Most of the current crop are intended to represent "unity." All symbols represent unity, in a sense—they imply belonging, manifest group identity. Even peace signs are a kind of loyalty check. But there is nothing more amorphous and complex than the supposed unity of 300 million people. Suddenly we are all supposed to be thinking as one, facing one direction—holding candles and humming a snippet of "Amazing Grace."

While grass-roots symbolism may be earnest, the culture belongs to consumers, and our communication is a matter of mass media. Grass-roots ideas quickly become products to be copyrighted and sold. UnitySymbols.com sells necklaces, T-shirts, and even dog collars combining symbols from twelve world religions — "symbol wear for the unique individual." Symbols of unity are also symbols of marketplace competition.

In the bitterly funny film *Wag the Dog*, in which a marketing team manufactures a phony war to distract attention from a presidential scandal, Dustin Hoffman plays a movie producer. The phony war is over and now the phony prisoner of war, William Schuman, must be brought home. He asks Willie Nelson to scrap the war songs and write something else for the occasion.

"I need a new song, okay? A 'good old shoe' song. It should be a ballad of loss and, uh—and uh, you want to help me?"

"Redemption."

"Loss and redemption is very, very good!" beams Hoffman.

Nelson grumpily agrees. "What key do you want it in?"

Soon there are truck drivers wearing T-shirts, pairs of old shoes are dangling from telephone wires, and the song is on the radio: "Good old shoe, good old shoe, stand up straight and proud the way he taught you to."

Symbols are speech—inherently political speech. There are no neutral symbols in mass culture; they exist to express an agenda. Displaying the flag or carrying candles is not so different from standing on a street corner and passing out pamphlets. Each symbol contains its opposite, too.

If a symbol promotes unity, then anyone without the symbol can be seen as divisive. Dialogue becomes disagreement. We have lately seen a deliberate avoidance of political dialogue; politicians have been counseling each other not to engage in debate. The pressure to display "unity," symbolic or real, is potent, almost censorial. One needn't disagree; spread the symbols around widely enough, and doing nothing becomes suspicious.

In a time of confusion, we fear things that give us cause for second thoughts. Clear Channel, the world's largest radio network, gave its stations a list of 150 songs to consider keeping off the air. The list includes songs that mention flying, falling, airplanes, and explosions, but also many songs of consolation and love: "Imagine," "Bridge over Troubled Water," "What a Wonderful World," and even "O-bla-di, O-bla-da." These are included, apparently, because thinking about peace and reconciliation now might make it more difficult to think about war. In an odd juxtaposition, "God Bless America" has been the patriotic song of choice at public gatherings, because our national anthem is "too evocative" in its images of war and bombs.[1]

The recent "America: Tribute to Heroes" concert broadcast by multiple networks was a remarkable bit of working-class symbolism from its opening: Bruce Springsteen in jeans and a T-shirt on a plain stage lit by many candles. The hint of gospel, Tom Hanks, Clint Eastwood, Billy Joel with a firefighter's helmet on his piano, other celebrities working the phones—an admirable bit of just-plain-folks salesmanship.

Symbolism is an inherently reductive act, but symbols themselves are often flooded with complex ironies beneath their surfaces. The Pentagon is either the symbol of our liberty or of our brutality. The World Trade Center towers were either symbols of our prosperous free-market economy, or of our malignant globalization. Neither will be allowed to simply be seen as buildings filled with people. Even what to call this time is a loaded question. Is it a tragedy, a crisis, an attack? Is it "nine-eleven" or "nine-one-one"? An "Attack on America" or—as CNN currently has it in red-white-and-blue framed subtitles—"America's New War"?

Flags means "us." Turbans and beards mean "them."

The actor James Woods recently reported the suspicious behavior of several Arabs with whom he shared an airplane's first-class cabin. They neither ate nor drank, he said, and didn't even "make themselves comfortable." Such behavior in a world of abundance is a symbol of difference: they have strange ways, different values— an immutable symbol of "other." (That an Arab may not *feel* comfortable on an American airplane right now was not considered.)

The most powerful symbol we have is still the flag, an image

1. *The New York Times*, September 19, 2001 sec. E, p. 6.

laden with irony. Flags were traditionally used in war; they are meant to show conquest as much as community. (For a lesson in unity and division, consider the enduring potency of the Confederate flag.) A cable company recently handed out flag pins to its employees, forcing the news anchors and reporters to explain that journalistic ethics would be tainted by such displays. But the fact that they felt obliged to explain the absence of the symbol only empowers the symbol with meaning.

Everywhere I turn now, I see stripes, stars, and combinations of red, white, and blue—streamers and ribbons that look more like school colors at football games than anything else. But how many Americans realize that Cuba, Russia, Slovakia, North Korea, Cambodia, and twenty-four other countries have red, white, and blue flags?[2] Or that the abstract designs of modern flags derive from ancient Islam's influence?

The desire to be united is a powerful one; symbols come to the fore now because we want so much to believe that we are united, that shorthand is all we need. Of course we need more than that to find a way forward. We must pity others' sorrows as well as our own; we must witness for each other as we struggle through this time of turmoil. It does no good to reduce that struggle to lapel pins and bunting. We are bound together as human beings, in a way we can't escape.

One definition of unity is the absence of diversity. But another definition of unity is the pleasing harmony of many parts forming a whole. Unity does not equal sameness, and difference does not equal division. If anything echoes the real meaning of "America," this is it—from Peru to Manitoba. It is quietly astounding that we

....

2. Thailand, the United Kingdom, the Dominican Republic, Fiji, Iceland, South Korea, Chile, Yugoslavia, Western Samoa, Costa Rica, Liberia, the Marshall Islands, France, the Czech Republic, Luxembourg, the Netherlands, Panama, Norway, Paraguay, Serbia, Laos, Australia, Puerto Rico, and New Zealand all have flags using these three colors.

can talk to each other at all; this miracle of multitudinousness is what I want to celebrate now.

The United States was founded as a plurality. It has flourished as such—a unique nation of free and often contentious expression, astonishing diversity, a mix of views more heterogeneous than any in history. We are many tribes from many lands, and our real unity is that in the United States we are allowed to be unique. If we are talking about patriotism, what I love most about my country—what stirs my heart when I hear "America the Beautiful"—is not that we are so much the same in this country, but that we are all so wonderfully different, and still here.

Late September, 2001

Out of the Fires, What Renewal?
John Daniel

ON SEPTEMBER 11, 2001, AND DURING THE WEEKS THAT
followed, I turned where I usually turn for solace — to the natural
world. There is a consoling sanity in the tall Douglas firs that surround our house, a reassurance in their loft and rootedness, their
composure, the way their boughs stir in the wind or don't stir. There
is health in the quick current of our small creek. There is rightful-
ness in rain and sun, perfection in the rasping calls of chickadees
and the yammering of flickers and the steady, dark-eyed gaze of
a black-tailed deer. There is an ungraspable majesty in the movement of daylight into dusk and dusk into stars and moon. It is
good to remember — at times it is a salvation to remember — that

beneath and beyond and above our obsessive human busyness, our blaring noise and lights, our wars and murders and torture, there lives a universe of ongoing beauty that we can mar but never destroy. That's easy to write, of course, on this still evening when no storm wind is threatening to topple those consoling Douglas firs onto the house. When no earthquake is making a seismograph needle of my pencil and bouncing the house from its foundation, no volcano leveling trees and house and my wife and me in a searing pyroclastic blast, no wildfire consuming our acre. Over the long haul, the nature of nature is violence—exploding stars, grinding tectonic plates, battering rain, scouring glaciers, pounding breakers, gyrating tornadoes and hurricanes. Peace and permanence are illusions of my short and sheltered human life.

The redemption, the saving grace, is that every natural violence does some good. The animal that kills and eats lives on. Predation gives the owl keen eyes and ears, makes mice into subtle escapists. A flood may kill many creatures, including humans, but it renews a river's ability to sustain life by flushing sediment onto the flood plain, creating new pools and deepening older ones, and sweeping juvenile salmon out to sea in the spring. Fire, too, is a destroying creator. When allowed to burn periodically, it clears a forest of choking underbrush and fallen wood, maintains meadows and a spacious array of mature trees. The fiery explosion of Mount St. Helens totally destroyed major populations of flora and fauna, but twenty years later the mountain flourishes with fresh life.

Even catastrophe on a global scale is generative. Sixty million years ago a massive asteroid struck the Caribbean off Yucatán, raising a dense atmospheric cloud that suddenly chilled the planetary climate. Dinosaurs, which had dominated Earth for more than a hundred million years, died off. A small gnawing mammal survived, prospered in the absence of the great reptiles, and eventually became us.

So — it may seem unduly optimistic, an indulgence of one who lives a long way from ground zero, but the questions I've been asking since September 11 are these: What redemption might come of that horrific violence? What thickets of blinding underbrush may burn away? What possibilities may be given a chance to grow? In what form might our renewal rise?

One thing destroyed in those fires, though denial of its death may persist a while longer here in the West, was our American sense of invulnerability. Throughout our history we have worn our continental isolation and military prowess like an impervious cloak, but now we know it's not impervious. The Cold War threat of Soviet missiles was authentic but abstract. The missiles never flew. The impromptu missiles of September 11 were all too real, and we know, despite heightened security and a bolstered military, that there will be other missiles, in other forms. It is saddening to know that, but necessary. Invulnerability is an illusion of youth. We have been stripped of our blithe juvenile autonomy, made to realize that we live in relationship with other peoples in other parts of the world, that we know next to nothing about many of those peoples, and that some of them despise us enough to commit mass murder by suicide.

The first thing to rise from the rubble of our presumed invulnerability was a profound sense of American community. We all felt the wounds, even on this distant coast. As friends and family of those on the jets and those in the World Trade Center and the Pentagon entered their vigil of horror, friends and family here in the West and across the country sought each other's company to watch the incredible images, to share the disorientation of our shock, to speak of the unspeakable and thus, however falteringly, to accept that it had happened. Our own had died, an untold number, in our own land. We were one people brought together in grief, more unified than at any time since World War II.

As I sang along to "The Star Spangled Banner" at a public gathering two days after the attacks, I heard certain phrases as if for the first time—"bombs bursting in air," "our flag was still there," "the home of the brave." By then we knew that many in the home of the brave, in the smoke- and dust-choked streets of New York, in northern Virginia, and in at least one of the doomed aircraft, had indeed acted with superb courage, the kind of courage we hope for from ourselves in our best moments but doubt we are capable of. We heard the stories of American heroes. The perpetrators, bold and audacious as they had been, were cowards. Long before they seized the airliners they had already vacated their lives, given them up to the cause of killing as many Americans as possible and to their own perverted hope of heaven. The rescuers, who very much wanted to keep their lives, gave them up to the cause of saving as many others as they could. Their sacrifice made human beauty out of the fires of hell. They ennobled themselves and their country. The American flags raised in the rubble of lower Manhattan and draped from the gashed Pentagon moved me as the flag had never moved me before. They marked our solidarity as a wounded but unbowed people.

Through the fall and winter, though—it's March as I write this— the flag has come to mark something else. In my rural portion of Oregon, it flies from mailboxes and fence posts and the doorways of homes. A paper version, sent out in the Eugene newspaper, is now taped to the windows of countless cars and pickups, mounted in storefronts here and in town. Flag stickers and refrigerator magnets abound. For a time the red, white, and blue was boldly printed on grocery bags from our supermarket. Wal-Mart, I have heard, put out a line of star-spangled diapers. A schematic Stars and Stripes, captioned "Baseball Remembers," hovered in the upper right corner of television screens during the major-league play-offs. Similar images have ghosted telecasts of other sporting events, and all the players in all the events have borne a flag patch on hat or uniform. The flag flew and occasionally still flies in television commercials, in newspaper and magazine advertisements, on billboards and the signboards of businesses. Over the weeks and months the spontaneous displays of Old Glory at the time of the attacks became something cheaper, something manufactured in mass.

Certain phrases—"God Bless America," "United We Stand," "One Nation Indivisible," "Proud to Be an American"—have proliferated like the flag, with the same effect. The language loses force, becomes background, an aural and visual Muzak. A farm store I pass on the way into town had this for many weeks on its signboard:

GOD BLESS AMERICA
PIG FEED $9.95

The storekeeper did not intend to devalue that three-word phrase, yet how could his use of it have had any other effect? Those who design and print grocery bags meant nothing ironic when, beneath the image of the flag, they printed "UNITED WE STAND" in quotation marks. They misused the punctuation in a very common way, meaning only to add emphasis to the sentiment, but unwittingly they pointed straight to the heart of the matter. Those slogans have been reduced to prefabrications that the culture quotes to itself automatically.

I don't doubt the sincerity of individuals who make such utterances and gestures. (Businesses are another matter—to invoke the flag in advertising, and with it the memory of victims and the pain of survivors, is offensive.) But I can't escape the feeling that even the expressions made by individuals are as reflexive as they are heartfelt, signs of reaction more than renewal. It's as if with these automatic gestures we wrap the flag like a thick, tight bandage around our wound. A bandage can aid healing. But a bandage, if applied thoughtlessly or prematurely, can hinder healing, too. On this coast, well removed from the personal losses suffered by many in the East, it seems that we have skipped quickly out of shock and pain into a spell of hypnotic patriotism.

For some, there is anger in that spell. I, and many others, reacted angrily on September 11, and to have done so was only human. We had been attacked, ferociously, in our own land. Anger has spurred our government to search for and bring to account the planners and enablers of the attacks. I am one of the many who support that limited aim and the use of force in achieving it. The American people and the families of the dead are entitled to justice, just as in Oklahoma City seven years ago. It is miserably unfortunate that securing justice in this case requires making war in Afghanistan, but the Taliban left us no other effective option. It is not a bit unfortunate that the Taliban have been routed and that music is sounding again in the streets of Kabul.

But anger that seeks justice must be disciplined and thoroughly focused, like a hawk plunging on a snake, or it destroys its end by its means. The civilian casualties inflicted by our own airstrikes have damaged the justice of our cause, and our government has compounded the damage by denying such casualties—or offering only belated, perfunctory regrets—and by advising American media that to publish or broadcast news of civilian casualties would be tantamount to aiding the terrorists. The Attorney General of the United States did injury to justice when he angrily suggested that Americans who do not support every aspect of the war on terrorism are themselves allied with the terrorists. He was referring to those—I am one—who take exception to such practices as trial by military tribunal of noncitizen suspects and indefinite detention of persons suspected of the least connection to terrorist activity, such activity defined in the broadest and vaguest of terms. Twelve hundred foreign nationals, almost all of them Middle Easterners, were rounded up after the attacks and imprisoned—without evidence, in almost all cases, of any crime more serious than a minor immigration violation. Six months have passed, and several hundred are still detained.

This clear-cutting of the Bill of Rights is not renewal but protracted reaction. It is anger hardening into policy, the flag that should protect dissent being used to smother it instead. This, sad to say, is nothing new in American history. It was reactive anger against immigrants, foreign nationals, and those who seemed foreign that fueled the violent suppression of industrial unionism from the Great Railroad Strike of 1877 through the first half of the twentieth century, that set off the Red Scare after World War I and railroaded the execution of Sacco and Vanzetti, that rationalized the red-baiting of the McCarthy era and other excesses of the Cold War. Almost anyone who dissented from government policy on the Vietnam War or was active in the civil rights movement has experienced some degree of reactive American anger. Many dissenters acted in anger themselves, and our society was ripped asunder.

No doubt some in my region subscribe to the with-us-or-against-us rhetoric now emanating from the executive branch of the federal government, but the good news is that many do not. On this coast the shameful memory of Japanese-American internment camps lingers like an open wound, and we tend to be fairly touchy about civil liberties. I am proud of three Oregon municipalities—Portland, Corvallis, and Ashland, our biggest city and two small towns—for refusing to cooperate with the FBI's interrogation of some 5,000 foreign nationals throughout the country. The three police departments advised the bureau and the Attorney General that Oregon law did not permit them to question individuals on their views and associations when there was no evidence they had committed a crime. Such restraint is admirable and in the best American tradition.

Locally, the belligerent comments I heard or read in the days soon after the attacks have subsided. In meetings, hearings, and letters to the editor, in casual conversations in markets and the post office, people are once again talking about issues that traditionally have concerned them—school funding, whether to build a new highway, conflicts between economic development and environmental quality. I take this as a sign of healing, a necessary recognition that what was important before September 11 is no less important today. It is not a sign that September 11 has been forgotten. How could we forget, even if we wanted to? It means that we are taking a middle way, most of us, between denial that the attacks occurred, on the one hand, and obsessive preoccupation on the other. We, like others everywhere, are trying to understand what our long-term response should be.

And, just as we do about schools and the environment, we disagree. I know many who strongly oppose the limited military action I support, and I know some who favor the much wider war that the government seems intent on waging, which I—barring major new attacks—cannot support. Honorable men and women *do* disagree, vehemently at times, and do so without impugning the other's patriotism or humanity. Dissent is the genius of a free society. The public seems to understand better than the Attorney General of the United States that a broad and vigorous diversity of views is not weakness but strength. In nature, healthy ecosystems prosper not because they are uniform and simple but because each is a complex equilibrium of diverse elements always adjusting and evolving. It is precisely the system's diversity that gives it the resilience to recover from natural calamity. It is uniformity, as in an even-aged plantation of trees or a food-crop monoculture, that impoverishes a system and makes it vulnerable to catastrophic disruption.

The public also seems to understand better than its leaders that the debacle of September 11 demands something more of us than acquiescence to a mushrooming military budget and a willingness to use our credit cards more frequently. Our armed forces may succeed in neutralizing Osama bin Laden and al Qaeda, but force cannot in itself bring us peace and security. Neither can sky marshals, beefed-up border guards, and other homeland security measures, necessary as those may be. If we ever doubted that there is deep and widespread anger toward our country in many parts of the world, we cannot doubt it now. We need to protect ourselves from that anger, but at the same time we need to recognize it, to engage it constructively, to ask what conditions, perceptions, and U.S. policies give rise to it and how they might be changed. The present human world is like a vast forest parched in summer, loaded with dry fuel, vulnerable to every lightning strike. A fire once begun can spread quickly to any part of the forest. Our need is to reduce the fuel. That will be far more difficult and will take much longer than dropping a few daisy-cutters and launching smart missiles. The rest of the world also has an interest in justice, and "justice," as Oregon poet William Stafford once wrote, "will take us millions of intricate moves."

Anger is dangerous because it is easy. It is the great simplifier, like a forest fire at full roar. As we work to understand the anger against us, it may be that our own anger will ease, and it will be then that reaction can give way to renewal. When the fire has passed, the slow intricacies of rebirth begin. Fireweed and lupine poke up through the ashes from seeds dispersed by birds and wind. Insects follow. Shrubs and grasses return, thriving in the openness of the burned-over woods. Deer follow the shrubs and grasses, a cougar follows the deer. Fungi rethread their gossamer skeins throughout the soil, delivering nutrients to roots. Voles eat the spore fruit of the fungi, and voles, in turn, are eaten by owls that nest in the larger surviving trees. The trees where the owls' descendants will nest are seedlings on the forest floor.

Any act of any one creature or thing—bumblebee, rain drop, plodding raccoon—is surpassingly small, but each may contribute to the renewal of the natural community. How can our own renewal occur except in such small ways, beginning at home in our own communities? How, except by speaking a kind word to one we dislike or who dislikes us? By examining ourselves for our biases and listening carefully, respectfully, to those who disagree? By not fearing and shunning strangers but opening ourselves to what we might learn from them, might learn only from them? By troubling to understand, as thoroughly as we can, the full cost of the comfortable lives we live—to our communities, to the natural world that sustains us, to other peoples of the planet? By demanding more of ourselves and of our government than reactive anger and patriotic display, more than the hardening of defenses and the waging of war? By honestly asking what our country contributes to the global community for good or for ill, and how we might give more of our best—more of the courage and selflessness of the September 11 rescuers, more of the generosity of the millions who spontaneously gave blood or money or materials, more of the old-fashioned readiness to pitch in and go to work for those in need that has always been our strength?

Natural renewal after fire or flood just happens. Renewal, like violence, is the nature of nature. But our own renewal won't just happen. It will take millions of intricate moves—acts of faith and forbearance, acts of restraint, acts of boldness, acts we cannot forsee, acts that may flower and bear fruit long after we are dead. It has frequently been said since September 11 that everything has changed. We say it, I think, because we don't know what has changed. Right now, it seems to me, the answer is little. Violent attack with great loss of life and counterattack with still more loss of life are the oldest stories in human history. Nothing much has changed. But much could change, if we want it to.

When sorrows come, they come not single spies, but battalions.
WILLIAM SHAKESPEARE | *Hamlet*

What Remains
Colleen McElroy

the light is all wrong
too cold too silver gray
the sun is hot
too low in the sky
too close it seems
your skin burns
through shatterproof glass
this is how it begins
anxiety dancing
in beads of light
the quarrel of crows
too loud too long
you wait for the fog
to burn off late
afternoons it never does
a skyline fractured
everything a little off
center and closing
what remains
blessings left uncounted
a single golden
moth speckled wings
dotted with false moons
flush against
a smoldering earth

Forsaken
Colleen McElroy

where have the birds gone
have they flown to other
islands lesser or greater
Antilles or cays tucked away
and squared against attack
have they scattered there
the seeds of destruction
propagating faraway
places with human rage
where do they fly when skies
are swallowed in dust clouds
turning noon into hellish
storms of midnight
when do they cease to sing
left to imitate the whistles
of mortars before they shatter
the silence   do they warble
the moans of the dying   where
is spring   how do seasons change
without swans robins sparrows
do feathers molt in the rain
of ashes colors burnt
in patterns of girders
laid bare   when do the pigeons
take flight explode from narrow

ledges give up the peck and nod
peck and nod that makes us believe
all in God's kingdom is good   who
takes the last shot that picture
perfect photo prize the cracked
beaks broken backs the glass
eyed stares talons open and hawks
measuring their final descent plumes
ablaze with insufferable madness

Due
Michael Byers

THE SUMMER BEFORE THE ATTACKS WAS A BUSY ONE around our house. My wife was pregnant with twins, and she and I were busy writing and making a living, scratching together an income as best we could while we prepared the house for the babies. This meant converting my office into a nursery—steaming off the purple floral wallpaper, knocking out a wall, painting, prying out all the paint chips that had fallen into the cracks behind the woodwork. A modest job, really, but with everything else going on it took a few weeks to complete. At least, we told ourselves, we weren't remodeling the whole house—which is what our neighbors across the back fence had been doing. We were friendly with these neighbors—the Rudolphs. They themselves were new parents, and presumably just as busy, but their remodel had been a much lengthier and more impressive project. For months their yard had been occupied by countless workmen, huge piles of debris, and the neighborhood had been filled with the sounds of saws and sanders and whatnot. But by June it was almost done, or so it appeared from across the fence.

The Rudolphs' house had been a smallish old cottage sitting high above its street—a nauticalized, blue-shingled Cape Cod, with two stories and a sharply peaked roof. Over the course of a year they gutted the interior, refitting it with new wiring, new plumbing, and new drywall. They sanded and refinished the floors. They rebuilt the kitchen. A new Viking stove, with hefty industrial hardware and quick-action burners, was muscled into place. They built a new fireplace of fieldstone. From our deck we could see the new French doors that opened onto the new brick patio, where, if our neighbors wished, they could sit on their new benches and wave at us from across the fence. Salvage lumber, reclaimed from old factories and warehouses, had been remilled and replaned to make their trim and cabinetry. And an entirely new third floor gave them a view of the Sound, the Space Needle, and the skyscrapers downtown. It was, from what we could tell, a very nice job. Costly, we imagined, but probably worth it, if you had the scratch to spend. Harry and Gina Rudolph's son Walter was not yet a year old, and from across the fence we could see him being carried around the new yard, where the landscaping was still being finished.

There were suddenly a lot of children in the neighborhood last summer. Our neighbors down the block had an eighteen-month-old daughter, who periodically appeared on our sidewalk in red tights, carrying an umbrella. "Singing in the…," her father would begin, and Frances would oblige, after a moment of cautious thought, with "Rain" — and then make a gentle little flourish with the umbrella, a motion of such unpracticed grace it seemed a gesture from another, vanished era. A woman around the corner had adopted a Chinese baby, whose round face appeared behind their plate-glass window now and then. A new couple two doors down from us had arrived with a young daughter and a son. And our neighbors to the north had six kids, aged eight to seventeen; after dinner the six Harrisons played basketball together in their wide, meticulously paved driveway, in carefully arranged games of three-on-three. They played with a silent, calculating intensity, so well did they know one another; for long minutes the only sound was the basketball pinging, pinging, pinging — then an exclamation, followed by another lengthy, scuffling silence.

And by June of last year my wife Susan was six months along. The twins would be our first children; their official due date — in one of those coincidences that stare you blankly in the face forever afterward — was September 11.

We'd known they were twins fairly early on, and by June we knew we were having a boy and a girl. We had not been expecting twins, to say the least, but by June we'd recovered from the initial panic. Mostly. Still, every now and then the notion of double parenthood — the feedings, the diapers, the ungodly cost — would hit us again.

"Holy shit, we're having twins," one of us would say.

"Holy shit, you're right," the other would answer, not exactly kidding. "What the hell are we going to do?"

Well, we didn't know, of course. Twins are medically classified as a high-risk pregnancy, even if you're perfectly healthy. This meant Susan spent a lot of time visiting her doctor at the university hospital, and I spent a lot of time accompanying her. Every three weeks or so my wife and I would show up in our Accord, get our parking validated, sit for a while in the waiting room surrounded by other somber pregnant women and their silent, attendant husbands, then be admitted back into the examining rooms. As the months went by the twins grew from pulsating white dots to bulbous commas, to salamanders, to proto-humans with arms and legs they could use to punch and kick each other. It was as though they were approaching—as the spring and summer passed—from across an expanse of desert, appearing on the horizon as bright specks in February and gaining detail as they grew nearer. The fact that this process was so commonplace did not make it any less fascinating.

Though as a writer I was trained to value the precise and the particular, I found myself entirely satisfied with my mushy, universal feelings of wonder and overjoyed expectancy. And why not? Occasionally the ultrasound would play at just the right depth and one of the twins' faces would swim into focus, a charming bland mask, gray on the monitor screen. Then it would slide out of view again, leaving us completely speechless. What could you say to that? What would suffice? During some visits the doctor would listen for fetal heart tone, and on these days the room was filled with the roaring background noise of my wife's body—which was then interrupted, when the microphone was angled the right way, by two bright, rushing heartbeats, full of obvious will and intention, like signals picked up from the depths of space. How reassuring that sound was, and how strange! How vital and unfamiliar these sounds were! But really everything was strange, and vivid; every week my wife grew bigger, more uncomfortable, and more awkward, and fewer and fewer of her clothes fit. "I just want you to know," she would say, hefting herself up the stairs to the newly-painted bedroom, "that this is not my body."

In an effort to mitigate our total ignorance, we were taking a series of twins classes at the university hospital's Multiples Clinic. A dozen couples were enrolled with us, all pregnant with twins, all as nervous and excited as we were. The trick was—as Cheryl the instructor would tell us constantly—to carry the babies as long as possible. Twins are born, on average, four weeks early. So our September 11 due date was just a date—like any other due date, just an approximation. But we wrote that date over and over again that summer, on the hospital forms, in letters to friends, and on our own calendars. For us, September 11 represented the forty-week mark, and as such marked the outer limits of possibility. A long shot, in other words. The best we could hope for. But we were optimistic. And the longer you carried your twins, the better the outcome was likely to be. Born too early, the babies would have underdeveloped lungs, immature nervous systems, an assortment of other difficulties. After thirty-three weeks you were considered more or less safe. Anything before about twenty-eight weeks was dangerous. Born before twenty-five weeks, the babies would likely die, or be badly injured: blind, retarded, or brain damaged.

Everyone in our group knew these terrible, frightening statistics, and we were all counting the weeks until we were out of the woods. Before every class, each woman would announce how far along she was—like drunks, I sometimes thought, reporting how long they'd been sober. And we were seeking that same kind of communal reassurance, I think; we wanted to know that someone else had done it longer than we had. The longer you went, the more precarious and difficult your pregnancy grew. Women carrying twins got more pregnant, faster, than women carrying singletons. At twenty weeks you started getting constant heartburn. At twenty-four weeks it was almost impossible to sleep. And by twenty-six weeks almost everyone had begun having contractions, which— if they were strong and persistent enough—had to be managed with drugs.

The class was held under the skylights in the big open waiting room of the Multiples Clinic, with the cushioned chairs gathered in a half-circle. It wasn't exactly a social occasion. When the class was over, at nine at night, everyone was tired and ready to go home. But the atmosphere was always friendly. We grew to recognize our classmates, and to root for them. The big fireman from Edmonds was mortally afraid of needles, and had to get up and leave the room during the epidural demonstration. The tall stylish couple from Wallingford—the woman in black, the man in gray—seemed to be breezing through their pregnancy with the same aplomb we imagined they showed in everything else. The chatty people from Whidbey Island, the quiet people from Bellevue—we were all ignorant together, which gave the room a nice, comfortable, congenial feeling. It was sort of like a language class—you went in feeling like a dummy, and laughed a lot at yourself, and came out feeling a little less dumb.

And of course none of us knew anything at all. How exactly did you breastfeed twins? How did you get them from the house to the car, pulleys? Sherpas? How did you shop for groceries? Where could you get cheap baby clothes? What were the odds of having to get a c-section? What are the dangers of terbutaline and magnesium sulfide? What does a contraction feel like? Come here, feel my belly, is this one, or am I just really pregnant? What does the Neonatal Intensive Care Unit do? What if the water breaks early? What do I do if I'm on bed rest? How the hell do you take care of two babies at the same time? We were all desperate for information, and for most of us, it was all going faster than we thought possible. I think we all sensed the day approaching: an ominous, inevitable feeling, when everything—we imagined—would change forever.

IN JULY OUR NEIGHBORS THE RUDOLPHS HAD A HOUSE party to celebrate the completion of their remodel. My wife was seven months pregnant by then, very heavy and uncomfortable, and getting around was difficult. And we had a twins class that night, so we couldn't stay long. But we wanted to see the Rudolphs' house up close, and we didn't want to pass up any opportunity for socializing, because we knew such occasions would be hard to come by after the twins were born. So we drove around the block. Harry and Gina's house was up a long flight of concrete stairs, which we climbed, slowly. Their yard was still disassembled. Wood chips stood in slumping piles everywhere, and the soil was still raw and tracked with footprints. But the exterior of the house was newly painted—a very pretty dark green with white trim. Inside everything smelled of fresh varnish and new wood. Every wall was flawlessly smooth, and the refurbished floors were shining.

We could hear people upstairs, so we slowly mounted to the second floor, where my wife stopped to catch her breath again. Then up one more flight of stairs to the new third floor. This was a big white open space at the top of the house, with the new balcony overlooking the street. A big party was in progress. Harry was passing out plastic cups of wine. It was a bright, sunny, summer evening, and people were admiring the house—going from room to room with cups in their hands, feeling the woodwork, trying out the sinks, opening the new windows. The work had taken months and months to complete, and now here it was, on display. And it was not disappointing. They had hired the best plumbers, the best designers, the old woodworkers who really knew their stuff. Harry gestured at the banister: "Look at the joinery!" he exclaimed. "And, oh my god," he cried, seeing Susan, "look at you!"

A dozen people stood on the balcony, plastic cups on the railing. From out there you could see everything. The high-rises downtown, still lit up from the day's work; the Space Needle with its winking red light; the gray plate of the Sound; the Olympic Mountains fifty miles away across the water. Someone brought a chair for Susan, and together we sat and passed the time, here at the top of the house—at the top of the city, it felt, in this new-built, posh, wonderfully extravagant construction, on the balcony that seemed to cantilever itself over the neighborhood. We all looked west across the water. We felt happy for Harry and Gina, who had been carefully lavish in building the house they wanted. The wine was very good, as it always was at their house. "They're kicking," Susan said, hand on her belly. "They can hear the party."

"So can the whole neighborhood."

"Your wife," Harry said, appearing out of the crowd, "is one hell of a trouper!"

"You're damn right I am," she said. "Great house, by the way."

"Isn't it amazing!" Harry cried. "Look! Look at that!" He faced the beautiful city, the sun in his eyes. "That's where I live, brother!"

And at that moment I, too, felt privileged to be there, an adult in the city of my youth, about to be a father, enjoying my neighbor's prosperous new view. It was fun to be around Harry, who was friendly in an honest, straightforward way I found admirable. I was feeling, as you can on summer nights like these, that the world was largely a benign place, that whatever difficulties arose would be faced by other good humans like yourself, that the future was a place of increasing brightness and levity, and that I would have a part in it, and so would my children, whatever they turned out to be. We left twenty minutes later, but the feeling lasted as we made our way to the twins class. Susan was thirty-one weeks along—almost out of the woods. She was uncomfortable, and the contractions were constant, and getting stronger. But the twins were growing well, and she herself was healthy.

But there was bad news. The quiet couple from Bellevue had lost their twins. Juliette's water had broken over the weekend, and labor had come on in an unstoppable rush. At twenty-two weeks their twins—identical girls—weighed fourteen ounces apiece. They had each survived for a little over an hour. The couple had wanted everyone else in the class to know why they weren't there that night, and why they wouldn't be coming back. "I've got their e-mail address," Cheryl offered, "and they said they'd like to hear from you."

What happened? we asked. What had caused it?

"They don't know."

Why did her water break?

Cheryl shrugged. "They don't know yet. They're looking into it."

Had she been having contractions?

"No," she said, "not as far as I know."

There was an appalled, ghastly silence. We were all picturing it, I think. That moment. The devastating, heart-sickening realization that you were giving birth much too early; the panicked drive to the hospital; the tiny bodies, unable to breathe or see; the terrible bright array of lights, the doctors working desperately, the crushing, crushing sadness. What on earth would you tell people? How would you survive such a thing? Nobody in that room could say a word; we didn't know one another well enough to commiserate. But we all imagined ourselves there, briefly—oh, how clearly we could see it! how vividly we could all imagine it!—and then together we put it out of our minds, as well as we could.

OUR TWINS WERE BORN IN EARLY AUGUST, FIVE WEEKS early. By September 11, they were long home from their brief stays in the hospital. Healthy, happy, the whole thing. I was up early that morning, heard some puzzling reports on the radio, went down the hall, turned on the television, and saw Manhattan covered in the dust of the first collapsed tower. I went back into the bedroom to tell my wife, found the three of them in bed— found my family, peaceful, at home, all of us just beginning something. I woke my wife to break the news. We had been planning to celebrate the day— nothing big, we'd just wanted to mark it, to remember it, as the day when we'd all arrived, finally, at the day of safety. Instead we spent the day watching television, hearing the eerie, absolute emptiness of the sky, having passed on that day—as we had always imagined we would—from one world into the next, new one.

New York Cover
Susie Bright

This is my blanket
My daughter called it a blankie when she was a baby
Now I feel babyish and call it the same

You can get underneath my blankie, like so—

Or I can embrace you with it—

You'll feel warmer
You'll feel babyish
You'll fall on top of me like an exhausted lover, under
    my cover, and
I'll feel the weight of your world crumble on top of me.

We'll both feel safer, in a blanket
Even though nothing has changed
Your side will be by mine and that's the final place I want it

This side
Of my blanket
Is the soft part, the part you hold against your cheek
When all the other soft parts get blown to bits

And this side
Of the blanket
Is the fuzzy part—
The side that stays fuzzy even when the picture elsewhere
    gets all too clear

Here's the dark part of my blanket
The place where I wanted to rest my eyes forever—
But my memories leaked in, like sunlight,
And my eyes grew so red they'll never sleep again

I wish I could make the bad smell go away with my blanket
The smell of gypsum and flesh and ashy shock
I could wipe it off the face of the earth, I could wipe myself
    off the earth,
I could tell you why all the loose ends ended up that way,
If I had one more chance, one more yarn, to make it
    right this time

I have a fantasy about America
It's made out of whole cloth
I guess there's no excuse for it

I have a love
For a big city
That took me in its arms and
Covered me
With blossoms and snowflakes and soot as thick as grease

I have to stop talking about you as if you're dead
I know you're only bleeding, and you'd welcome my dry hand
I'm covering you in white linen
When you're ready to defy me in red silk
I tell you I'm ready to take you in tatters
And you tell me to stick a needle in my mouth if that's the way
    I'm going to act

Okay, I'll shut up

Instead of blessing you and damning you,

I'll just cover you
The way I'd like to be covered
So close, so bound together, so sooty and greasy
That nothing will ever tear us apart

Santa Cruz, September 24, 2001

Dark and Light
Amy Gerstler

That which is mine is dear to me, and his own is dear to everyman.   —Plautus

Meanwhile this disheartening war goes on.... It seems to me that nothing could make one so despondent about human nature and the world, who was inclined that way, as just such a war as this, coming at this time of the day in history.
—Phillip Brooks, 1870

MY FATHER AND MOTHER ARE FIRST AND SECOND GENER-ation Americans. Their forebears were Russian and Eastern European Jews who fled the old country before they or their families were wiped out. When I was growing up one of my parents' main goals was to keep our home life undeviatingly pleasant. They were pretty rigid about it. No talking about unhappy subjects. No complaining. Morbid interests must be shunned. Politeness is of paramount importance. Anger is never appropriate.

Some of these traits may be common to their generation, reflecting shared values and experiences. Their values my parents were happy to espouse, aphoristically and often. Their difficult or painful experiences (or anybody else's) they absolutely didn't want to talk about. A kind of cheerful fatalism emanated from them like fog from a fog machine. No sense dwelling on the negative, the traumatic. No use even mentioning such things. There's nothing to be discussed or done. Smile, and soldier on. Of course I gravitated in the opposite direction. I'd skulk about the house with a volume of Kafka tucked under my arm, brooding about how no one would ever understand my wild, dark mind except Franz himself. Just my luck that the only guy I really wanted to date had died of lung disease in 1924. My mother shook her head at me as she would at a lost soul.

To this day musical comedies, baseball and basketball games, and uplifting movies remain my parents' favored entertainments. The tragic, the seedy, the aberrant, and the abject, which have always fascinated me, were to be militantly resisted, as news, or as art. To watch depressing films or read dark-themed books is to give in to sickness. To honor darkness with your attention is to invite it to infect and kill you, in their view.

My folks' insistent lack of interest in the gritty side of life not only caused me to be hopelessly drawn to depictions of it; it made me impatient with them. As a teenager, I felt I was more broadminded than they were. My tastes were worldly and sophisticated. I was tough. Interested in the entire range of human behavior. Ready to contain every complexity. Unafraid. They weren't. That was all there was to it. Perhaps these illusions are typical of my generation.

September 11 made me think differently. My tastes haven't changed. I still adore Kafka, but my parents' attitudes toward dark art make a kind of sense to me they never did before. When I spoke to them after watching the twin towers being destroyed over and over again on TV, all morning long, they were very collected. I was the one beside myself, sobbing. I had no tolerance for the news images at all. Although I've never had much stomach for "real" images of tragedy, as opposed to fabricated, highly artified ones, this inability to watch the news without becoming hysterical took me by surprise. Far from feeling that the TV coverage had something to teach me, as I had in the past, I felt assaulted beyond my capacity to endure or comprehend. A friend told me he had to explain to his seven-year-old that each time the tape of the destruction of the twin towers was shown, the event wasn't happening anew. I identified with that kid. I'm not proud of my reaction. But the fact is that initially all I could think about was escape. I started telling friends I was moving to Australia or Canada. Did they want to come, too? The images I was presented with of September 11's events had outstripped my suddenly very limited ability to contain them.

My husband had the opposite reaction. He was glued to the TV for the next several weeks. Every morning he devoured the *New York Times*. Suddenly he was reading foreign papers online, trying to get information that was being underreported or swept under the rug in the American press. Sensibly and understandably, he wanted to be informed. He is often more of an adult, and braver than I. Overloaded, I fled the bedroom and its prerecorded screams night after night, closing several doors to muffle the sounds of replayed mayhem, and installed myself on the couch.

My father was very calm when I called on September 11. He'd fought in World War II, he gently reminded me. Pearl Harbor had been a turning point for him. He had seen and lived these kinds of images firsthand. Consequently, I numbly realized, he never wished to steep himself in secondhand reflections of strife. He'd had plenty of the terrifying and wanted to avoid anything that remotely resembled it. If he was going to the movies or reading, his agenda was clear: he wanted to be cheered and heartened. He had no hunger to contemplate suffering or angst in reproduction, however poetic.

I am not saying that graphic news coverage is wrong, or should be curtailed. And I'm not inveighing against dark or transgressive art, either. Far from it. I'm simply acknowledging that September

11 ignited, for me, firefly-like sparks of sympathy for decisions my parents made long ago about how they wanted to live. Limits they wished to observe. These sparks continue to flit through my thoughts. My parents' limits are not mine, but I have newfound tolerance for their urge to keep darkness at bay.

This is a simplistic epiphany, and I consider it a failure in my own thinking and education that it didn't hit me years sooner. The poet Charles Simic recently wrote in *Artforum* magazine that "As an immigrant who grew up in that world [war-torn Eastern Europe] I could never comprehend the thrill of movie audiences in this country at the sight of wholesale killing and bombs exploding in some action movie." He could have been my father talking. If I'd formerly thought my parents' insistence on keeping things "light" at all costs meant they lacked a certain intellectual depth or emotional courage, I am now in the interesting position of feeling that I completely misjudged them. Among the most positive outcomes of September 11 may be the large and small opportunities, imperatives, really, to think and act differently. I am starting small. "Light" does not necessarily mean "lite." "Dark" does not always mean "most true or profound." At least I hope not. My appreciation for true, enlightened comedy has increased a thousandfold over the past few months. I bless it and consider it holy.

It remains to be seen whether we humans can learn from our bloody, repetitious history, whether we can enact some form of global humanism before we goad ourselves, and this lovely planet, into extinction. But I promised myself if I wrote this, I would talk only about my own family, and not give in to the temptation to preach. I am not informed enough or ready to sermonize. What I want is to learn more and change.

"This is only the beginning," my father said quietly when I called on September 11. His voice was grave but not shocked. Despite closed doors, I could still hear taped explosions and yelling from the bedroom. I hoped Benjamin wasn't overdosing himself on horror in there. Childishly, all I wanted at that moment was for my softspoken father to keep talking, to say anything, and for the balm of his dear, familiar voice to drown out the TV's yowling and punditdrone. Terrible things happening every day in Afghanistan and elsewhere in the world are no less horrifying or important than the fiery collapse of the twin towers.

January 2002

If There Were No Days, Where Would We Live
Primus St. John

When the Norse spring began
Freya rode her horse across the world
scattering flowers
this story echoes into Lady Godiva
who lifted the burden of the tax
by riding naked
but horses also bring
the death they've seen
the dragons
who live under the hills
the spider-women
living in canyons
and in the war
I felt the girth
and the fit of the reins
of death ...

The heart line begins
on the thumbless side of the palm
traveling horizontally under the fingers,
when it is clear & deeply etched
you have deep emotions ...
so the war is over, my love,
and we have killed enough of them,

torched their homes
trampled their fields
mutilated their arms
burned their legs
harvested their ears
and wore them like dark pearls
drove them crazy
made night a sure sign
of death
their schools, lost canyons
with nothing blowing through them
and an exact count of
dead mothers
dead fathers
dead children
and all that was given
taken away.

What do you do now
with the hunger
and the poverty glaring in their faces?
St. Theresa
would have probably kissed it,
but we were not saints
we were soldiers
hiding in the enemy's world.

How many times
must I be dipped into the water
to be a child again?

There was a village
where children loved to play
with kites.

You came to it over a hill
and the first thing you saw
kites—
red and blue birds
multicolored dragons breathing fire
bugs with fat wings
and fat noses.

The kite maker was an old woman;
I loved her wrinkles.

I found out
if you come at the right time
of year
she'd be flying kites
to a dark-haired child
with huge eyes

They say she has re-created
what she's lost
from the little pieces
she puts back up into the sky...

Catastrophe and the Widening Human Heart
Primus St. John

AS SOON AS I HEARD THAT THE PLANES THAT FLEW INTO the World Trade Center towers came from Boston, I called my daughter. When she has to go to Los Angeles on business, she usually takes those early direct flights from Logan International. After three rings on her phone that seemed like an eternity, she answered. "Old Man," she said, "you came in third. Mom and May already called." We bantered for a while and then hung up.

On Wednesday night she called me back. "What are you doing?" she asked. Oh, I'm just sketching out a short article for the *Oregonian*. "About what?" The terrorist attack. "Which brain are you using? The goofy Dad one or that poet one of yours?" You tell me.

I've always thought of the Trade Center towers as arrogant phallic assertions of financial dominion. The first attempt to blow them up in 1993 suggested that there are those who want to symbolically castrate American might. Terror has a voluptuous nature, too.

I have been noticing how suddenly our own might can be turned into our own excruciating suffering and loss. Terrorism is very frank about pain. Suddenly my daughter shocked me with this remark: "You know, Dad, it's strange. I can acknowledge the outrage some people around the world feel because of the policies we apply to them, but today is the first day, as a black person, I've ever felt like an American without that double-consciousness thing. Ironically, the agency for that feeling came from outside our borders. I am the same target as every other American citizen. We're all on the killing ground together. I'm scared and I'm pissed."

Catastrophes always surprise me the way they widen the human heart. People running down the stairs in the towers helped anyone who needed help, and the firefighters kept going up. People helped people simply because they needed help, and not because of who and what they are.

On the stairway of one of the greatest centers of commerce, the bottom line became people, not money. Watching the TV coverage and reading the papers these last few days, it seems to me the great temple of potency, the great center of might, is the human heart.

Since Tuesday, it seems that the large hole where the towers used to stand is being filled by something more substantial than steel and reinforced concrete—the hands and hearts of people working together.

The great danger of terrorism is how it draws opponents into serial retribution, creating a passionate history and tradition of revenge. It is meaningful to count our dead, but it is also meaningful to count our living. In times like these we need the courage and power of the heart, not of the weapon. We need to talk about and deal with what we will not bear, and do what's really needed. We need to steel ourselves by preserving all the living, even our enemies.

A Crack in the Earth
Barbara Earl Thomas

"My world will not end." But worlds—entire nations and civilizations—do end.
I repeated to myself, "My world won't end." But how could I be so sure? I don't
know. For a moment I wondered ...

—Langston Hughes, on the eve of World War II
I Wonder As I Wander: An Autobiography

ON SEPTEMBER 11, I WAS IN THE GRAND CANYON ON THE
Colorado River so far from the rim of the world that I would not
learn for nearly five days of the World Trade Center destruction
by hijacked planes. I would not witness the spectacle of exploding
metal skin engulfed in billowing plumes of smoke nor see the endless televised repeats. I would be Rip Van Winkle, far away as if in
a dream but not asleep.

I left Seattle on September 7 and headed for Flagstaff, Arizona,
to meet up with my fellow travelers. I was one of three invited
writers-in-residence on a specially organized river trip. I'd been
preparing for weeks. There was the list of projects to finish, equip-

ment to buy, and inertia to overcome. There was too much to do at home; why should I go anywhere? I have this thing about travel, especially air travel, that makes me want to clean my house, mow the lawn, finish my projects, and burn my journals. I've never developed a fondness for flying though I like to travel. I inherited some of this hesitation from my family, who were part of the Negro Migration from the South to the North in the early 1940s. They came to Seattle by train. After that they stayed put. Aside from an occasional car trip, they didn't want any more excitement.

I know I have far more chance of dying in a car than in an airplane. Yet, if I don't get home, I want things in order for my family and friends whose calls started a couple of weeks before I left. With each call I'd laugh and make light of my trip to the river that most of my family thought was just a crazy idea. Any fears they harbored for me about the airplane were trumped by the fact of the river. Most of my relatives didn't know how to swim and, as a vacation, a trip on a raging river without showers or proper toilets had nothing going for it. We joked and bantered, but underneath the conversation was a serious current acknowledging who and what we were to each other. We exchanged words, but in the silences we laid our prayers. And at the end there would be the "Now, you be careful out there on that river. Okay?" I'd say, "Yeah, yeah, you know me, no crazy stuff. I'll be fine." I'd say this knowing that whenever we parted for any reason, what we really wanted was the very thing we could not give each other: the certainty that we would see each other again.

This was my third river trip and perhaps my last. Of the three trips, two had been writing assignments and one a film project. On my second trip a year and a half earlier, I had managed to flip out of a small paddleboat with seven other paddlers. I descended into a whirlpool of chilled water with darkness all around me. When I tried to surface, I came up under the boat and thought,

"This is it." How many times could I do this and still have the odds on my side? But there I was, back again.

Unlike my previous trips, the river was Depression-green-glass clear and not the muddy color of its name. I saw all that was hidden beneath the normally milky surface. Tree branches, boulders, and whirlpools were clearly visible. On this trip, the water ran so low that we would eventually lose two motors and be caught temporarily on rocky piles.

We put in on Monday, September 10, a sunny clear day. There were a few clouds but no hint of rain. We numbered twenty-four, including the crew. We traveled from Washington State, Florida, Texas, Wyoming, and New York to be in the Canyon on the river. The night before, we dined together at Marble Canyon Lodge. There were a couple of parents traveling with their adult children, businessmen, writers, entrepreneurs, and retired people. I am a writer and a painter. I knew from prior outings that even as few as we were, we would soon form even smaller subcommunities based on interests and personalities. Much was familiar in my return to the river: the painted hills and desert terrain, the smell of the heat baking the brush, and the relentless roar of the river. There was a serious lecture from the boat crew about river safety and etiquette. We would be in the Canyon for seven days and out of contact with the world. If we hurt ourselves or got lost, help would not be immediate. We were charged with keeping an eye out for one another. Down here our group was all we had. Coming from cities where telephone, television, voicemail, and e-mail were ubiquitous, it seemed, even on my third trip, like a fairy tale that a person could be so out of touch. The isolation was part of why I came to the Canyon.

Spirits were high as we scrambled for life jackets, sized up the boats and boatmen, and chose a raft. Though I commented to my traveling partner, Ruth, that maybe it was all of the difficulty of getting out of town, but I felt like I wasn't all there, that part of me was stuck somewhere on the road between Flagstaff and the river, still waiting to arrive.

On the evening of September 11, we set up camp, ate dinner, and finally lay down under a mantle of stars. When the first airplanes appeared, I didn't see them. The airspace above the Canyon is normally a no-fly zone. But soon some of the lights that I thought were shooting stars transformed themselves into several tiny faraway airplanes. They crisscrossed my slice of sky, mixed in with the stars, the Milky Way, and space debris. The next day I asked if others had seen the planes as well. We talked about it, said it seemed strange to see the airplanes especially at such an early point in the trip. We concluded it probably had something to do with our being in the Grand Canyon Park proper, that the planes must have been there on Park business.

For four more days we traveled through layers of geological time. The Vishnu Schist, Bright Angle Shale, and the Tapeats Sandstone. The shades of green in the Sandstone were multitudinous. More than I could hope to remember, though I tried to record them in the back of my brain, breaking them down by the colors needed to re-create them when I returned to my studio. We examined petroglyphs, wondered at the people who had lived there, pondered what had happened to them. Their cultures had survived under such physical hardship, thrived and then disappeared. We saw grain storage caves in impossible places and remnants of long unused trails.

It showered. There were rainbows. Peregrine falcons flew overhead. We counted our days by Bighorn Sheep, Mule Deer, Ringtail Cats, and Kangaroo Rats. We set absent wristwatches to Golden Eagles, Condors, and Striped Kingfishers. We were kept at attention by Scorpions, Black Widows, and Collared Lizards. In a class by themselves were the Canyon Pink Rattlesnakes, one I mistook for a cinnamon roll as it lay curled up on a rock right in front of me. It was only when it moved that I realized a cinnamon roll had no reason to be there. I took my leave and let it have its rock.

We ate. We slept. We woke each morning to the trill of canyon wrens and an icy cold river that had successively dropped several inches from the day before. I wondered if at this rate there would be enough water left in the river to get us through the end of the trip. We went about our business.

It was Saturday, September 15, the sixth day of our seven-day trip, our last night in the Canyon. We'd set up camp and were preparing for dinner when one of the fellows in our group stumbled over to my section of campsite. He stood in front of my tarp and said, "Isn't it just horrible?" I paid little attention to him, because in prior conversations I had found him argumentative and a little arrogant. I'd seen him get into a disagreement with some of the boatmen about some detail of their boating. Fair or not, I thought, here is a rich guy who needs to be in charge even when there is nothing for him to be in charge of. One night during a camp-side reading he'd whipped out a huge cigar and lit up. After that I took to ignoring him. And I ignored him now as he stood in front of me. I didn't look up. I noticed his feet; he shifted from one to the other. He was flushed. Maybe he'd had too much sun. "I need a beer," he said. I thought, "He's run out of beer and he's here to mooch one." With nothing to offer, I continued to shake the sand from my day-pack. One of the other women finally offered him one of her beers and asked him what was wrong.

"You know," he said. "The Trade Center and the twenty thousand people killed." I jerked my head up and glared at him.

"You know," he repeated.

"Know what?" I said. "What do you mean, we know? Know what?"

Making a sideways-nodding gesture with his head like he was

pointing back up the river, he continued, "That guy back at Havasu Canyon. What he said."

We'd passed a number of hikers on the trail but I'd talked to none of them. Cherie, Page, and Ruth moved closer.

He said, "Afghans or Arabs hijacked airplanes and destroyed the World Trade Center. Twenty thousand people are dead."

"What the hell are you talking about?" I said. At this moment I fiercely disliked this man.

He repeated his story, this time more slowly, articulating the details. Though I was not sure I believed him, I took the fact of the telling as a bad sign. As he continued, I started to shake. I felt the urge to go to the bathroom, to evacuate my body and myself from this moment, to make room for something that seemed far too enormous for me to contain. The Canyon pressed in on me. Audacious, ridiculous, out of scale. I wanted to shrink it down to size, get it out of my face, put it in its place. But the Canyon stood insistent like a regal giant, removed from my concerns. Still beautiful in its shape and color, it responded to the slightest change of light as if magic were second nature. I must have been praying out loud because Kathy, a woman with a sweet Texas drawl, grabbed me by the shoulders and told me to hold on. She said, we don't know anything for sure. At that point, I had fallen to my knees and felt myself sink into the sand.

Tom, our guide, we learned later, had also heard these rumors but had chosen not to tell us until he had details. Hearing our discussion, he gathered us together. As he spoke, he neither confirmed nor discounted the story. Tom said he would make a satellite phone call once he found a place on the rocks where signals could get through. Until then, he said, we should consider that we had no real facts. It was the first time on the trip that I knew there was even such a thing as a satellite phone and that this was the way contact was made with the outside world. And still this was not instantaneous. For two hours we waited. A usually boisterous campsite fell eerily quiet, the roar of the river magnified.

By the time we reassembled, the sun had dropped behind the cliffs. Their craggy edges leapt skyward cutting a sharp silhouette. The heat was oppressive. Visibly shaken and holding a scrap of paper on which he'd written the facts, Tom delivered the news that five days earlier four planes had been hijacked. Hijackers drove one into the Pentagon. Two others were driven into the World Trade Center in New York City. He said it was caught on television as it happened. There was startling footage of the Trade Center's collapse. It was thought to be the work of Osama bin Laden and his group of terrorists. There was talk of as many as six thousand lost. All airports in the country were closed and the military was on alert.

From this crack in the earth I felt the world break open. Out of it poured an exposed center. There was a hard silence and then searching looks. Words failed us. Like seagulls caught in an oil spill, we floundered, awkward, embarrassed, unable to take flight. With Tom's news, we'd lost our last chance to have this be a cruel misunderstanding. I sensed that we'd lost something else but I couldn't put it into words. I startled myself when I said, "I don't know if we are tough enough for this."

"Are we at war?" I asked.

"It's possible," Tom speculated.

How could we not be?

I looked at the three women among us who had lived through Pearl Harbor and World War II. In lantern light, our skeletons shone through thin layers of skin, the fragility of skin and bones luminous. We were prefossil shadows moving on the earth as if we barely existed. Who were we now? If the world above was so changed, how could we be the same?

The silence was broken when Joyce, one of the stockbrokers,

let out a scream. "Oh my God, all the people I'm responsible for! And I'm here. What am I doing here?" She wailed and rocked back and forth, head in her hands. There in the center of camp was our table, covered with steaks, potatoes, assorted salad items, and a cake in honor of a fiftieth birthday. It seemed like a prop from another time. Should we eat the cake or leave it? Allison, mother of two, a doctor and AIDS specialist, said, "I wanted to be on this river for my fiftieth birthday. I am here and I will have my birthday." She took the cake, cut it, and handed it out.

From the shadows, Cherie, a writer whose daughter and husband were in New York, said, "I know it may not be appropriate but I was supposed to read my story tonight. And I would still like to read it. If that's okay." We nodded and sat. She stepped forward into the light and read a story about her husband and a trip they had taken to Egypt. It was at a beach on the Red Sea at Sharm al-Sheikh where her husband emerged from the water after snorkeling. She said he looked overtaken as he walked toward her and handed her the goggles. With great urgency he told her that she must go out that moment to a spot in the water that he indicated. She knew she needed to go. She dove into the water without explanation. There she hovered on the surface above a great coral reef. In a phenomenon of light and the sun's angle refracted on the water, the coral was illuminated in just such a way that it transformed the coral into a magnificent underwater cathedral. It glistened like stained glass windows, with high vaulted ceilings and gilded curves. She said, "Had I not trusted my husband or hesitated even a moment to question, I might have missed that vision."

Now she'd given it to us to hold and to tell. I looked around at each face. Who were these people about whom I knew nothing and everything? Intimate strangers. Distress and calm passed among us like food and stories. At one moment I was the consoled, the next the consoler.

"Is this what it felt like in 1941?" I asked.

"Yes, but this is different," one of the older women said.

"How?" I asked.

"Just different. Maybe the reasons back then were more clear," said another. "But no matter, you gotta stand up. You can't let people make you afraid. That's how they win." They who? I thought.

A woman behind me whispered, "You have to believe in the heartland. We have a very strong heartland, it will pull us through." This was a case where I understood every word in the sentence but I didn't understand the sentence. Someone started in with "God Bless America." Then we all sang. I sang hard and loud and hoped for release. None came.

In our group there were several businessmen; a couple were stockbrokers. The Trade Center had particular meaning to them. There were also four young men. If there was a draft, they would all be eligible. Two of the four were brothers. They were in their mid- to late twenties, thick-limbed, beautiful to look at. What would this mean to their lives and the lives of the girlfriends that'd come along? I remembered Ruth telling me that just after she and her husband married, he went off to active duty in World War II. Neither one of them expected that he'd return. Besides the girlfriends, also along on the trip was their father, grandmother, and the grandmother's best friend. Though the women, both nearly eighty, moved slowly, they came along on every side hike, no matter how difficult, aided by son and grandsons. Hand in hand, this family stretched itself around the cliffs on narrow pathways like a string of pearls. What would they be without those boys? A broken, mismatched set? A damaged heirloom? They weren't mine to give but I didn't want to give them up.

I understood struggle and dying. Any one of us could fall ill or be in an accident at any moment, but that seemed like a random mix of distant possibilities. This death felt close. Everything else fell away. What did it mean to be at war? If we were at war and whoever "they" were "were here." And it seemed they were. What would I need to protect my family? A knife and a gun? All I could think of was the footage I'd seen from Vietnam and World War II. Gun blasts and near misses. Houses leveled and fire everywhere. Were people up there fighting in the street? Would I be strong enough to go for days fighting? I'd come into this world only a few years after the end of World War II. My birth father, who died when I was barely three, had fought and was wounded in that war. My second father fought in Korea, where he nearly froze to death. War had no romance for me, but I had the urge to fight.

I wanted to get out of the Canyon right at that moment, to put my family in a circle with the youngest in the center. Surround them in fury and fierceness, swell up like a puffer fish, and blow fire until I had created a moat of safety around them. I wished I were younger and stronger. Would there be rationing of food, water, and gas? What would we have to give up to be in this war? I counted myself lucky to have lived so long in the world without a major world war. Was the jig up? Had my odds finally run out? And what of the people in the Trade Center and on the hijacked planes? The families, all the last words and promises lying there in the dust and debris. Unthinkable.

By Sunday evening, September 18, after a helicopter, a small twin-engine plane, and a three-hour van ride, we were back in Flagstaff. Filtered through scrub pines, the light of an autumn evening looked hazy but normal enough. Our hotel on approach was intact. I could tell nothing from the driveway or random placement of the cars in the parking lot about what to expect in the hotel. We unfolded our cramped, dirty bodies from the van. Would there be a shower? As I crossed the threshold of the Marriott, aromas of food wafted from the restaurant. There was the murmur of voices from the dining room and lobby. As I trudged past, carrying my backpack full of sand-laden clothes, I scanned the rooms. This told me nothing. There was a television. It hung, unwatched, over the bar, the sound muted. A constant ticker tape of narration paraded along the bottom of the screen: AMERICA'S NEW WAR. There, on split screen, was a newscaster on one side and a fully engaged Madeleine Albright on the other. Was she still Secretary of State? It was only Sunday. Were they already interpreting the interpretations?

I watched the two heads mouthing words, soundless. I imagined they repeated the previous days' events, listed one after the other in ever more intricate loops, the stories of planes, hijackers, and box cutters. Next I knew they would show the film, the amazing footage. The astounding proof that gave no reason beyond the fact of its happening. I decided at that moment that if my absence meant that I was not to be there with my family and friends as it happened, I would not watch it. Not then, not later. It wasn't to avoid reality. It was there whether I saw film clips or not. What I wanted was to resist being pulled inside another's viewfinder, after the fact, trying to make sense out of this tragedy by gauging the force of the plane's impact or the amount of time the towers took to fall to earth.

I would start from where I was. For five days I'd lived without the knowledge. For two days I'd lived with the attack inside me fueled only by imagination. Slept with it in a faraway place. Imagined my own death as a puny nothing. Understood in flashes how a mother might give up her child to a passing stranger, as she walked toward her own death, on a chance that the child might survive. I'd seen my life in the layers of shale and schist. Worthy, but no more or less important than anything else. Maybe that's what the Canyon does. Wears you down and brings you together at the same time. Nothing is constant. The evidence of change is everywhere; it's written on the walls, miles deep and centuries thick. It's all in flux, the sand, the birds, the water, the lizards, and the light.

AS I BOARDED THE PLANE ON MY FINAL LEG HOME, I thought of our last morning on the river. The wind kicked up fine canyon sand. It clung insistently to our skin. We scrambled without talking. There was no reveille for the last rolling of the sleeping bags or dismantling of the tents. But a raven lurked at camp's edge. Fearless, he waited for one of us to turn our back. He needed only a moment to swoop in and seize a prized object. Beyond him was the river. To our astonishment it had risen during the night. For the first time on the trip, the waters met the sharp imprint of the shore's high waterline. It was as if the rising signaled a mud letting. Unlike all the days before, the river no longer ran clear. Overnight, without warning, it had changed. It now ran a dense muddy red. And a riverbed once visible disappeared, boulders, tree trunks, ominous crags, gone. We launched our boats into this new river and traveled the short distance over a reality no longer seen, only imagined.

On Hate
T. Coraghessan Boyle

FOR THE PAST TWO MONTHS I WAS HIDDEN AWAY IN A
remote part of the Sequoia National Forest, finishing a new book,
working through the morning and early afternoon, then wandering the silent, unpeopled Sierra in a long waking dream of freedom and tranquility. Yesterday, on hearing the news of the attacks
on New York and Washington, of the pornography of hate and
violence and all its myriad repercussions, my first thought was to
return to the Sierras, to get as far away as possible.

But there is no return and there is no place far enough. I keep
rehearsing, with the novelist's compulsion to inhabit a scene, the
particular pedigree of horror that must have infested those airlin-

ers, the individual fears, the final meaning of giving up one's life and consciousness forever. The powerlessness. The despair. The annihilation of hope and compassion. And then I feel my own latent violence and hate raging up in me and can think of nothing but vengeance, blood vengeance, which is exactly what the terrorists want me to feel. Catholic and Protestant, Arab and Jew, Serb and Croat, Hutu and Tutsi, violence breeds violence, and once initiated, there is no end to the escalation.

This attack was ingenious. A group of terrorists without troops or conventional weapons was able to exploit the weakness of a free society in which all individuals have the right to pass freely, without fear or suspicion. They saw a way to convert our principal means of intracontinental transportation into two-hundred-ton bombs and were able to visit carnage and loss on a society that has never known it domestically, not even in fighting a four-year war for domination of the planet against Nazi Germany and Imperial Japan.

This was no car bomb, no individual spraying a parking lot with automatic-weapon fire, no act of random violence. This was a commando raid, unimaginable in its conception even to the minds of novelists and screenwriters, let alone of the military experts we assign to protect us, an attack so vicious as to make us all quail before the imperative that drove it: how could anyone hate so much?

Sadly, I think we all now know.

It Keeps Happening
Vern Rutsala

We've lived so long with either/or—
until now things were always
this or that, our distant wars sealed shut
with dates and however bloody,

history danced on to the next step,
but now the ambiguous ashes
keep falling, those planes aimed
like darts, and no matter how we blink

it keeps happening. We edge toward
the lives inside just before the crash
then wince away. Out here we remember
the ticking sound of that gray snow

from St. Helens but this ash keeps falling
from the calendar and the date never moves—
neither ending nor beginning, maybe
only the middle of a story without end.

And this is new for us, this swimming
among questions without answers
and we feel something like a cosmic
pull to the endlessness of space

but snap back again to seats inside
those planes, to desks in offices.

We want to turn off the TV, we want
to start the day over but it keeps happening.

Brought up as we were with either/or,
we know the next step in the bloody dance—
distant lists of casualties— and we'll
go on breathing in this ash that keeps falling.

When we remember that we are all mad,
the mysteries disappear and life stands explained.

MARK TWAIN

Seven Letters
Joshua Clover

DEAR MOVIES:

Well it was a good run. It was your century though the motorcar
New York incarceration the Holocaust Elvis the atom bomb population as a concept Coca-Cola communism made a go of it. Frank
O'Hara had a brief but phenomenal century during which he
wrote at least three great poems for you: "Ave Maria" "Poem (Lana
Turner has collapsed)" and "To the Film Industry in Crisis" ("in
times of crisis, we must decide again and again whom we love").
I went to you again and again for several reasons it was a way to be
with other people but not speak to them mostly they bore me. Not
only Hollywood but Parisian films were very popular in my part

of the century even if you don't include *La Jetée* there is still *In girum imus nocte et consumimur igni* ("and the people and the use we made of time all this constituted an ensemble very much like the happiest disorders of my youth"). But mostly Hollywood it was you who were a great joy mechanical reproduction Marilyn Monroe of thee I sing the artificing of the image rose over the century a poppy in the garden of immediate reality. When I was homesick I went to the movies when I wanted sex lazily then the movies when frightened when tired when too cold to sleep outside once in Boston still I loved you less than music. In New York September 11 having just flown in from Paris I did not sorrow as much as when Kurt killed himself I accept full responsibility for this failure and hope we can move on. War movies of Hollywood I am trying in particular to take you seriously as inventions not just as tesseræ in the dream we are trying to dream of life during wartime. In war movies of late there is some distant abattoir overrun by clans factions or tribes the Americans don't really appear there to engage the enemy because it can't be known this is extremely important because repeated. Undecideability of the bad guy movies are trying to fly into disorder but it's against their nature if *Black Hawk Down* had lost the half-hour of exposition Hollywood cinema could finally have given us abstraction as the Great War gave us the third dimension (Apollinaire): Mogadishu Violence Abstraction. At some point there was no music on the radio angry enough so I stopped listening for that but I kept going to the movies this was around Kurt's death late in the century. My first thought when the south tower came down was for the film industry in crisis movies had been superceded more or less right on time.

DEAR OCTOBER 18, 1977:
    Recognized two of you suddenly: "Arrest 1" and "Arrest 2" painted from photographs in *Baader Meinhof: Pictures on the Run 67–77*

Astrid Proll with details lost Andreas Baader bleeding in the garage lower left Holger Meins's clothing on sidewalk lower center indistinct in your version "pictures are dull, gray, mostly very blurred, diffuse" (Robert Storr). Then your Gudrun Ensslin portraits "Confrontation" 1–3 spectral demoralizing from Proll's photos where she looks like a hippiechick. At arson trial 1968 Ensslin unbearably sexy a female Rolling Stones nine years and four days before her death by hanging October 18, 1977. Series hung in New York 1988 now returned as part of massive Gerhard Richter show 2002 currently biggest artist in world. It's important to put things in sequence recently feeling this very intensely it was last year just before September I understood the Beaubourg thinks Richter is the Angel of Death of Painting while walking fourth floor hallway contemporary era out of representation. Catalog for *October* given to me just recently by Ange Mlinko while Proll photos from Kay Kimball after visiting my tiny apartment Jean du Bellay 1998. When things happen in order they're events some days you watch the same few seconds over and over.

DEAR SHOPPING:

I buy expensive clothes for specific events and also sometimes when I am so far from home I cannot imagine ever being seen but enough about me let's talk about you. This is the greatest year of your life. The Mayor by the middle of that week told New Yorkers that what they could do was go about their lives go to the movies go shopping. This spread quickly and soon the President was saying it. You had been rising up to us for a very long time but something had been holding you barely beneath the surface like a face under latex paint. The grander ideologies. Now you are full risen and shopping is a national duty. In nostalgia shops there are those posters telling us to buy war bonds but now anything will do the money gets where it needs to go the love letter that is always delivered.

DEAR ANDRÉ BRETON:

I wrote you a poem.

Chreia

At this time there was an expectation of terror meaning cops in kevlar and the green civic garbage cylinders sealed with discs of steel.

At this time the new train ran to an underground forest sheathed in books.

This time many years after the towers near the sex of the city were found to be twin cruets of jizz and sang.

We all floated with the same specific gravity in the constantly moving stream of money as of this time.

As in time of strike there was quite a bit of garbage loose in the street not like an orang-utan in the Rue Morgue but it eddied and whorled at the edges of the seductively weeping stream.

I was riding a swan to the underground library or having sex with a swan under a shroud of words.

As of this time we kept a copy of the city in the library and another in the ether.

Constantly offered as a time of therefore but with a feeling of as.

Kevlar and carbines and garbage reduplicating into the quotidien in the time of the Plan Vigipirate.

Not more people in the street but more intensely as in the time of a transit strike promenading behind the veil of speech.

Around this time we thought of the skyline as new nature.

And through it flowed the invisible milk as through the ether and the sewers the milk of capital.

There was an expectation in everyday life.

It gathered in the dead spaces beside the endlessly grieving stream.

Of milk jizz and sang in the time of garbage in the vale of lang.

The shining order the burning simulations there are more of it.

DEAR BAADER MEINHOF (HUT RECORDINGS 1996):
After September 11 you were the only record I wanted to hear
made under the name Baader Meinhof by Luke Haines who is also
The Auteurs and Black Box Recorder printed on the compact disc
made in Holland THIS IS THE HATE SOCIALIST COLLECTIVE. Wanted to hear "Mogadishu" tablas and toy piano something like being
invited into a fever ("Captain Martyr Mahmoud says it's a twenty-
four-hour flight when the fireworks hit you Mogadishu on a beautiful Saturday night"). There's a song you could dance to "There's
Gonna Be an Accident" sprung synthetic bass giving way to sibilant violin and guitar the second verse begins "Do you remember
Petra Schelm?" No I don't though research tells me she was a hair-
dresser killed in a shoot-out 1971 after joining Red Army Faction.
In another song "The Petra Schelm Commando" appears elsewhere
"The Holger Meins Commando" from this I learn tradition of using
the name of fallen comrades I find this beautiful. An ecstasy. And
then at the last second of "Accident" very startling the bass comes
back much louder the bomb in the reggae song but before that
middle of second verse the moment which makes you decide at
which end of the sentence you imagine yourself standing: "you're
going home in a fucking ambulance."

DEAR MARJORIE PERLOFF:
Somewhat cool in November meaning the top up very disappointing on the rented convertible out to Pacific Palisades to find
you ("drive west young man" instructions said). It was hilarious

what you were saying about Adorno when we passed his former house strange fellow living above the ocean writing about astrology that's not how we think of him mostly. Mostly we didn't talk about your public letter exchange with the other famous intellectuals "had it coming" is a bit of a charade so is "The man who takes care of our garden." It was not the beginning not the ignition of some terrible technology the attacks were not the end of history (which also had a fine century) the argument it seems in the *London Review of Books* (now the debate must be everywhere this being one thing that terrorism means hijacking the discourse) was whether September 11 was a middle moment. Not whether it was deserved nor defensible because neither but was it narratively exchangeable? If not airplanes then something else is the question I suspect everyone in for example Gaza understands the concept they have all come to believe Chekhov-like gospel. America if you have an air war hanging above the mantel in Act I it must go off by Act III ("I had done no writing at any point when the U.S. was not bombing someone" says Juliana Spahr) everyone hustling for high ground from which to espy that moment before the first feeling of therefore. Marjorie I loved your house some Schindler and Lloyd Wright to it but the rooms in strange relation to each other torqued by the hillside a mystery of Los Angeles I kept thinking and the L.A. Basin spread out below us and the proscenium sun.

DEAR ROBESPIERRE:

When was terror not the order of the day?

Jilly
Stacey Levine

WHEN WE ARE SAFE AS INGROWN TREES, NO ONE SPIES
or comes close along. With a mountain of wreck slightly visible
through our window, each evening is tin-blue, tamped-down. We
have formed an anxious attachment to dawn. Jilly sits in her arm-
chair late, saying nothing, reviewing cases; I steal near, arrange
myself; I wait; the storm is not yet over, and so I believe it is time
for she and I to grow into each other, and become just the same—

Jilly never stops working; junior partners are loaded with propul-
sion and steam; she still barrels through the turreted streets downtown, quipping with colleagues, grabbing a drink, stopping to

observe holidays, to pray; from our home in the sky I watch the city with an insect's expert gaze, waiting for her to return, to sit with me. They say it is wrong to live for another person, but on most of these days I am helpless to stop it—

If necessary I will make her tea from rust, her dinner out of clay. After an event comes a mineral silence: the silver vase on our table, a flat evening of TV. At night in the bed I grow down, down, into the basement floor of my parents' home in order to fly away from them again, then again; Jilly listens softly as a moth breathing soot—

I still cannot believe she is all right. Jilly returns from work, lies in bed, tries to pray her way into the safest places: but god contains worms, I say; I laugh. I leave our apartment to buy an oak mule chest, more linen, a hurricane lamp. I wake before the pigeons who purr to Jilly in her sleep, telling her my clinging is not bad, that it makes me more who I really am—

Jilly bought a gargantuan vehicle as large as a small house, its flanks protected by curving blue metal, its exhaust pipe a vulgar hose pouring white volumes of fog, and upon this hose I must at times affix my own mouth, in order to live more dutifully, I think, alongside the world's continuous broadcasts of dust and adult greed—

Soon we will have a granite-topped counter, a crystal pitcher; I prepare dinner. It was always difficult to interpret, but Jilly's favorite food is creamed corn. She goes to her desk to pray, shutting me out; if her moods are unclear, I begin to lose my own shape.

At the table there is little to discuss; we eat chicken with silent fervor, then sweet popcorn and a creamy drink; the TV reports a man with a prosthetic face and knees—

Jilly buys a phone for her vehicle, then drives all Sunday, no destination in mind; I sit nearby, a blur in a tennis bracelet and skirt. Odors seem to fly from our bodies, it is hard to say: dust, sugar, brine, the mingling of the city's sweat and the opposite of this odor: sense. Shifting lanes, Jilly worries aloud that god's furthest edge is weak, that it might not contain enough strength; the vehicle's comfort leather makes us slump; I say we will grow closer as if one person, safe this way, no effort to it, and I believe we have the room to do it—

Long ago, Jilly was a chemist, boiling solutions and investigating salt; she sought something vapory from the world, then found me; she awakens with soft alkaline eyes like mine, a drape of dark hair behind her neck; when she leaves for work I am pasted to the window again, unsure what is part of me, what is not—

All these complex mental processes to glue Jilly inside me, or else keep her from getting out. She has had little occasion to be angry with me: I bought two pair of underwater shoes and a new dinnerware set. To depend on her meticulously is correct; to implant myself with the simplicity of corn; water follows the shortest possible route and only runs downhill; it effaces itself in the brightest sun—

She goes back to work in the dust-burdened city, built and rebuilt by ants; she will return aloof, worried about the most distal parts of god, his failure to intercede with the warring earth; I pile macaroni on a plate piece by piece. I dust our library, the new bookcases reaching as if ladders to our vulnerable roof; last year,

Jilly had a certain shape; she survived and now she is different; my shape changed likewise, but I don't care because Jilly made it—

The purplish night makes us thirsty for air; I do what she wishes, and all things that come naturally to her and nothing is wrong; the city has no sleep; and tonight, there is Jilly standing nude, worry the very currency of our bedroom; I hold her wrist in my fingers very late, feeling the velour of our uncertain, empty legs—

Through the transparent bedspread I see our pale skin, our postponed smile, and something wholly inviolable.

Your Name Here
Beth Lisick

THE BURNING WAS THE THING THAT REALLY SURPRISED her. How so much burning could happen so fast. Rachel had always taken a certain pride in the peaceable kingdom that was her digestive system, but then, eight months pregnant and wide awake at 3 a.m., she was wrenched by an internal fire chunneling its way from her stomach up to her throat. She wondered if the expression "acid reflux" appearing on television and in magazine advertisements was a new thing or, in typical fashion, had she just started paying attention now that it applied to her? The only other term she had heard for describing such a thing was "l'bob," a word taught to her one afternoon in junior high by her boyfriend as they held hands in the quad under the ginko tree.

"Man, O Manishevitz," he said. "I keep l'bobbing that enchirito I had for lunch."

Without much prodding, he explained that it stood for "li'l bit of barf." At the time, she thought it would have been so romantic if he had invented the word on the spot, just for her, but she was too shy to ask. Now, twenty years and no subsequent mentions later, she could be fairly certain he had.

What really bothered Rachel, at that moment, wasn't so much the l'bob, but the alarm. Edmund the Chicken Guy would be picking her up at 5:30 a.m. and she could tell he was the type to mean sharp. She was supposed to be waiting for him on the front stoop. How could she do this on no sleep? She had almost promised to whip them up a batch of banana nut muffins for breakfast, but luckily she bit her tongue, having finally learned that lesson. How many times in her life had she indiscriminately promised her editor or her doctor or the dry cleaning lady a jar of homemade pesto or a tray of pralines only not to follow through. She liked the way it sounded so magnanimous and quirky in the moment, like something a waif in a French film would do, *Next time we meet, I shall bring you a plate of buttery madeleines*, but Rachel also knew she used these promises as a crutch when wrapping up conversations. When she finalized her plans with Edmund the week before, she just left things at "See ya Tuesday morning" or something she was reasonably sure she could deliver. Her impending motherhood was definitely making her face up to some of her tired old shit.

Edmund the Chicken Guy was her last assignment before maternity leave. (Maternity leave. Now that was a joke. She worked as a columnist for the city's largest daily paper for six years at this point, but because she was an independent contractor, she didn't get so much as a modestly priced seasonal bouquet or an e-greeting out of them. She figured it was the price she paid for having a decent, steady writing gig, but she still enjoyed complaining about it to anyone who would listen.) The column was called "Your Name Here" and the schtick was that each week she'd go on some kind of minor adventure and write a thousand words about it. It could be anything from fly-fishing with rehabilitated Crips to driving monster trucks with drag kings. One week she'd appear as an extra in a Jennifer Lopez movie and the next she'd spend the solstice with pagan astronomers. Gun shows, doll shows, dog shows, boat shows, mall openings. This week was tame. This week was chicken.

Edmund the Chicken Guy was one of those local celebrities along the lines of Mary the Pot Brownie Lady or Raj the Mango Lassi Man. He supplied fried chicken to just about every corner store in North Oakland and South Berkeley, including Family Town, the shop run by a Yemeni family on Rachel's corner. Even Beatrice Daniels, the world-renowned food maven, waxed on about Edmund's chicken even though it wasn't free range.

All Rachel had to do that morning was help fry up chickens and go on some deliveries. She was already positive the column would wind up a bit treacly, too heartwarming, but that was pregnancy for you. Crying at the long-distance commercials and bursting into tears when she felt the little invader kicking her in the ribs in the middle of the night.

Maybe it was 4:30 a.m. when she decided to forget about trying to sleep anymore. She leaned over her husband, snapped off the alarm and then lay back down. Ezra was snoring again. She kicked him a bit, hoping he would wake up so she could ask him to bring her some baking soda and water for her stomach. He stopped snoring, but didn't stir. The room was yellow from the streetlamp and she looked at his face awhile, before rolling her huge, ripe body out of bed. It took her a few tries to work up the momentum to propel herself into the bathroom. Sitting on the toilet in the dark, for what must have been the sixth time in as many hours, the utter irrefutability of what was happening to her hit a new level. Forever someone's mother.

The house smelled like last night's calamari steaks. It was fishy enough to cement her lingering quease and Rachel was reminded of what she'd been telling her friends since she found out she was pregnant. If you step foot in my house one day, she said, and it smells like a combination of sour milk, maple syrup, and diapers, don't be afraid to tell me. *I want to know.*

About five 'til five she went out on the front porch and waited for Edmund. September still felt like summer, even at this hour. Rachel listened for the boat bells out in the bay, but she couldn't hear any that morning. It was too bad. Hearing sounds from the water made her feel like she lived somewhere exotic. She decided Berkeley may have been eccentric, but it was hardly exotic. Her belly jumped. The baby had the hiccups again and she thought maybe she'd call her brother in New York and tell him about it. She had a bunch of free long-distance minutes on her cell phone and he'd be awake by now, wouldn't he? And wasn't his birthday coming up? The anal, uptight Virgo. God, she had been so relieved when she found out her son's due date fell well inside Libra. One Virgo male in the family was enough. Forget it.

Why was her hand clamped so tightly around her coffee? Her hands were bloated. Was she nervous? She still didn't feel like a journalist. She felt like her job annoyed people. Instead of looking at it like she was giving Edmund some publicity or she was letting her readers know about a cool small business, she felt invasive. She figured Edmund would much rather be going about his daily routine without having to drive over there to pick her up and be shadowed all day long.

A big, blue step van came rubbering up the street. No logo or anything. Rachel could hear muted slow jams coming out of the open doorway and proceeded to hoist herself off the porch.

"Hey, Edmund!" Her cheeriness sounded phony and she knew it.

"How you doing this morning? How's that little basketball?" he said, nodding his head at her belly.

"All right. I'm all right," she said getting in. "A little sick, I guess."

"Hope you like the music," he said. "This tape's been stuck in here for five months now."

A man's voice sang, *Give it to me. Give it to me. Give it to me.*

"One song," Edmund said.

"There's only one song on the tape?" Rachel said.

"Cassingle."

HIS KITCHEN WAS A TINY INDUSTRIAL SPACE IN EMERY-ville with a metal roll-up door, and as soon as Rachel walked in, she said something she felt stupid about. Something like, "So this is where Edmund's famous fried chicken is made!"

"Yep," he said, glancing around the space, nodding. And then, "Are you all right?"

She sat down on a stool and let out a big sigh.

"You know, we don't have to do this today." He went to the walk-in refrigerator and came out with a stack of boxes. "If you're too sick."

Instead of making chicken and taking notes, Rachel spent the rest of the morning lying down on a cot in the kitchen while Edmund gave her the play-by-play. *Now I'm pulling out extraneous quills*, he was saying. *Now I'm getting the batter ready. Fresh fat! That's the key!* Rachel kept drifting off to sleep, dreaming about the baby. In her dreams the baby could always talk. He was always making demands.

"Dead as dirt out here," Edmund said once they got back in the truck with the chicken. "Dead as dirt!"

Give it to me. Give it to me. Give it to me.

THE CHICKEN MAN HAD HIS VERY OWN SOUND TRACK. Rachel opened her eyes and looked out the door. It didn't feel like lunchtime on a weekday. There was usually a line of tech workers with badges around their necks standing outside the juice place. It was like a national holiday the way the stoplights went on changing for nobody.

"I'm taking you home," he said. "It'd be bad for business if you delivered during a delivery."

Rachel had to look at him to see that he was teasing her.

"Or more likely, if I threw up," she said, brushing a sweaty strand of hair from her forehead. "Let me just stop in at Family Town with you. Just so I get an idea what the deliveries are like. I can extrapolate from there."

"Extrapolate, huh?"

"Okay," she conceded. "Make shit up."

He laughed. "You can make up all the shit you want. As long as it's good shit."

They parked the truck in the green zone in front of the corner store and Edmund hauled out a tray of chicken.

It wasn't until they got up close that they noticed the metal gate was locked, but the glass door behind it was open.

Edmund peered in and saw Amir and the two Mohammeds, father and son, sitting behind the counter watching TV.

"Open up in there! I got your chicken!"

The teenager came and unlocked the gate.

"Hey, Mohammed," Rachel said. "What's up?"

"Can you believe it?" he said. "Did you see?"

Edmund set the tray on the counter and Rachel walked over to the cash register and looked at the screen. New York. She felt the baby's head rotate in her pelvis like a small globe turning inside a cage. It had always been a strange sensation and she silently marveled at the fact that she had almost grown used to it.

Requiem with Marinara
Michael Hood

AFTER THE SHOP-WORN DAYS UNDER THE DOG STAR OF
August, Indian summer brings airs of change. Also dahlias, sun-
flowers, and the little-old-lady miracle of hydrangeas purpling up
from lime-green. There's a preponderance of zucchinis: we ran-
sack the cookbooks for ways to eat the plentiful blossoms of their
unborn. It's a fat time.

Except for some inedible shrubs in my yard that I largely ig-
nore, tomato vines are the only life forms I'm fully responsible for,
unless you count two middle-aged cats as fat and sedentary as I.

Growing tomatoes is a challenge in the Pacific Northwest. The
sun is unreliable, spring doesn't always show up; summer nights

can be cold and sometimes it rains for the whole month of July. We always feel blessed living here—that's one of the rules. But God's abiding love doesn't always provide warmth—at least not the kind that shortens the growing season for Mediterranean fruit-bearing flora.

We try to trick God or at least try to help Him by seeking out tomato varieties hybridized for Siberia or buying electrical gadgets that warm the soil. We fashion personal greenhouses for each precious plant with fabric developed for camping on the moon. We feed them imported seafood more expensive than we'd buy for ourselves and swear by techniques thought up by old women in Wisconsin. The earliest tomato gets the biggest prize, but large and perfect fetch bragging rights, too. As often as not, we lose the battle, reaping only a few or ones blighted or puny.

It's a sport, a challenge; keenly competitive between suburban men, I'm told, but I don't do it competitively—I hardly know my neighbors. I live in a quiet, well-groomed city neighborhood of single-family dwellings, isolated in my writerly life. Sowing, reaping, and playing in the dirt is a way to exercise a part of my brain that otherwise would be as flabby as my old body.

Calendar note for Tuesday, Sept. 11, 2001: *Start tomato sauce.*

After all these years, I've got it down. I cut back the bushes, leaving only the tomatoes that promise to ripen in the few sunlit weeks left. With the leaves gone, the thick naked vines blacken in their wire cages but are loaded with dark green fruits turning orange and red, none smaller than a golf ball.

The kitchen table is full of red ones, ripe and ready. I've peeled the onions from a huge bag that I've bought; I've husked a pound of garlic. There's a bag each of oregano, marjoram, and basil leaves torn from the stems; and fresh bay leaves from the mountain laurel in my next-door neighbor's yard.

I have two restaurant-sized pots I drag out every year. The

shorter one is for dipping the tomatoes into boiling water for peeling. The other is heavier and taller and is for cooking the sauce. I have a long-handled wooden paddle that reaches the bottom so I don't burn my fingers. I make the sauce in batches as the tomatoes ripen, putting it in jars, giving it away, and eating little else for weeks. It's a major ritual of my ritualized life.

The phone rang early that morning and woke me. It was Kathryn.

"Turn on the TV," she said.

I got up and stumbled into the living room and saw the towers, one smoking crazily like a trick cigar. I sat down transfixed.

The phone rang after the second one was hit. It was Kathryn again.

"What are you doing?" she asked.

"Watching," I said.

"Can I come over?"

"You can help me make my sauce," I said.

"Okay," she said.

We're friends of maybe ten years. A pretty woman, my age; conservative in nature, liberal in politics; given to wearing sweats and her long hair clipped up in a calculatedly messy French roll. Most of what she's about is calculated; she's into cycling, recycling, composting, a women's book club, and fundraising for Planned Parenthood. She's a consultant of some kind; she lives nearby. We speak frequently, but rarely in person—it's one of those caffeinated phone relationships born of the neediness that comes of working at home.

We've talked a lot, but not really talked. Her Corgi, Bernie, died last year, she wept on the phone. My daughter had a cyst, I fretted, she sympathized—that sort of thing—a few real things shared, but never in the same room at the same time.

I opened the back door and in she came, wearing prefaded bib overalls, a dark blue T-shirt, and the rubber clogs she wears in the garden. She looked small and obviously upset. I put her to work smashing the garlic with the flat of a knife as I dipped colander batches of tomatoes into the boiling water. I dumped each batch onto the long counter, then we gripped with thumb and paring knife and zipped off the curling peel from the little Xs I'd cut in their bottoms.

From the tiny screen of my kitchen TV, the horror came in batches from New York in the repetitious manner we've come to expect in crises from the town crier of national TV. Coiffed heads apologizing for any moment of dead air. "Over to you, Bill." The crushing footage rolled over and over like a porno loop, the marauding planes plunging into and deflowering the skyline; a money shot of fire and sparks. The same smudged, terrified people mouthing the same words and running the same streets with the same shock and disbelief. The towers came down, one by one.

Barely speaking, we cut the onions. First in halves, laid cutside flat on the table, then down-slices an inch apart; next, one or two horizontal cuts not quite through the core; then the final vertical chop that makes the half-inch dice.

To Northwesterners, New York is a kind of steak, the home of the Yankees. We don't have collective disdain for New Yorkers like some in other parts of the country do. We're so far away in so many ways, we're not mad at New Yorkers for the usual complaints: arrogance, xenophobia, rudeness—all this is lost on us. The exposed humanity of those scared and bedraggled brokers, executive assistants, and janitors was no surprise—not to us.

The sounds in my kitchen were knives against the cutting boards, buildings crashing down, screams. A cat sat on a chair earnestly watching our every move, hoping something edible would fall to the floor.

We caught the coiffed minds coming off their tethers, ever so slightly, ever so professionally. A choke-up, an eye-wipe. "Over to you, Bill." An interminable procession of cooler heads relieved the anchors: retired military men, former officials, authors of the odd book previously ignored, now vitally significant.

Death and onions. We wiped our own tears with the backs of our wrists and the clean corners of our aprons. We couldn't look at each other, Kathryn and I. Be-aproned and stinking of onions, we held on to our precious composure; fearful on a fine sunny day. Far away, death and destruction, yet closer than ever before.

Kathryn put down her knife, hands folded over it on the cutting board. I stopped and looked up. She was staring at me, her eyes awash.

"Martin?" She said my name like it was a last breath; I opened my arms and she fell into them. We stood hanging on to each other for I don't know how long; shaking and sobbing as one; gulping full-throated, snotty, tearful, and sweaty in the hot kitchen. It was about losses: the lives, the illusion of safety, yesterday.

I snapped off the TV; "Let's sit down."

I started toward the living room, but she said, "Let's go to your bedroom and get away from the glare."

The bed was still unmade from my leap up from the yesterday that was only this morning. I pulled the cover up, and kicked off a cat. She stepped out of her clogs, pulled the shades, closed tight the curtains, and shut the door. It was like night in the room, with just enough light to see her open and tear-streaked face.

We lay down and I held her for a long time in the cool dark. We didn't talk, but after a while, she shifted her face around and we kissed; the first thing we'd ever done that wasn't painstakingly platonic. Timorous at first, it slowly became a real kiss. Then we were kissing with forty years of tongues and lips; putting our hands inside each other's clothes and grabbing each other like ten thousand feared dead. There was the fire of lust and desperation. It was a great relief.

Our clothes came off piecemeal, and then it was all wet membranes and fistfuls of hair; our clunky old bodies straining; voices crying out in pleasure and despair. She made no flattering noises and I responded in kind. I just wanted to crawl into the warm hole of her and not come out until Christmas morning. She sought her own kind of oblivion and found some, I think, though I don't know the specifics. As I said, we'd never talked much and we didn't start then.

THE PICTURES FROM THE PENTAGON CAME WITH THE brusque warmth of garlic browning in good olive oil. While smoke rose from the capital, Kathryn rubbed the herbs, I seeded and chopped the tomatoes. Local coifs feared for the Space Needle, and the onions smelled glorious as they smothered in the pot with the herbs and the garlic.

The sauce, its aromatic parts finally assembled, simmered on the stove. On TV, the planes defiled the buildings again and again; talking heads droned on and on. Kathryn and I lay in our dark refuge and fucked like crazed weasels.

I PUT ON MY OLD ROBE, AND A POT ON A BURNER FOR THE fettucine. Kathryn's hair was uncalculatedly down and she wore an old butter-yellow Arrow shirt of mine. She shoved the tomatoes aside on the table to make space for forks and spoons while I grated reggiano, tossed bibb leaves with oil and balsamic. We sat down to huge plates of pasta with the fresh, bright red sauce ladled from the cooking pot.

"Pass the cheese," I said.

I'D STAND AT THE STOVE LADLING SAUCE INTO JARS; THE planes still flying, the people still crying and running. She'd come up behind me and put her hand inside my sauce-spattered robe and say, "come" in a voice so different than I'd ever heard out of her. She'd lead me dreamy into the darkness and the damp bed. We'd start another session of lips and hips and soft hardness groping up one side and down the other on raw knees and abraded elbows and with sore tongues. We demanded control and relinquished it with equal ferocity. It was the honesty of fresh tomatoes and splayed-out flesh begging and demanding. Her old breasts, my old belly. We jiggled, we quivered, we were alive. *Mangia*!

THE SAUCE SIMMERED DARKER AND RICHER. WE DIPPED bread in it and ate it with pancetta. We poured it on orrechiette and tossed it with penne. There was plenty of cheese.

And so it went as the sun went down, then up, then down again. Despite everything, summer still slid slowly into fall.

We had a lifetime together in two days; a successful marriage without courtship, promises; nor cycle of illusion and disillusion. We never took each other for granted; hopes were un-had. It was love all right, true and pure—we just used it all up. We climbed each steel hill of here and now, to lie breathless and famished at the top, then plunged down the other side again.

There was submission and sadness and safety. There was anger. It was wild neurological consolation. It was ecstatic relief and distraction, a clamoring to quell the flames of fear and the fear of flames.

Once, after we'd stopped thrashing and calling out, I sensed she was crying though I couldn't see her face in the darkness.

"Are you OK?"

"No."

"What's the matter?"

"It's the baby," she said.

I didn't have to ask what baby. And she didn't have to say, because every baby was heartbreaking that day. The dead baby, the orphaned baby, the baby who'd have to hear the story sooner rather than later. She wept for the baby who'd live in the ashes, or grow up in the hostile scar where a skyline once was. She cried for the baby we'd never have.

I felt dismal and reached up to pluck a nipple between thumb and forefinger.

"Hungry?" I asked.

"I'm starving," she said.

In violence, we forget who we are.

MARY McCARTHY | *On the Contrary*

The Real War
Ken Kesey

I COULD HAVE WRITTEN THIS BETTER ON SEPTEMBER 11, the day it was happening, if I could have written.

Everything was so clear that day, so unencumbered by theories and opinions, by thought, even. It just was. All the newborn images, ripped fresh from that monstrous pair of thighs thrust smoking into the morning sunshine. All just amateur cameras allowing us to witness the developing drama in sweeping handheld seizures. All just muffled mikes recording murmured gasps...

Now, more than a week has passed. The cameras are in the grips of professionals, and the microphones are in the hands of the media. Bush has just finished his big talk to Congress and the men in suits are telling us what the men in uniforms are going to do to the men in turbans if they don't turn over the men in hiding. The talk was planned to prepare us for war. It's going to get messy, everyone agrees. It's going to last for years and probably decades, everybody ruefully concedes. Nothing will ever be the same, everybody eventually declares.

Then why does it all sound so familiar? So cozy and comfortable? Was it the row after row of dark blue suits, broken only by grim clusters of high-ranking uniforms all drizzling ribbons and medals? If everything has changed (as we all knew it had on that first day) why does it all wear the same old outfits and say the same old words?

Because we are talking about not just war, this time, but about the war above the war; the Real War. This war has already been waged and it's not between the U.S. and the Taliban, or between the Muslims and Israelis, or any of the familiar forces, but between the ancient gut-wrenching bone-breaking flesh-slashing way things have always been and the timorous and fragile way things might begin to be. Could begin to be. Must begin to be, if our lives and our children's lives are ever, someday in the up-heaving future, to know honest peace.

True, the warriors on our side of this Real War seem few and flimsy, but we have a secret advantage: we don't fight our battle out of Hate. Anger, yes, if we have to, but anger is enough. Hate is the flag the other side battles beneath. It is the ancient flag of fire and blood and agony, and it waves over the graves of millions and millions.

Our side's flag is a thin, air-light blue, drifting almost unseen against the sky. Our military march is a meadowlark's song among the dandelions. And our Real War rally isn't given any space at the United States Congress.

Where can you hear it? Lots of places, if you listen. Across

Dairy Queen counters. In careful post office talk. In e-mail is where I've been hearing it, for days now, and the entries are getting clearer and more numerous. At first only ten or fifteen. Then fifty or sixty. And this morning, more than three hundred!

Here are a few chunks and pieces that I printed out:

This bit from *Charles Daniel*'s e-mail (it came on the first day): "I'm still in a state of shock to see the Trade Towers fall and the Pentagon, the very symbol of military power in this nation, on fire. It's like watching a science fiction movie…"

From *Michael Moore*: "Will we ever get to the point that we realize we will be more secure when the rest of the world isn't living in poverty so we can have nice running shoes? Let's mourn, let's grieve, and when it's appropriate, let's examine our contribution to the unsafe world we live in. It doesn't have to be like this…"

Valerie Stevenson: "Of late, I've tried to adopt a philosophy of loving everyone unconditionally. Tuesday morning that went out the window as feelings of outrage, revenge, and retribution flooded my soul. Then I realized just how easy it is for these terrorists to control my feelings…"

Deepak Chopra: "Isn't something terribly wrong when jihads and wars develop in the name of God. Isn't God invoked with hatred in Ireland, Sri Lanka, India, Pakistan, Israel, Palestine? Is there not a deep wound at the heart of humanity?"

Apache Lani: "This insensitivity allows people to live in comfort, bubbly making judgments about others' welfare that has absolutely nothing to offer toward societal progress, health, or even self-respect. I know in my heart that our country is guilty of the above…"

Usman Farman: "I was on my back. This massive cloud that was approaching. I normally wear a pendant around my neck, inscribed with an Arabic prayer for safety, similar to the cross. A Hasidic Jewish man came up to me and held the pendant in his hand and looked at it. He read the Arabic out loud and what he said next I will never forget: Brother, if you don't mind, there's a cloud of glass coming at us. Grab my hand and let's get the hell out of here!"

Radio Havana, Cuba: "…there is no joy here in Cuba at the events of Tuesday. No one is cheering or holding impromptu block parties to celebrate the most astonishing act of terrorism in history against, what has been for Cuba, an implacable enemy for 40 years. There is, instead, a profound feeling of shock, revulsion, and compassion—and very real apprehension about the cries for vengeance that emanate from every corner of the White House and the U.S. Congress…

Few doubt that Washington has just suffered the consequences of its actions across the globe. Even if Osama bin Laden is found responsible, the people of the U.S. should know that he was previously trained and used by the CIA in its war against the former government of Afghanistan. George W. Bush will seek to take the war to another part of the globe where more civilians can pay for the death of U.S. civilians without their blood and disfigured bodies being shown on CNN. No solution will be forthcoming in the destruction of those deemed responsible. The enemy will still be there because the enemy comes from within…"

J. Zwemer: "I am a former Marine, and would like to say that all that has happened is sickening to me. I feel that our gov't has found its way into yet another major conflict. This bloodshed has got to stop! I know it's hard to think of peace when there are so many reasons to be angry."

Carey: "…after my own street I walked one more block south, bringing me about five blocks away from the World Trade Center. There was a line of firemen, police officers, military, and press. There was little to see with the smoke. The most shocking thing, I realized, is that there is an entire area of downtown that is abjectly unlivable and terribly dangerous. There is what I would estimate to be 10 square blocks of utter human suffering.

I have been told by a lot of people in the past 48 hours that they love me. Listen to the gift I have been given: this tragedy reminds me that I get to travel this Earth understanding how loved I am. Thank you, all."

Greg: "I don't like the word 'retaliation.' I think 'law enforcement' is the proper term. Most of the people in Afghanistan or Iraq or wherever were just born there and try to live the best life possible under the circumstances..."

The Dalai Lama (to President George Bush): "On behalf of the Tibetan people I would like to convey our deepest condolence and solidarity with the American people during this painful time. I am confident that the United States, as a great and powerful nation, will be able to overcome this present tragedy...It may seem presumptuous on my part, but I personally believe we need to think seriously whether violent action is the right thing to do and in the greater interest of the nation and people in the long run. I believe violence will only increase the cycle of violence."

Carolyn Adams García: "If the Islamic peoples of the world are pushed into coalescing and cooperating against a common enemy that has no respect for them and their culture, we will be in a war with over a billion people. People we have been training and selling weapons to, so that our own warplanes, guns, and missiles will be used against us."

Tamin Ansary: "I am from Afghanistan, and even though I've lived here for 35 years I've never lost track of what's going on over there. Some say, why don't the Afghans rise up and overthrow the Taliban? The answer is they're starved, exhausted, damaged, and incapacitated. A few years ago the United Nations estimated that there are 500,000 disabled orphans in Afghanistan—a country with no economy, no food. Millions of Afghans are widows of the approximately two million men killed during the war with the Soviets…We come to the question of bombing Afghanistan back to the stone age. It's already been done. The Soviets took care of that. Make Afghans suffer? They're already suffering. Level their houses? Done. Destroy their infrastructure? There is no infrastructure. Cut them off from medicine and health care? Too late."

Lama Zopa Rinpoche: "May all the people's hearts be filled with loving kindness and the thought to only benefit and not harm. May the sun of peace and happiness arise and may any wars that are happening stop immediately."

Suzie and Robert: "We pray for those who imagine themselves to be the sole owners of the knowledge of God. Let the shroud of hatred be lifted from their souls, the veil of bigotry be lifted from their eyes, and the fire of anger in their hearts be quenched by the healing love. We pray that our leaders be guided to those actions that are just and will spare the lives of innocents. We pray for comfort and healing for all those who were injured and the families and friends of all those who lost their lives—and we pray for a global unity in which there is recognition of God as love, love without condition, love unending."

Lauren and Rick: "As I was passing the firehouse this guy stuck his hand out to my dog's nose and she licked his hand and he said, 'Thanks, I really needed that.' I looked up and there stood a man crying, gently…"

There's a bunch more, but you get the idea. All openhearted e-mail. And all certainly slanted, because they were sent to our *intrepidtrips.com* Web site. These people know who we are and what we believe in, and it can't help but make you a little proud as well as a little humble. But it's more than that.

Well, I can remember Pearl Harbor. I was only six but that morning is forever smashed into my memory like a bomb into a metal deck. Hate for the Japanese nation still smolders occasionally from this hole. This 9/11 nastiness is different. There is no nation to blame. There are no diving Zeros, no island-grabbing armies, no seas filled with battleships and carriers. Just a couple dozen batty guys with box knives and absolute purpose. Dead now. Vaporized. Of course we want their leaders, but I'll be damned if I can see how we're going to get those leaders by deploying our aircraft carriers and launching our mighty air power so we can begin bombing the crippled orphans in the rocky, leafless, already bombed-out rubble of Afghanistan.

As the Dust Settles: Three Essays
Peter Coyote

Pausing for Thought
September 18, 2001

Now that the initial rush of grief and rage has abated a bit, I must acknowledge a growing unease about the rhetoric of retaliation and war I hear unanimously from our leaders and a too uncritical media. Since Congress has now authorized the President to spend as much as he sees fit and to punish whomever he likes, it seems important to request a deliberative pause to consider what a "war against terrorism" means and implies.

A "network" is any group of people who align themselves for a common purpose. Tim McVeigh and Terry Nichols (and three others the government could not make a sufficient case against) were a "terrorist network" pursuing a vengeful agenda. What could soldiers or bombs have accomplished to inhibit their capacity to act? Like the Olympics bombing in Atlanta (where the perpetrator is still at large, by the way), the terror in Oklahoma City occurred in our own country, where we speak the language and spend more on domestic intelligence than many countries spend on their entire economies. What makes us think "a war" will be more successful in places where we are constrained by enemies and political realities; where we cannot put espionage agents on the ground, and do not know the language, customs, and terrain?

It is an understandable impulse to desire vengeance when hurt, and it is in this sense that I understand many of the declarations of the President and Congress. Nevertheless, one must ask—does retaliation serve the best interests of our people? If not, what might? It appears that bin Laden secreted "sleepers" into America who lived invisibly until they were activated to a task. The nineteen men who so traumatized us did not fit our comfortable profile of addled and "brainwashed" men. They were self-organized, multilingual, educated, technologically proficient warriors of fixed purpose sustained for years before sacrificing themselves. Knowing what they cherished enough to die for would be the most reasonable place to begin any counter-terrorist response, would it not? Lacking that knowledge, what logic indicates that military campaigns in the Middle East will make us safe from such suicidal agents and not simply inspire new soldiers to replace those who have fallen?

No matter how deranged he may appear to us, Osama bin Laden has a goal and has devised a strategy to achieve it. To foil his intentions, we must at least understand them. The assertions of motiveless evil or simple jealousy of Americans propagated by the media does not suffice for an answer. Bin Laden, like Saddam Hussein, was once our ally, trained, armed, and funded by our government. We did not think either of them deranged and unstable then. Why have our relationships with both of these men soured? Why are Palestinians burning our flag? Why do so many in the Middle East apparently hate us so much? Might the problem reside in our policies there? Can average Americans identify and understand those policies?

When bin Laden asserts that America has little regard for the interests and lives of Muslims, unfortunately he has ample evidence to bolster his claims. He can remind Muslims how their cousins in Eastern Europe were denied arms to defend themselves against Milosevic's ethnic cleansing, and then bore the brunt of his genocidal fury when we initiated our bombing of Yugoslavia. Ordinary Palestinian citizens impoverished in Israeli refugee camps would need no urging to be convinced that the United States supports Israel too unequivocally, no matter how egregiously or even illegally Israel behaves toward them. It is tragically easy for bin Laden to offer himself as their fist.

In Baghdad alone, he could point to the 200,000 civilians like our own who died and the others who suffered as we are now suffering, from our bombing of a major metropolitan area. He can cite UN estimates that an additional 500,000 children have died of an epidemic of cancer from the million uranium-tipped shells we fired there, or from diseases related to our destruction of the civilian water systems. We make it too easy for bin Laden to be the avenger for their anguish and rage.

People with something to live for are not eager to commit suicide. What are the effects of our policies on ordinary citizens in the Middle East? If they do not support them, we must attend to their grievances if we ever hope to sever connections to the thugs claiming to represent them. Bin Laden argues that the West is anti-Muslim. What could serve his interests better than further violence levied against people already traumatized by us and our allies, proving that we are the enemy he says we are?

A "war against terrorism" has a nice ring, but let us not misunderstand that what is being described is a war against ideas and intentions, and these are not targets that can be bombed or burned away. This is a war for the "hearts and minds" of people we have underestimated and ignored for too long. We made a tragic and costly mistake in Vietnam by proceeding in ignorance of the culture, belief systems, and resolve of those we were determined to vanquish. I pray that we do not hurl ourselves into the same abyss again. It is not the way to honor our dead. It is not the way to live.

This piece was written in that first week after September 11, when the shock of being assaulted and the grief over our wounded prompted so many column inches of outrage and violent rhetoric from men who would never leave their offices. Having lived through the Vietnam War, I knew that others would pay the tab for their intemperance, and wrote this piece to call for a meditative pause to sophisticate and focus our response. While I fervently believe that a response was called for, I harbored hopes at the time I wrote this that the United States would work through the United Nations (and under world law) to assemble a truly multiracial, multireligious, multinational task force, so that any punitive expedition would be made in the name of civilization—and not merely Western civilization.

Words, Bullets, and Bombs

In 1994 Steven Emerson, a reporter and counter-terrorism expert, produced a videotape called *Jihad in America*. On the tape, recorded at charitable fund-raisers for Muslim causes in a number of American cities, Muslim clerics appeal openly for the murder of Jews and "death to America." Further footage shows young children at Muslim summer camps in the Midwest learning songs about becoming martyrs and killing Jews.

One should not judge Islam by its fanatics any more than they judge Christianity by the Ku Klux Klan. However, the bombing of the World Trade Center affirms that the devastation, death, and posttraumatic stress brought to America that day were direct expressions of such previously stated intentions.

Our courts have correctly ruled that even burning the nation's flag while demonstrating for political change is symbolic speech and therefore protected. Such acts are essentially an appeal to voters or legislators and inherently supportive of the democratic process. There is a critical difference between such speech and exhorting others to murder. Prudence requires of us the assumption that a person demanding our murder would do so if offered the opportunity. Hitler stated his intentions clearly in *Mein Kampf* and the cost of ignoring or dismissing them as rhetoric is obvious today. The domestic terrorists who destroyed the Federal Building in Oklahoma City and the Islamic terrorists who bombed New York and Washington were both nurtured in a broth of toxic, murderous speech. What separates a death threat from the act of murder is largely ability.

The demonstrations against the World Trade Organization (WTO) and inequities in the global economy were met with overwhelming force: tear gas, truncheons, rubber bullets, mass arrests, the raiding of group headquarters, and infiltration by provocateurs. Environmentalists, demonstrating peaceably, have had their eyelids pried open so that red-pepper spray could blister them. Such groups were raising legitimate policy issues and demanding that they be given wider debate. They were utilizing every available option to change public policy except violence and calls to murder those who disagree with them. Policy makers had determined that such groups were more fitting for surveillance and intervention than the home-grown militia members calling for murder and race-war or the local networks of Islamic terrorists or wannabes. There is an obvious and unsettling reason why such a disparity of attention exists, and it is probably because groups like the WTO protesters and environmentalists are open, democratic, consensus-oriented, and easy to infiltrate, while militias and terrorist networks are more difficult and dangerous.

Public safety would be better served if governmental hyper-vigilance was redirected toward protagonists and institutions that truly threaten our national well-being. Demonstrations that might alter the status of elected officials or challenge current distributions of wealth are not armed insurrections. Inciting people to murder, however, is a dangerous act and at the very least "reckless disregard for the safety of others." As such, it is no longer protected speech. The question of why people demonstrating for change are so aggressively targeted for intervention and people advocating murder and race-war are not is one that deserves wider public debate.

Lethal fringe groups are taking advantage of our carelessness, not our freedoms. Not all of these are Muslim, by any means. William Pierce's novel *The Turner Diaries*, found in Timothy McVeigh's car when he was arrested, prophesies "The Day of the Rope" when "race-mixers" will be hung from lampposts. One might have thought such local varieties of terrorists particularly vulnerable to infiltration by one of the government agencies receiving billions of tax dollars for such monitoring. Yet, after the demolition of the Marine barracks in Lebanon and two embassies in Africa, the destruction of the Federal building in Oklahoma City, and two attacks on the World Trade Center, one must question whether undue attention paid to a broad spectrum of social-change organizations has not diluted the government's capacity to respond to enemies of its people (to be distinguished from critics of its gluttons). Unsettling as it may be, it is necessary to speculate if these agencies are up to the task required of them, and if not, what steps and policies must be adopted to make them capable of deterring implacable and skillful foes.

It is time to distinguish between those who act to destroy our political system and those who protest to sway public opinion. Murderous thugs require surveillance and constraint more urgently than the hundreds of thousands currently detained for self-medicating with illicit substances, or infiltrated for trying to save old-growth redwoods or to protect domestic jobs. Guests who call for the death of their hosts need to be put out. Neither will occur while policy makers are strong-arming and muzzling legitimate debate to the degree that they overlook those building the bombs and loading the ammunition.

I wrote this essay for the San Francisco Chronicle *around the time the attack on Afghanistan began. I found myself amazed by the degree to which our own institutions float over the muddles they've caused, virtually immune to criticism. The destruction of Pan Am flight 103 and TWA flight 800 initiated not one but two airline safety hearings in Congress. Yet when the World Trade Center towers were destroyed I hadn't heard a single media reference to this fact, or that the recommendations produced by those hearings even existed. No one has hijacked an Israeli airliner since 1974. The technology and processes to ensure that safety are known. They are, however, expensive. Instead of spending the money to do the job right, we have initiated a host of modest, cosmetic procedures—taking the nail clippers from ten-year-olds, while baggage is stowed in the hold un-x-rayed.*

The same kind of thing happens in the realm of intelligence agencies, which are extremely effective at infiltrating nonviolent protest groups that are usually operating in the public's best interest by attempting to curtail the excesses of the nation's "manufacturing class." Now that 9/11 has raised the stakes, it seems to me more pertinent than ever to create clearer definitions and distinctions about which groups are and which groups are not enemies. Then we need to treat them accordingly.

Repeating History

There is a synchronicity between the 1973 oil crunch, the watershed event that began the dissolution of the selfless social activism of the 1960s, and the current tragedy of 9/11. Both the oil crunch and the destruction of the World Trade Center towers offered the uneasy authorities a "two-fer"—an objective situation requiring a political response—which simultaneously camouflaged a parallel political agenda not directly related to it. This would never pass public muster in ordinary times. In the case of the oil crunch, what was essentially a hiccup in global distribution systems was manipulated into a general public anxiety where Americans were led to doubt whether or not there was "enough to go around" to support the expansive, revolutionary experiments of the 1960s. Long lines at the gas pump deflected the focus from the society to the self, and became the environment in which the social contract, in place since the 1930s, might be reformulated under the guise of a national emergency to pull the rug from beneath the feet of an active, socially committed generation publicly reexamining priorities and standards of social behavior.

In current terms the horrors of September 11 were an objective fact requiring an expanded public dialogue about internal security as well as some armed response. Whether or not that response should have been orchestrated solely by the United States is arguable. I believe it should not have been undertaken so unilaterally, under the same principle that states that when someone kills your brother, you call the police and have the matter attended to under processes of law. Had we given the United Nations eight weeks to create a multicultural, multireligious task force to get the perpetrators, we would have been shoring up support for international law, and gone some way toward obviating our international "cowboy" image; but this is a position one can argue with honorably, and I cannot fault the administration for its response, I can only disagree.

However, administration proposals to return fifteen years of tax breaks to the nation's wealthiest corporations and to relieve them of any obligation to pay alternative minimum taxes, transferring that burden to individual taxpayers, bear the same relationship to fighting terrorism as giving your children's food to the neighbor's pit bull so that they can live in a neighborhood with vigorous animals. In both the 1973 and the current cases, an event was used to energize a parallel, fear-driven agenda, interrupting an ongoing debate that might have led to a more equitable and humane society.

Less than a decade after 1973, President Nixon was gone, and so was Ford. President Carter was politically emasculated and publicly humiliated for attempting to restrain the nation's oil companies from gouging their own citizens mercilessly. The next president, Ronald Reagan, generated a kind of cozy, avuncular camouflage for the polished steel skin of the corporate machinery that had placed him in office. The rapidly concentrating media giants were in lockstep behind him, spreading the message that material acquisition was good; greed was good. A pristine example of this philosophy might be David A. Stockman, Reagan's director of the Office of Management and Budget from 1981 to 1985. This man wrote a book detailing how the trickle-down, supply-side economic philosophies he concocted for his president were an abject failure, based on cooked figures. The book became a best seller, making Stockman wealthy despite the fact that his cockamamie theories had shattered the nation's fiscal stability.

Reagan-era media concentrated on discrediting the Sixties, and its political turmoil and dislocations, condemning the social activists as self-indulgent romantics. Generous impulses were everywhere subverted and short-circuited by naked appeals to self-interest, and the stock market rose to unparalleled heights, fueled by tax monies returned to the rich and dedicated to speculation rather than rebuilding the nation's industrial sector. The lure of instant riches succeeded in deflecting nearly an entire generation's imagination into thoughts of personal gain. Social protest virtually disappeared. Magazine articles investigated the lassitude of the current crop of students, and the Reagan-Bush continuum (despite or perhaps because of Bill Clinton's Blue Dog Democrat interregnum) continues unabated today, and is more robust for being on a constant "war" footing against yet-to-be-named enemies in yet-to-be-announced countries.

More of the nation's resources are being dedicated to weaponry and conventional weapons systems (having nothing to do with antiterrorism) than at any time since the Reagan years. Empty, expensive, public gestures like stationing soldiers and vehicles at either end of the Golden Gate Bridge, or confiscating the nail clippers of airline passengers while their un-x-rayed luggage is shoved into the jetliners' holds, are acts designed to shelter the political class from future criticism and to foster the illusion that they are doing something to protect the public, without spending their campaign contributors' money. This is the same political class, by the way, that deep-sixed the airline safety proposals generated by not one but two Congressional hearings investigating the destruction of flights 800 and 103, blown out of the sky a decade earlier. Months of investigation, millions of dollars, and concrete safety recommendations disappeared as certainly and finally as the airliners and the World Trade Center, leaving not even the slightest ripple of rebuke for the corporate minions in Washington who perpetuated that sleight of hand.

Meanwhile, during the most prosperous period in recent memory, the same people liberated forty million working poor from the supposed indignity of having to pay for food with food stamps. It is amazing that they could achieve that without debate or questioning how people working a forty-hour work week can be legally compensated by wages so low that they are unable to feed themselves! Laws passed in the public's name have declared to the world that it is agreeable to us to execute the mentally handicapped; that we will never capitulate to a World Court; and that the "American lifestyle" is not up for review, no matter how egregious its environmental consequences may be.

What does the enthronement of such public cupidity and malice do to the public spirit of our nation? What malfeasance is being done to others and to us in the people's name by those who pretend to act on our behalf while in the pay of others whose interests are inimical to our own? What might "coming forward" as a people to do something about this situation look like and entail?

We are currently ruled by a self-referential "political minority." The majority are those who have boycotted an unresponsive political system by refusing to participate. I say "ruled" advisedly, because the policies enacted by this class have addressed only the smallest percentage of "swing-voters" who will determine the outcome of an election by their allegiance to one or another hot-button issue that never affects the central swindle perpetrated against the people as a whole. The political class fights amongst itself to represent the employed, the educated, the investors, and the wealthy while they jettison the poor, the uneducated, the handicapped, the disenfranchised, and those of color to the pitiless teeth of their free-market religion.

Such a state of affairs is the obverse of generosity! Disseminating confusion is greed! Disenfranchising people is a selfish act. To create and support distribution systems for food, water, medicine, and vital resources that block most people from access is the institutionalization of selfishness. To confuse simple issues with corrupted, obfuscatory language is an act of black magic to concentrate power for the selfish. For the Democratic Party to cede the making of global war and the fighting of terrorism to an expanded National Security State and to presidential whim because they are afraid of his popularity, to quibble only over the few remaining domestic dollars, is cowardice in the extreme. It is self-interest proceeding to its inevitable conclusion of murder.

The self-serving fiction of the political class is that the public does not know and cannot follow the threads of their manipulation among the welter of conflicting charts, data, and polls! The question for us here—pondering such questions today, tomorrow, and into the indeterminate future—is for what purposes shall we raise our voices, and set our sights?

What does this have to do with September 11? The photo of the planet Earth from space has given us a graphic representation of interdependence. No nation is wholly good or evil, and there are subtle and complex webs of guilt and complicity that bind us to the forces that wreaked such horror on our people and our economy. For the first time in decades, America could speak as a "victim," could represent itself to its own citizens and to the disenfranchised of the world as truly understanding pain and loss. That is a vital gift that has opened the heart of this country in many surprising ways, and I would hate to see it squandered.

Unfortunately, I am seeing all too much "business as usual" from the politicians and very little representation of what citizens think, see, and feel. The only concrete suggestion I can make is that the "crotch" of the dilemma is campaign financing. When politicians work for the people, they will represent them. It is that simple. Until they do, like us, they will continue to work for whoever pays them. As long as the interests of those who pay them are not congruent with the interests of the vast majority, we are laying the seed for future 9/11s, future disasters, and future suffering. In the interest of initiating dialogue I would propose the following four steps toward a cure:

1. Full federal financing of all federal elections, including a ban on soft money.

2. Free prime-time television air time for all qualified candidates, in return for which:

3. All candidates agree to appear on each network in unstructured, town-hall-style debates, where the audience is free to question them.

4. The same tax deduction for individuals and tax-exempt corporations that is currently offered to for-profit corporations for "disseminating information," often against the interests of the average person.

It's my belief that if the above changes were made, within a decade we would have an entirely different political environment, one in which "two-fers" would be unnecessary, and where harm done to others (in our names) would only be done with our express permission. It's a dream, I know, but so was America in 1776. The post-September 11 behavior of our leaders indicates to me that the dream is still far from fulfilled.

By the time I got around to writing this last piece, which, like the others, was conceived as an op-ed piece, the national madness was in full swing. The Patriot Act was gouging a furrow through the principles on which the nation had been founded, and for which countless thousands of its sons and daughters had died. The political class was rolling over at an unprecedented rate of speed, offering the president carte blanche to run the war anyway he chose, because they were afraid of his popularity. The obvious use of "parallel tracks" reminded me of the 1970s and the time when Ronald Reagan and conservatism began their nearly total control of the media and public policy vocabulary. I was getting cranky by this time. Everywhere I looked people who should have known better were abandoning their principles and power as if they could easily be retrieved once things "calmed down."

Anyone who has ever tried to train a dog, or discipline a child, knows that freedoms, once extended, are very difficult to take away. It is a normal response to chafe at a tightening leash or parental discipline. And yet, I am watching a nation, terrified into insensibility by one terror attack, whole-heartedly colluding to turn their country into an armed camp, their airwaves into propaganda for the military and its escalating budget, while their civil liberties are being scrapped along with other industrial wastes. I write these pieces not because I think that they will be effective in turning the tide of such craven thoughtlessness; I write them because it is the only way I know to remain human, and to ensure that an alternative voice remains alive.

On Recognition and Nation
Diana Abu-Jaber

TEN DAYS AFTER THE TERRORIST ATTACKS I WAS ON CAM-
pus preparing for the start of school when the clean-cut young
man approached and handed me a flyer. He looked me in the eye
and nodded as if we'd conducted a business transaction. And then
I looked at the flyer; it called for, among other things, "a rounding
up and questioning of all Arabs." My first thought was to tell him
he'd confused me with someone else. He hadn't realized I was
one of the ones he wanted rounded up.

But after I climbed the four flights of stairs to my office, I found
the same flyer slipped under my office door—the same door that
bears my very Arabic name. For some time, all I could do was stare

out my office window at the tiny sliver of sky that shows through the skylight. I remembered that when we lived in Jordan and I was a little girl, there was a woman who used to take care of me who was from a place called Palestine. She used to say: "In times of great calamity, clear your eyes and make your mind like a pond of water."

Years later, I read nearly verbatim the same words of advice in a novel written by an American writer. It was like coming across a juncture of insight without culture, a moment of mutuality and recognition. I grew up with people always telling me who I was— based on clues like the color of my skin or the sound of my name, but I often had the sense that they weren't really looking.

Even now, I'm frequently told—sometimes insistently—that I don't look Arab. I'm told that I look Russian or French or Irish or Greek or Italian. I don't take it too personally, though I sometimes have the sense that people simply don't want me to look Arab. Just the other day, while discussing the frightening fallout of the attacks, a good friend asked, "You don't think of yourself as Arab, do you? I don't!"

But sometimes things aren't so clear. Even though I've spent most of my life in America, five years ago I was again living in Jordan. An American friend and I were driving through the open countryside and at one point we decided to explore the courtyard of one of the crumbling medieval castles scattered around Jordan. The place appeared to be utterly abandoned and desolate; there was a large rusted padlock on the door. The wind came ringing high over the desert plain, and for miles around the only movement seemed to come from a pack of yellow dogs trotting toward us from the far horizon. Their eyes were soft and their mouths hung open in natural smiles. But then we realized that a man was walking with them and this man had a powerful, rigid face, the aspect of someone who's spent his nights watching the stars and animals, who hadn't learned how to govern his internal state in order to please or comfort other humans.

He approached us with his pack of dogs and the closer he got the more thunderstruck his expression. He finally stopped, raised one hand and pointed at me. My pulse was leaping in my throat. Wind roaring in our ears, both my friend and I stood stock still, unsure if we were intruding. But then his expression seemed to break open and he quietly said, "Anissa?" My grandmother was named Anissa, but she had been dead for more than thirty years at that point. We then learned this man had known her when she was a young woman living in Amman. No one in my family has ever told me I resembled my grandmother—a woman who died before I was born. But here, years later, and miles away from Amman, this stranger crossed an empty space, squinted through sand and wind, and recognized something.

It's a rare and lovely experience to feel like someone really has seen you, and it's become more essential than ever for us to try to do just that. We mustn't allow the rage, hatred, and terror churned up in the wake of the horrific attacks to tear at our fabric as a people—as members of a nation or as members of the world. Film and television, among other media, have urged viewers to regard Arabs, as well as African Americans and Native Americans—indeed anyone with dark skin or non-Christian beliefs—as suspicious, dangerous, and even evil. In the wake of terrorism it's natural to feel frightened, angry, and disoriented. But to honor our dead and to strengthen our living, we must draw together, recognizing our mutual humanity. We must be at peace—at the very least—with ourselves as a nation if we ever want to live in peace with the world.

Today when I enter the little family recreation center at the foot of the hill where I live in the suburbs of Portland, Oregon, I overhear one of the mothers bantering with the front desk staff, saying, "I just wish they would round up all the people with Mohammed and Abu in their names and take them away." She looks up at me; she doesn't know why I'm staring at her. She doesn't know who I am and I do not recognize her. Every day since the terrorist attacks, I've heard comments like these—a chilling, blind rage that wills people into being "Other." How desperately we want a simple world, a place in which people are innately good and others are innately evil—how desperately we want to believe that this basic dichotomy will explain why those others do things like hate Americans and attack them. But this is a child's wish for a make-believe world.

The woman who took care of me when I was a child once told me the story of the tower of Babel. Its creators were punished because they stopped listening to each other: the tower was a monolith, a prideful, fixed eye that stared only at heaven and tried to forget about the earth. Now I think of America, our love of the big, loud, beautiful, of machinery, wealth, industry, flight. How we may forget the people standing on the earth.

This is a strange and painful time to be Middle Eastern and American—a time when some people are buying American flags because they're frightened not to fly them. My Aunt J., who also lives in a place called Palestine, once told me: catastrophes can bring out the very best and the very worst in people. Some people become better than they naturally are and some become much worse. That is why you must not judge ahead of time or expect too much in either direction.

Remembering this makes me hope that there's an opportunity for us to be better, to feel more deeply, to see each other and ourselves more clearly. If only we will look.

We Have Met the Enemy, and He Is Us
Jess Mowry

THE TITLE OF THIS PIECE IS, OF COURSE, A QUOTE FROM the late Walt Kelly, who drew the comic strip *Pogo*, and it is, perhaps, Pogo's most famous line. It's certainly one of the most truthful, and definitely one that applies when it comes to the United States falling victim to global terrorism.

Or maybe I should say, FINALLY falling victim.

No, I'm not implying that the U.S. "got what it deserved" after over a century of exporting its own terrorism to the world, because I have no sympathy for anyone, any cause, any religion, or any government—including our own—that would murder innocent people. I haven't forgotten the people of 9/11 in writing this, and there can never be any justification for the terrible events of September 11, 2001.

But misplaced revenge and retaliation won't bring back even one of those thousands from the dead; and the innocent people and children the U.S. government is presently murdering in Afghanistan are no less important to me than a banker, secretary, or janitor at the World Trade Center. The needless death of even one child in the poorest of countries, whether from starvation or some stupid bomb, should shame us all as human beings.

I'm writing this essay a little over a month since the tragic events of 9/11, and after nearly four weeks of the U.S.'s so-called "War on Terrorism", which has consisted, thus far, of attacking and bombing one of the poorest nations on earth, a nation already so ravaged by wars and internal terrorism that there is very little left to destroy. The U.S. news media has proudly proclaimed, and not once but twice in as many weeks, that "we have destroyed the Taliban Air Force"—which was, I believe, two actual airplanes—and "we now have mastery over the skies in Afghanistan."

This might be funny if it wasn't so pathetic, something worthy of a *Pogo* satire: the richest nation on earth systematically destroying what is left of one of the poorest in tragicomic "retaliation" against mostly innocent people and kids. I've heard talk of "bombing Afghanistan back to the stone age"—a waste of bombs, really, because it was already there, thanks mostly to the U.S. in the first place.

But maybe I should tell you where I'm coming from…a generation caught between two extremes…the conformist Eisenhower, paranoid McCarthy, Cold War period of the 1950s, but really too young to have become much involved in the hot Vietnam War, hawk or dove political stances, Civil Rights and Black Panthers years of the mid- to late 1960s.

I was three years old when President John F. Kennedy was

assassinated. This was also the year that members of the Ku Klux Klan—one of America's own groups of terrorists—bombed a church in Birmingham, Alabama, murdering four little girls. Even though I grew up in West Oakland, California, the birthplace of the Black Panther Party, I was only about ten when they were being terrorized, murdered, and bombed by the U.S. government. I knew Bobby Hutton slightly (an "old kid" of sixteen, who was murdered by police—shot in the back—at age seventeen), but I was only dimly aware of world events. Still, like most kids in Oaktown, I knew who the terrorists were—the cops—and we waged our own youthful war on them in the same way young Palestinian kids throw rocks at Israeli tanks.

My teen years were spent mostly in the "nothing 1970s," when Nixon was out and Carter in, when the Vietnam war was a bad memory, when Disco ruled briefly and most black music was happy and silly…before the Reagan years when the CIA began using cocaine to finance its covert terrorist operations, and crack (coincidentally?) began flooding U.S. inner cities and a lot of black music changed to brutal, self-hating, often hopeless "gangstuh-rap." I remember well that change of atmosphere, and it coincided perfectly with the coming of Reagan and his corporate masters.

Now it seems they are back in the saddle.

Virtually every article, essay, letter to the editor, talk show guest, or talking head I've read or heard for the last solid month—no matter how far right, far left, U.S. media, or foreign source—begins by condemning the terrorist attacks on the World Trade Center and Pentagon as inhuman, despicable, and so forth. In this I agree with all my heart.

However, these acts have also been called "cowardly," at least by our dubiously elected (selected?) President, and on this point I disagree. I wouldn't say that what these people did was brave—in fact, I don't know what to call it—but I think we must ask ourselves how people could hate the U.S. with such desperation and fury that they would give their own lives in an act of mass murder? I wonder how many U.S. pilots who are in Afghanistan dropping bombs at the moment would crash their planes and die for this "cause" if ordered to do so by President Bush? Not many, I think. In our culture, what might be called a "suicide mission" is seldom without some chance for survival. Perhaps this is some sort of measure of our society, though I'm not sure what it indicates. On one hand it might show a greater respect for human life, but on the other, you might say it reveals a lack of religious or moral faith... that unlike the early Christians in Rome, we aren't willing to die for our God(s) or beliefs, either in the jaws of lions or at the controls of our billion-dollar bombers.

Maybe desperation is the key element here? After all, throughout history, suicidal desperation has been the last resort of people who've been oppressed and beaten down until they have no other recourse. Suicide attacks are often the only weapons the weak CAN use against the strong, or a seemingly invincible oppressor. It was suicidal desperation that caused almost a thousand Jewish men, women, and children to die by their own hands or throw themselves from the cliffs of Masada rather than be captured by the Roman Army in A.D. 73. It was suicidal desperation that caused many African men, women, and children to jump overboard from the slave ships and drown rather than live their lives in chains. The Japanese kamikaze pilots of WWII were another example of suicidal desperation; and it matters not if their cause was just, only that they believed in it so strongly that they were willing to sacrifice their lives. Buddhist monks doused themselves with gasoline and died in flaming agony to protest the U.S. war in Vietnam. I haven't heard of any Israeli suicide bombers in recent history— only that many oppressed Palestinians are willing to sacrifice their lives this way because they feel they have no other choice. Seems to me a truly "civilized" or "good" nation would ask itself what it had done to make people this desperate?

Back to the subject of Gods and religions, I can't help but think that if God was really on "our side" then nobody would hate us but evil people. The religion of Islam and the Muslim people certainly aren't evil; though just like any other religion there are always false priests and raving fanatics trying to twist God's Word around to make it serve their own hateful or greedy agendas. And I definitely wouldn't say that the Christian religion was the "best" or the only "real" one on earth…after all, the Ku Klux Klan calls itself a "Christian organization," and its members have terrorized and murdered thousands of innocent people and children since the Civil War ended. Come to think of it, isn't it usually "Christian Right-to-Lifers" who fire-bomb family planning centers, sometimes murdering innocent doctors, patients, and occasionally, ironically, unborn babies as well? If people actually read the Bible instead of letting other people tell them what they say it says, they would discover that Jesus never taught or believed in violence, hate, killing, revenge, or terrorizing people.

Fact is, there's been more hate, murder, killing, pain, suffering, conquest, exploitation, slavery, genocide, terrorism, and starvation on this planet caused by people who call themselves Christians than by any other religion in history. Seems to me that if people really believed in the teachings of Jesus, not only wouldn't they do this stuff, they wouldn't let other people—or their government—do it either.

Maybe this goes back to that saying, "If you're not part of the solution then you're part of the problem"? And it's always a lot easier to be part of the problem, because all you have to do is nothing, just sit on your couch and watch people and kids get murdered on TV…at least only what the U.S. government will let you see … because it's currently buying up all the civilian satellite photos of

Afghanistan to prevent the public from viewing the unpleasant things it's done. And, of course, the corporate-controlled news media won't be complaining about censorship of the so-called free press in this country.

As a matter of fact, I heard Dan Rather, the "anchorman" of CBS's so-called news, say he would "get in line behind the President." Makes me wonder what he's "anchored" to...the Pentagon perhaps? It sure doesn't sound like independent journalism or freedom of the press to me...sounds more like he knows that if he doesn't lick the bloody combat boots of his corporate masters he'll be fired. If all the news the U.S. public gets is from TV, then it's being lied to.

In other words, business as usual.

Ah, yes, business. The drumbeat of America. The U.S. is undoubtedly the most powerful nation on earth today, but it is far from being the "greatest." It uses its power to make itself richer and to terrorize other countries into doing what it wants or giving it what it wants. It is also the largest seller of weapons in the world, as well as the biggest exporter of terrorism to other countries... though like all bullies it prefers to prey on the small, the weak, and the defenseless. Indeed, the U.S. has seemingly become the "Evil Empire" that former President Reagan once called the U.S.S.R. back in the 1980s.

"If you aren't with us, then you're against us!" foams Bush. Sounds as if he gets all his lines from old Western movies, though personally I think he missed his last rabies shot.

Of course, he's not really in control of the government anyway, being just a front for the real corporate power that got him "elected" on forty-nine percent of the vote. In one way that's probably a good thing, because he's such a monumentally ignorant, hateful, and nasty little man that it's easy to see the power that's really behind him.

Naturally, he's not a complete idiot, and some of his stupidity is feigned for the public…no one could be moronic enough to honestly ask, "Why do they hate us," or actually believe that "they" hate us because we have democracy and blue jeans, that THIS creates suicidal desperation; but it certainly eases the public's mind and keeps them from asking that question of themselves.

Could it be possible that "they" hate us because the U.S. makes up only five percent of the world's population, but it uses up twenty-five percent of the world's resources? Or, maybe they hate us because the U.S. has refused to attend, or has walked out on, so many conferences about human rights and environmental issues such as global warming and ozone depletion, demonstrating to the rest of the world that it doesn't give a damn about other people or about killing this planet.

Sure, the U.S. gives millions of dollars in aid to a handful of poor countries, but only if it thinks it can get something from them. And even though it gives millions in aid, it simultaneously spends BILLIONS on weapons, figuring out new ways to terrorize and exploit other nations. This concept is akin to our current plan of spending billions to simultaneously drop cluster bombs and food packets (called "Snow Drops" in typically Disney-grotesque lingo) on the same innocent men, women, and children.

I believe there are more than five million people in Afghanistan—people and kids who are starving to death at this moment—and the United Nations can't deliver real food to them while the U.S. is waging its so-called "war on terrorism"…which is a form of terrorism itself. So what good are a few thousand food packets? Especially when Afghanistan is reportedly the second most mined country in the world (thanks partly to us) and if those kids run out to get those "Snow Drops" they stand a good chance of being killed or maimed.

Let's turn things around and pretend that Afghanistan is bombing the U.S. Now, if you saw your family or children get killed, would you want to eat the food that Afghanistan dropped? Shish-kabobs, for example, since we're basically dropping peanut butter and jelly? And remember these people did nothing to us, just like those people in the World Trade Center did nothing to them. Perhaps the dead understand and forgive one another, but it seems to me that for those of us living, all this will do is make some people hate the U.S. even more. And right now there are millions of people all over the world who hate the U.S.—people who didn't hate the U.S. before it started this stupid war.

Speaking of stupid, the U.S. is about the only country in the world with "smart bombs" and stupid kids...kids who are taught virtually nothing in school about the rest of the world or about the other people and cultures in it. We're a nation of flag-waving xenophobes. But, of course, stupid and miseducated people are easy to control, as many governments have discovered throughout history.

By the way, did you ever consider that if bombs were really "smart" then they wouldn't explode at all?

The U.S. government says it will punish any nation that "harbors or supports terrorists and terrorism." Seems like it should start by punishing itself. The U.S. has exported its own brand of terrorism all over the world for decades, such as training death squads in Haiti, in Nicaragua, and of course training Osama bin Laden and the Taliban, too. Speaking from experience, I can attest that it certainly terrorizes people of color within its own borders with police brutality, harassment, and murder.

As I mentioned, it's interesting that crack started flooding U.S. inner cities at the same time the CIA was using cocaine to finance its terrorist operations in the 1980s. Could the CIA have created the market for crack to make more money, and also to disrupt, demoralize, and divide the black community, promoting self-hatred and black-on-black violence to keep us under control and bloat a burgeoning privatized prison industry? Oh, heavens no, we're the good guys on the white horses, remember? We just ride the range, occasionally defending Truth, Justice, and the American Way.

It's also interesting that the so-called "Northern Alliance," which the U.S. wants to support in Afghanistan, is the world's biggest producer of heroin. Don't be surprised if smack starts pouring into our inner cities if the U.S. wins its stupid "war" and puts the Northern Alliance in charge. I say "if," because no other nation in history has managed to conquer and hold Afghanistan for very long, including the British Empire and the former Soviet Union.

In my very first book, *Rats in the Trees*, published in 1990, I predicted that "guns, gangs, drugs and violence" would soon be moving out of the ghettoes and into white suburbia. Does anyone remember Columbine? There was yet another act of suicidal desperation by someone who felt they had no other choice. So, let's see how this prediction holds up a year from now.

The plain unadorned truth is that the U.S. will set up and support the most evil and corrupt dictators and governments in other countries just to be sure it gets what it wants. And it will help those dictators murder and terrorize the people and children within those countries…including, of course, Afghanistan.

Albert Einstein once said that you can't have the same people who created a problem solve the problem. This is pretty much true when it comes to terrorism…the U.S. can never stop the terrorism it created by making more terrorism. But that's exactly what it's doing right now.

For instance, the U.S. often points out that poor countries don't have democratic governments so they "need U.S. help." The real truth is that a poor country can almost NEVER have a democratic government when a superpower is messing with its internal affairs. Why? Well, imagine that the U.S. was a poor country and Haiti (for example) was a rich superpower. Now, Haiti wants something from the U.S.—oil, most likely—so it postures and puffs that black people, an ethnic minority, are being oppressed in the U.S. Then it starts selling those black people guns and other weapons, and sends in advisors to train them in how to terrorize and overthrow the white-controlled government. This, of course, starts a civil or guerrilla war in which thousands of innocent people are killed or starved to death (merely "collateral damage"). Then, if the black people win, Haiti doesn't care WHAT kind of government they set up as long as it will sell them cheap oil. It's really that simple.

The U.S. has been doing this kind of thing to poor countries for over a hundred years. It's not, however, the same kind of imperialism that the British Empire (for example) practiced when they invaded a country to further their own interests. When European powers took control of a poor country they had a sense of responsibility with their imperialism, they believed it was important to "civilize" the nations they exploited. They built cities, railroads, highways, factories, hospitals, schools, and universities. They established an infrastructure. Yes, the people were subjugated, but they sometimes ended up better off in the long run. These imperialist countries exploited the poorer nation's resources—oil, gold, lumber, diamonds, etc., and/or its cheap labor—until these riches were used up or exhausted. Finally, when the poorer country had nothing left worth exploiting they "gave" it its independence and walked away. Yes, they left it poor, but they also left the infrastructure they built. And sometimes a nation can rise upon that.

However, the U.S. plays a different game, shows no similar sense of responsibility. Its form of imperialism began shortly after the Spanish-American War when it found itself winning Cuba and other former Spanish possessions, as well as needing coaling stations around the world for its rapidly expanding merchant and naval fleets. Instead of building or improving a poor nation's infrastructure, the U.S. simply set up ANY kind of government, no matter how brutal or oppressive it might be, or how many of its own people it murdered or starved, as long the U.S. got what it wanted. This policy hasn't changed much in over a century. With this form of imperialism, the U.S. doesn't have to invest anything — commit itself, so to speak, on a humanitarian level — by building railroads, highways, schools, hospitals, and so forth. (A good example of this was the U.S.'s long occupation of South Vietnam, during which they mainly built military bases of plywood and tin, which were already falling apart when the U.S. withdrew.) Even "better," the people of that country stay poor and uneducated, left to fight amongst themselves instead of banding together against this exploitation.

You probably read in your fifth-grade school books that the reason the U.S. never tried to build an empire was because it was "good" and "believed in freedom and democracy for all." This is mostly nonsense. The real reason the U.S. never tried to build an empire was simply because it was a lot cheaper to start a civil war in some poor country, back the side it wanted to win, then set up a government that would give it whatever it wanted.

So why did it "help" a country like Haiti (for example), which is the poorest nation in the Western Hemisphere and has no resources? Simple: Haiti was once seen by the U.S. as being the "new Taiwan"…a country with a cheap labor force where kids could be put to work in sweat shops for about eighty cents a day while stitching that new pair of Fubu jeans that cost you eighty dollars. And Haiti is just one example of this kind of exploitation.

Or, say that a poor country doesn't have any resources, but it happens to be "pretty," like many Caribbean and Central American nations. The U.S. will set up the government it wants, through peaceful coercion or otherwise, and build fancy hotels and resorts, basically turning that country into a nation of cooks, waiters, maids, servants, and prostitutes.

You might say that it's better for a poor child to make eighty cents a day sewing your hundred-dollar kicks than to starve to death. And there is a sad sort of truth in that. But the problem is that you have created a nation of slaves that are dependent upon you. You are keeping them one day away from starvation or food-riots, and they aren't free to build their own society. Furthermore, children who work all day in sweatshops obviously have little or no time for getting an education.

That's another good reason "they" hate the U.S.

Now, as I write this, the U.S. is trying to overthrow the Taliban government in Afghanistan to put the Northern Alliance in power, even though the Northern Alliance exports heroin and will probably be just as brutal and oppressive to its own people as the Taliban were. Is the U.S. doing this to "stop terrorism"...or could the magic word be "oil"?

It's certainly no "military secret" or "Internet rumor" that in 1997 the major oil companies—Standard, Uniocal, Exxon/Mobil—invited representatives of the Taliban government to a meeting in Texas. The gist of this meeting was that these companies wanted to build a pipeline across Afghanistan to exploit the rich Caspian oil reserves, and they wanted the Afghan government to be stable so that rich investors would put money into the project. The Taliban leaders were told, in effect, "let us carpet you with gold or we'll bury you with bombs."

It's also no secret that there were plans in the Pentagon to begin bombing Afghanistan in October 2001—BEFORE the 9/11 attacks. In addition, the FBI had an investigation underway that might have prevented the attacks of 9/11, but were told to stop because it was messing up the pipeline negotiations. The head of the

FBI resigned in protest. He became head of security at the World Trade Center, and was killed in the 9/11 attacks.

Black folks have a saying—"things that make you go hmmm."

Another reason "they" hate us is that the U.S. doesn't seem to think of itself as just one country in the world; instead it thinks of itself as BEING the world, and can do anything it wants, including violating International Law.

For instance, before the U.S. government had even proven that Osama bin Laden was guilty of being behind the events of September 11—and I guess we'll have to take their word on that—President Bush screamed for his blood, "dead or alive," and ordered him assassinated. Whatever happened to "innocent until proven guilty," or "due process of law"—the supposed mainstays of U.S. justice? Even the Nazi war criminals received fair trials. If indeed he is guilty, then by International Law he should be brought before a world court, not lynched by U.S. terrorists in the same way my own people were lynched by the KKK. I get the absurd image of Bush parading down Wall Street with bin Laden's head on a pike...though I doubt if that image is absurd to Bush.

Ultimately, it doesn't really matter if Bush actually achieves his sick little dream, because he and his corporate masters are creating thousands of future terrorists right now with every orphaned Third World child whose parents or family were killed by their bombs.

Yet another in the top ten reasons why "they" hate us is U.S. corporate terrorism.

Did you ever see those Chevron (Standard Oil) TV commercials where Chevron says its people "care" about butterflies, animals, and the environment? If it really "cares" then why did it have its own private army run bulldozers over people's villages in Kenya to get them out of the way? Then, of course, there were Boise-Cascade's incursions into Mexico, terrorizing the peasant farmers to get lumber, and supported by U.S. bombs and aircraft. There are countless examples of this kind of U.S. corporate terrorism, all of it sanctioned or aided by the U.S. government.

The fact that the U.S. has continually supported Israel's terrorism upon the Palestinians hasn't helped much, either. Again and again the Israeli Army invades Palestine, murdering and terrorizing innocent people and children, leaving those people no other recourse than suicidal desperation, while the U.S. turns a blind eye. Just whose "Freedom and Justice" does the U.S. protect?

The fact is that the U.S. is a longtime expert at terrorizing and bombing poor countries. If you'll read up on history you'll find that, since the end of wwII, the U.S. has mainly terrorized people of color, often called "The Global South." A partial list of countries that have been bombed by us in the last fifty years would include: Korea, Cuba, Guatemala, the Belgian Congo, Peru, Chile, Laos, Cambodia, Vietnam, Grenada, El Salvador, Nicaragua, Panama, Iraq, Iran, Mexico, the Sudan, and now Afghanistan. Did any of these countries attack the U.S.? Nope. And the people of Afghanistan certainly weren't responsible for the terrorist attacks of September 11, 2001.

Yet Bush has the nerve (or monumental stupidity) to call the U.S. a "peace-loving nation"! I believe Nikita Khrushchev often used this same expression during the Cold War era to describe his own Soviet Union. Echoes of the "Evil Empire" again?

The very same day that Bush asked U.S. kids to donate money to the Red Cross, the U.S. bombed a Red Cross food storage warehouse in Afghanistan! And, when it's not actually bombing poor countries of color, the U.S. usually has economic sanctions against them, starving their people and kids because that country won't do what the U.S. wants.

I don't know how you were raised, but my father taught me that actions speak louder than words. Presently, the U.S. has economic sanctions against Haiti (again, the poorest nation in the Western Hemisphere). Why? Because the Haitian people held a free election and voted in a government the U.S. didn't like. In the Sudan, the U.S. bombed the country's only pharmaceutical plant. It said it had "made a mistake," but did it offer to help rebuild the plant? Nope. So, if as a result, you watched your wife, your kids, or your parents die of some disease that doesn't even exist in the U.S., wouldn't you hate the U.S., too? If you saw your family starve to death because of U.S. economic sanctions, or get killed in a bombing raid called an "unfortunate mistake," or "collateral damage", then wouldn't you hate the U.S., too? Maybe to the point of suicidal desperation?

Again, I'm not trying to imply that terrorism and murder done by the U.S. on innocent people can ever justify revenge in kind… but Bush and his masters seem to think so because they judge everyone by their own brutal standards.

Is the U.S. so "good" that it doesn't "deserve" this kind of hatred? Is the U.S. so "pure" that it should be sacred or inviolate from having parts of its cities reduced to rubble…something that has happened throughout history in virtually every other nation in the world? Even if we set aside the skeletons of slavery and the slaughter of Native American people as sins of a distant past, the U.S. is one of the only two supposedly "civilized nations" in the world today that still has the death penalty. It executes kids and retarded people…especially in President Bush's home state. Did you know that never…never…in all of U.S. history has a white person been executed for murdering a black? If you keep these facts in mind, then maybe it isn't surprising that it seems "okay" to the U.S. government to bomb, exploit, and starve "lesser races" all around the world.

The U.S. is also the most violent nation on earth in its movies and entertainment media. Even its children look like they're dressed for war these days: indeed many are actually killing each other with real guns and bullets. Yet we say we are "good" and should be immune to the horrors we wreak upon others.

"Freedom and Justice for all"? The U.S. government just gave billions to the airline industry—huge corporations—to "help" them now that lots of people are afraid to fly, yet it never offered a penny to all the working people who got laid off. Now it's supposed to be "patriotic" to travel and spend money. Business as usual.

The U.S. government has said many times that it can't afford "welfare" to help its own poor, that it can't afford to improve our schools…so how can it afford billions upon billions for this hateful "war on terrorism"? The U.S. once declared a "War on Poverty" within its own borders, but it seems to have surrendered that war without ever firing a shot.

Are the majority of people in the U.S. "bad" or "evil"? Of course not. They are just miseducated and lied to. At worst they are simply ignorant when it comes to knowing about the rest of the world or what really goes on outside their own formerly "safe" borders. They are ignorant because public schools in the U.S. don't really teach anything about the rest of the world, just like the corporate news media doesn't give them any real information.

"Freedom of the press"? In 1987 there were more than fifty companies that owned news services in the U.S. Today there are six—all huge corporations. Think about it. Freedom of the press only works when the presses WANT to print the truth.

The U.S. COULD be the greatest country on earth for helping poor people and promoting real peace, and it could still make a healthy profit while doing so. But instead the greedy corporations who run the U.S. choose to terrorize and exploit other countries and their people. Basically it's all about money.

Speaking of which, did you know that President Bush's father, who was president during the Gulf War when the U.S. first started bombing Iraq (and has never really stopped), has money invested in bin Laden's family business? Did you know he's been a guest of the bin Laden family? Did you know that the Bush family has money invested in a huge corporation (Carlyle Group) that builds and sells weapons? And some of the same weapons were sold to the same "terrorists" the U.S. is supposedly bombing right now. I believe that's called a "conflict of interest" at best, while at worst it's supporting and aiding terrorism, yet I haven't heard of anyone freezing the Bush family's assets or investigating their interests.

Now the U.S. government wants to censor the Internet and spy on its own people, take away their rights and read their e-mails (more than it does already) to "protect us," despite the fact that the First Amendment to the Constitution states that Congress shall pass no law abridging freedom of speech.

If we take this a step higher into International Law, we should remember that it was said at the Nuremberg Trials that all human beings have an obligation to try to prevent immoral acts committed by their government—to at least stand up and speak out against such acts. Ah, but they were talking about what happened in Nazi Germany, right? How could that apply to the good old U.S.A.?

Consider a few parallels between Nazi Germany and what's going on in the U.S. right now…

#1: Nazi Germany thought it didn't have to obey any International Laws or treaties. #2: It singled out a group of people and a religion to persecute and blame for its ills. #3: It filled its citizens' minds with lies and false propaganda to frighten them and make them hate its "enemies"—real or imagined, foreign and domestic. #4: Its government controlled the news media and entertainment industries. #5: It spent obscene amounts of money on weapons of war and a military that it claimed were only for its own defense. #6: It had an internal police force (a form of "Homeland Security") to arrest and harass anyone who spoke out against its policies, or anybody it decided to label as a "terrorist" or a "threat." #7: It steadily chipped away at the rights of its citizens to question or to protest against what it did in their names. #8: Its leader seized far greater powers than the Constitution originally gave to his office. #9: Its leader was an internationally ignorant man who was intolerant of anyone who didn't share his own racist and xenophobic beliefs (although Adolf Hitler was better educated than Bush). #10: It wanted to rule the world, force its will upon others, and exploit the people and resources of other countries.

Here's an interesting quote:

> Why of course the people don't want war. Why should some poor slob on a farm want to risk his life in a war when the best he can get out of it is to come back in one piece? Naturally the common people don't want war: neither in Russia, nor in England, nor in Germany for that matter. That is understood. But, after all, it is the leaders of the country who determine the policy and it is always a simple matter to drag the people along, whether it is a democracy, or a fascist dictatorship, or a parliament, or a communist dictatorship. Voice or no voice, the people can always be brought to the bidding of the leaders. That is easy. All you have to do is tell them they are being attacked, and denounce the peacemakers for lack of patriotism and exposing the country to danger. It works the same in every country.
>
> —Hermann Göring, 1938

Do you see much difference between Nazi Germany of the 1930s and '40s and the U.S.A. of the present? We don't have mass concentration camps and ovens…yet. Although stock in the U.S. prison industry is increasing in value right now, in anticipation of all the new "criminals, traitors, and terrorists" that the government is going to catch and lock up with its new expanded powers of suppression.

It doesn't take an Einstein to figure out that if you keep building prisons you're going to need prisoners to fill them.

When all is said and done, it would seem as if the U.S. is really a luxury the world can no longer afford…a big, greedy, stupid, racist, insatiable, all-consuming bully. I would suggest that this leaves the U.S. with three basic options for the future: One, join the world and use its power and riches for real freedom and justice for all; two, attempt to conquer the world and try to hold on to an empire (which has never worked for long in all of world history); or, three, destroy the world…something it's very capable of doing…with the philosophy that if we can't have it all, then no one else should have it either.

Judging from past history, which of these choices do you think Bush and his masters would make?

Of course, if you're blindly, wave-the-flag-and-bomb-the-bastards patriotic, then you've been brainwashed into rejecting the first choice, you THINK you want the second, but you'll probably end up with the third. Remember that when you're dying of radiation poisoning, anthrax, bubonic plague, or skin cancer. Also remember that it was made right here in the good old U.S.A.

I'm sure some "patriotic" people will say, if you don't like the U.S. then leave it. And go where? There doesn't seem to be many places left on this planet where one could escape U.S. terrorism, exploitation, or its bombs.

As I mentioned at the beginning of this piece, I knew who the terrorists were when I was just a little kid; and to paraphrase Walt Kelly's Pogo, I have met the enemy and he is U.S.

Elegy to a Betrayer
by an Outlaw Prophet
Floyd Salas

Dedicated to George W. Bush

When the cock crows twice
and the finger of a maid
pounds like a gavel
ache for my wishbone in your breast
for I foresaw this

Yet I wear no crown of mocking thorn
nor sun on my brow
with disciples of stars in the suck of its orbit

My halo is the bad breath of the dispossessed
There is vinegar in my blood
For clad in prickly robes of woolen ash,
shackle scars and stigmata
the blemish of one burning hand
raised as high as the green fingers of a Sunday palm
left fingers crossed
the knot of tongues cracks the seal of my lip
quakes the grim still of the square
Its many pebbled verbs ricochet like sling shot
from the Goliath mace
the hilt of the sword that is worshipped as cross

For I sound the omen's sigh
There is a beast in the market place
a brick-fleshed idol with chalk bones
plumed and vested
in the mail bonds of patriotism
banners of blood
and streamers
of sheer white
Break his legal joints
Dismantle the linked letters of his laws
that fetter the revolt of conscience
bind the spirit
in the hip-high shafts and labyrinths
of the martial code
sacrifice sons
stunt man's spine

Because I cannot love the Christ
and this Caesar too
I submit to my fate
and so must you

You will find it easy
For in the breast cage of most men
neither love's dove
nor spur of hate
but hawk of fear!

And when the draft and rumor of war
sharp as a saber's swipe
rips my robe
reveals the cuff burn on my wrist
the convict twist of my ankle

the pimple's taint of whore on my groin
my cut-purse girdle
surely you'll swear
I mask a traitor's face
One eye is odd!
No Sunday riser
Does he believe in God?

But I will be an easy prey
and in the noon light of an open square
with a bending ear and turning cheek
I'll welcome the chapped snare
of your seduction there

Then when the cock crows twice
at the blasphemous wound cramped in my palm
ache for my wishbone in your breast
for I foresaw this

When Elephants Fight, the Grass Suffers

Floyd Salas

Speech for War & Peace reading sponsored by PEN Oakland
Pearl Harbor Day, December 7, 2001

WHEN THE BOMBS LANDED IN AFGHANISTAN, I KNEW
what to expect. I'd already lived through the war hysteria of World
War II and had been taught to hate the Japanese. I'd lived through
the repressive Eisenhower-Dulles regime of the fifties that followed the Korean War, the so-called McCarthy years, in which a
middle-aged, white female elevator operator would see the red
cover of my novel, *The Brothers Karamazov* (a religious tome if ever
there was one), notice that it was Russian and probably communist, and warn me before I got out not to read subversive literature.
When an insurance investigator asking about the neighbor next
door would say, "And, of course, he doesn't belong to the Commu-

nist Party or anything like that, does he?"

I knew how militarism could make everybody suffer and had been an unwilling martyr for smoking pot, hunted nearly all of my adult life for smoking a joint on Saturday nights, and for being a student peace activist in the early days, 1960 and 1961, when a fellow female activist learning of my plight said, "Well, at least you're being hunted for a good cause and have the big boys watching you now."

I knew what it was like to have my phone tapped and my house bugged and every deep association I ever established with another person, including *every member* of my family, be corrupted by the FBI. I knew what it was like to be driven out of three colleges in the Bay Area alone; anything to keep me from becoming the writer I wanted to be and writing about the subversive, unconstitutional acts of so-called peace-keeping forces. And they were right, because two of my novels, *Lay My Body on the Line* and *State of Emergency*, both published by NEA funds, were about just that: the corruption of the student peace movement by the FBI.

I'm talking about the subversion of the constitution by the Military-Industrial complex, which we learned and were warned about in Eisenhower's final speech upon leaving office when, believe it or not, he named the sources of true power in this country. The only democratic thing he ever did as president.

We have two enemies: bin Laden and the very same military-industrial complex. Bin Laden will shoot us on sight and the military-industrial complex will take away our liberty and make us poor.

The Republicans stole the election by keeping black people away from the polls in Florida and through the actions of the elections chief who counted only the votes she wanted to count so she could be true to the Bush who was governor, son of the ex-CIA chief president, and brother of the Bush who had been barred from stealing from the stock market for seven years for ripping off sixty-five million from retired people, the same people the Republicans want to exploit by putting all of our Social Security funds into the stock market, so they can keep stealing, even our retirement money.

Then after they stole our election, they stole our tax money. Congress gave a tax rebate of $300 to me, and $300 billion to the oil companies, who are the robber barons of the twentieth century, as opposed to the railroad robber barons of the nineteenth century. It took them only ten months to put us in a depression and blow away nearly all the dot-com Silicon Republicans who voted for them. The mega-cats only help the mega-cats. They step on the small businessman, "out-compete him" they call it when they buy off the politicians, who are now giving them another tax break to stimulate the economy, their economy, not ours. They won't put money into programs for the poor, there's not enough to go around for that, but they will give another tax break to the big man.

That's the industrial part of the equation. The military part of it is to strengthen the military (and by that I include all police functions, whether international or local) and keep a good hold on any kind of dissent so it doesn't upset the status quo of the military-industrial complex. It's called complex, because it is a complex. And part of that complex is to create a war hysteria that will keep in line those politicians who might object but still want to get elected and don't dare appear unpatriotic.

This war hysteria is what made me hate Japs, not Japanese, that's too human, Japs, subhumans, as a kid. This war hysteria allows guys like Attorney General Ashcroft to get new laws passed to tap our phones and bug our houses and make us so afraid we don't dare open our mouths to complain. Some lousy politician even wants to cut all federal funds, in a so-called Patriotic Act, to all state and local governments, meaning Berkeley, that don't fly the flag.

At the same time, there will be secret trials so that the shenanigans of the prosecutors won't be exposed and the constitutional rights that have made this country great will be circumcised. And that's not a pun. The new DEA head has shut down medical marijuana shops in L.A. and warned doctors that they could lose their licenses if they prescribe pot to a cancer or AIDS patient suffering the ravages of their terminal illness. Calling it state's rights when they want the stolen votes of Florida but negating state's rights when it interferes with the profits of the medical drug makers or the cigarette nicotine-addict makers or drunk makers in the alcohol industry is also all part of the complex. They don't want people to be able to grow their own medicine or mild recreational drug, when alcohol is the worst drug in history, has destroyed more lives than all the other drugs in the world. And right here, in the Bay Area, our own Berkeley Repertory Theater is facing a National Endowment for the Arts cut-off in funding for planning to produce a play, "Homebody/Kabul," which is considered critical of the Bush policy in the Middle East.

Samuel Johnson said, "Patriotism is the last refuge of a scoundrel." Be careful of flag-wavers, they need to make a show to conceal their true motives from you. The last war led by a Bush was for oil and he brought a depression, too. This war led by a Bush is also for oil.

Malcolm X once said to some bright black scholastic students, "The most important thing you can do is think for yourself. Otherwise you will be going west when you think you're going east and east when you think you're going west."

The true subversives are not those who disagree with the official statements of the party in power, however dishonestly that party gained power, but those who subvert the constitution, what those flag-wavers in Washington are doing now.

Right now we have the Military-Industrial Complex in the

West led by a millionaire and bin Laden, another millionaire, and the fundamentalist Muslim religious zealots in the East, and we better think for ourselves or we won't know which way we're going.

In India they have a saying, "When elephants fight, the grass suffers." Both sides in this war are elephants, and in our case, a Republican elephant.

President Johnson, when he said he would not run for office again, began his speech by saying, "I am a free man, a citizen of my country, and a member of my party." He began with I am a free man, and I say that I am a free man and a citizen of my country and I will fight subversion whether it comes from a disgraced president like Nixon, a former head of the CIA like George Bush Senior, or a flag-waver like his dishonest son, Junior.

Ash Colors the Clouds

The Berkeley sky's patriotic
The rose stripes color the light blue
Maybe it's the war?

We sit in a serene scene and ponder
the beauty that comforts us
while bombs blast holes into the firmament
and adobe houses
and crush kid's skulls

This is called bad luck
or
superiority
industrialism carried to the zenith
in a painful blast
that blows your head off
your body apart

legs
where they don't belong
a child's skull
hollowed
and brainless

This is progress
That's what it's called
Revenge by the high and mighty

I can't sit still and only care for what comforts me
while death rains down
on other people

Ash colors the clouds
like an erasure
streaking out
the dying day

.

America United
Ishmael Reed

They are saying we should join hands and show
solidarity with our new friends,
that we should burn candles and sing, "God Bless
America," and "Amazing Grace," and stand tall
with Sir Rudolph Giuliani, the Mayor of New York,
the joker among racial profilers, under whose
rule 35 thousand Hispanic and Black men
were stopped and frisked.
"No one group should be targeted
as a result of the WTC bombing," Sir Giuliani said.
They say that we should link arms with the
killers of Amadou Diallo, shot 44 times while
minding his own business.
That we should march with
them to that gleaming City on the Hill, preceded
by the Albany jury that acquitted them, who
play Yankee Doodle Dandy on their piccolos,
fifes and drums.
They say that we should form a big strong line
with Sir Colin Powell who said that he's
against the bombing of civilians and buildings.
"I'm against the bombing of civilians and buildings,"
said Secretary of State Powell, MacWorld's Black Knight.
They say we show our gratitude to
the woman whom President George Bush, Jr. calls

Condi as in,
"Get me Condi."
Ms. Condoleezza Rice, daughter of the
Hoover Institute and Chevron Oil,
murderer of the Nigerian Delta people.
He calls upon her when he lacks the facts,
which is often.
Maybe we should send her a carton of
nail polish, hot combs, skin lighteners
and pocket mirrors to show
our gratitude, our affection.
She said that there was no reason for
the U.S. to attend the Race Conference in Durban,
South Africa.
She said that "We are a country that does not
judge people by their skin color or religious beliefs."
They say that we should bow our heads and pray along
with George Dumya Bush, who said that the
citizens of South Carolina should decide whether
the confederate flag should fly over the state capitol,
who said that every black man who was electrocuted
in Texas received a fair trial.
He said that he wanted the "evil doers"
"Dead or Alive," smirking, eyes squinting,
send them all to Boothill
which is how we do it in Texas,
why shucks, we're going to smoke
them out of their holes because
they're the bad guys and we're
the good guys so
you're either with us or you're
with them.

He said that he would bomb Afghanistan
as soon as Condi showed him where it was
on the map.
Bombs upon which they write, "Hijack this, fag,"
because they is the man,
they is civilized.
And they cluster bomb hundreds of men, women and
    children
because they are with them
And they bomb the Red Cross because
they are with them
And they bomb their hospitals and senior citizens' homes
because they are with them
And they bomb thousands of goats, sheep, pheasants,
donkeys and geese because they are with them
Osama bin Laden who, if he is a modem equipped
cave ogre, had his fangs, hooves and horns supplied
by American taxpayers.
If the Russians had built a bigger soccer
stadium we would have even more room
to punish women who read books and don't
cover their ankles!
Dumya Bush, bin Laden's comrade in oil, thinks
All I wanted to be was baseball commissioner
but hell being president is more of a blast than I thought.
Every time I open my mouth, thousands flee their
homes and head for the borders. When I visited Italy
a few months ago, the police beat up demonstrators
while shouting Il Duce. Who is this Il Duce? Get me
Condi.
They say that we should place flags in our
windows and join Dumya in his

crusade I mean campaign.
They say that we should bond with
the neo-confederates and All-American Union Busters,
Trent Lott, John Ashcroft, Gale Norton and
maybe join them in burning a cross because
that's what brotherhood means, doesn't it,
joining together
and standing around fires and stuff.
Won't generals Nathan B. Forrest, Robert E. Lee
and Stonewall Jackson, American patriots all,
be proud of us and
beam up to us from their permanent residence
as we stand shoulder to shoulder with Dixie.

I got it. Maybe we would fly the Stars and Bars
along with the Stars and Stripes to
show that not only is one country united
but both countries. I mean shucks,
two for one is a good deal ain't it.
Ain't that what they say at Wal-Mart.
They say that we should chant
USA! USA! with people
who shadow us down the aisles
of department stores, hassle us
for living while black,
who voted for propositions 209, 187
and 21, who try our children as adults
and place them in jail with predators.
They say we should chant *USA! USA!*
with people who say that it's the poor's
fault that they are poor.
They say we should chant *USA! USA!*

with people who drag us from behind pickup trucks
and beat us for taking a walk in Bensonhurst, New York.
People who
send our kids to special education classes,
who say racism doesn't exist,
it's just us playing the race card.
Why don't we sing, "America the Beautiful"
with those who red line
and gentrify us into oblivion.
Why don't we join Gov. Gray "Lights Out" Davis
who reduced our community colleges' budget
by millions
and Jerry Brown, The Imperial Mayor of
Oakland, in a recitation of
the Pledge of Allegiance.
I mean, police brutality is the price you
have to pay to get people to shop at the
Gap.
They say that we should stand with
Rev. Billy Graham,
Pat Robertson and Jerry Falwell,
Christian soldiers
who want to hammer the infidels.
"Why those people over there are
Manicheans. They see the world in
black and white," said Stephen Cohen from the
Brookings Institute.
They say that we should belt out a chorus of
Kumbaya with
Pfizer Pharmaceuticals, experimenters on
African children, applaud them
for donating to the recovery effort of those thousands

who perished at the WTC,
sacrificed on the chainsaw of ignorance and
arrogance, the twin bothers of mayhem and death.
They say we should give a warm patriotic
embrace to those who say they're fighting for
freedom abroad but deny us freedom at home.
They always say that
we're fighting for freedom.
They said it during World War I, World War II,
the Korean War, the Vietnam War and the Gulf War.
They say now Mose and Mosetta and
Li'l Abner and Daisy Mae,
Jose and Maria if you
die for us in the steaming stinking jungles
and in the mean Afghanistan winters
we'll maybe let you
have a grilled cheese sandwich at Denny's.

They say we should unite,
that we should display the flag,
wear red, white and blue headrags
and help rebuild Wall Street.
"More than two weeks after the
terrorist attacks, costume retailers
report that the good guys are out-
selling the bad. Grownups and kids
are bypassing black capes and picking
up patriotic gear such as Uncle Sam hats."
They say we should empty our pockets and max out
our credit cards on Christmas
to show our loyalty.
"We must not put our buying

decisions on hold. Go out and
buy cars, and automobiles, and
electronics, and appliances," said
the economist.
"The market is a forward-looking
beast. We must hunker down with
the Beast," she said.
"Santa is going to look a lot
like Uncle Sam this year," predicted
Monk Rivers, a spokesman for the
Mill Corporation, which operates 12
malls.
We should show our determination
to vanquish our enemy
by emptying our wallets.
We must hunker down with the beast
for this crusade I mean campaign,
Operation Noble Eagle I mean,
Operation Infinite Justice
I mean, Operation Enduring Freedom.

I mean—
as soon as we can find out
who the enemy is.
Their unpronounceable names.
Their strange customs.
Their scraggly beards.
Their writing that looks like
wriggling worms.
Their baggy pants.
The diapers on their heads.
By jiminy, I heard that these A-rabs

expect to be surrounded by
25 virgins when they blow
themselves to kingdom come.
They hate modernity.
They hate "The Pink Flamingo,"
Britney Spears,
theme parks, Diet Coke, corn syrup sucrose,
obesity and novels whose
length exceeds 500 pages.
Why can't they get with the program.

WHY DO THEY HATE US
Major David Letterman asked General Dan Rather
THEY HATE US BECAUSE THEY'RE EVIL
THEY HATE US BECAUSE THEY'RE ENVIOUS
said General Dan Rather from his blow dried and
tanned silver foxhole at Black Rock.
Let the president tell me where to go
and I'll show up, he said.
"We should invade their countries,
kill their leaders and convert
them to Christianity," said Admiral Ann Coulter,
the *Daily News*'s ersatz blonde.
We should join Dumya in his crusade
I mean his campaign as soon as we can
locate the enemy. It keeps changing
like a chameleon, it seems to always be
one camp or cave ahead of us.
What did the woman on C-Span say
on Sept. 23, phoning in to the *Washington Journal*
Where do I go to get the understanding of
what I need to understand

in order to understand the president
who wants to invade Afghanistan or is
it Pakistan
or is it Tajikistan or is it
Uzbekistan or is it
Turkmenistan.

I can't stand all of these stans.
Hey! Don't we have someone who can speak Arabic.
Hey! What happened to those shining
seas that were supposed to protect us
from all of this PC nonsense.
All I wanted to be was baseball commissioner.
Get me Condi!

The Radical Moment of Truth
Etel Adnan

FOR ME IT ALL STARTED WITH THE THREE MILE ISLAND nuclear accident in Pennsylvania, in 1979, while I was in New York. The sky then looked all white and panic was subtly running over the faces of the people. The fragility of a formidable city like New York was suddenly made apparent.

That night I couldn't sleep, not out of fear but because of the consciousness that we are in a permanently apocalyptic world. I kept getting up and scribbling (on the grand piano of my host!) little bits of visions, which became in 1982 a small book of poetry entitled *From A to Z*, because there were as many poems as the letters of the alphabet.

The attacks on the New York towers and on the Pentagon were even more ominous. It was as if the world had taken a sharp curve and went out of orbit. The psychological shock was felt around the planet. The United States, the most powerful country for more than a century is seen, by now, as the supreme father-image: loved, hated, or envied; whatever people think or feel about its universal presence and weight (including in outer space!), the U.S. is held responsible for anything and everything that happens. It has become the ultimate point of reference, the paradigm by which the world defines itself.

What happened last September is that the "father" had been hit and people fell into disarray, regardless of the complexities of the sentiments they nourish toward the U.S. Most importantly, they are fearfully awaiting "Zeus" to unleash his thunder, knowing what the awesome power of that retaliation implies, and knowing that they will all be affected, with or without their approval.

The danger resides in the fact that two angers and two fears are now facing each other.

The usually dominant powers are afraid of this new, vicious, and invisible form of aggression that guerilla tactics represent. This danger is fluid. It calls for massive retaliation and that, in turn, creates more fear, anger, and frustration. Two unknown elements, both explosive, are closing in on each other. How far will the "War on Terrorism" go and how far will the rest of the world go in its own reactions? We are sailing into the unknown. We should be worried, should mobilize our mental energies to address such an ominous situation.

Technology has created means for destruction too powerful for this Earth. Earth is a known entity, charted and limited, while our powers of destruction have become unlimited, going beyond what the Earth can sustain. In the event of a new World War there will be no safe haven for life, our own species becoming the most vulnerable of all.

Each one of us, wherever he or she is, should be concerned. Each one of us has the right (and the duty) to express the anguish and, hopefully, the desire for the peaceful resolution of any conflict. These problems are man-made and therefore must be solved by men. There is no "other" in the crisis we've reached, we are together, absolutely together, in what has happened and what will ensue.

This crisis is just the tip of a volcano that spits its fire. It isn't limited to just one kind of terror, but rather, terror in every field of activity; the terrors of poverty, epidemics, oppression, and extreme pollution of both the Earth and its atmosphere. They all have reached a danger point. They are not imputable to a single country but, in diverse proportions, to all the countries of the world. Therefore, they require coordination of all possible efforts. The archaic ways of thinking in terms of special interests are obsolete. We must, for the sake of sheer survival, place our values on the welfare of humanity taken as a whole.

I think that the human imagination has lain dormant for too long. Statistics are no substitute for thinking. Bankers are not counting hexameters. Money is not a means to happiness anymore but leads only to more money. We are losing our powers to be creatively foolish. Who could build Macchu Pichu today? Who could lose his or her mind for the *Venus de Milo*? The grants and awards systems have colonized even the poets. Who remembers Maiakovsky?

I will take the risk of recalling a particular event that took place in Beirut in 1974 (a long time ago, indeed). The Armenian community in Lebanon was commemorating the genocide their parents had witnessed during the last years of the Ottoman Empire. They asked painters to contribute a painting for the show they had planned at the Armenian Cultural Center. Many artists responded favorably. As I am also a painter, I decided to participate (I had gone back to Lebanon for a few years). I took a big piece of white cardboard and wrote on it with a brush and China ink this statement:

> When the Armenians will fight for the good of the Palestinians,
> and the Palestinians for the Armenians,
> there will not be genocides.

My "painting" was refused. That's not art, I was told. I said, But that is graffiti art! A page from an artist's book!

The committee was, in fact, scared, given the tensions that were already running high in Lebanon…and which led to the civil war we all heard about. Some people said that the statement was meaningless. In a flash of light, I had seen the whole tribal mentality of people at war or remembering war; their "intense" patriotism, a form of self-love that we glorify. Tribal mentality is rewarding but dangerous. Sometimes it has to be turned around. And when that happens we will experience a moment of moral ecstasy, a moment of togetherness well above any satisfaction tribal solidarity would ever give.

As for my "painting," some artists and journalists supported my view, made pressure, and it was finally hung.

Our formidable arsenal of technological know-how must be directed toward goals such as the eradication of poverty or the restoration of an ecological balance. To that effect, technology shouldn't be blamed because, after all, it is neutral; it is knowledge that can be used for the better or for the worst. It needs to be enlightened by our capacities for love. I do not mean "love" in a general sense, but in its specific manifestations: love for people of any color, race, or creed, even love for the "enemy" when he isn't harmful anymore, love for the Earth whose generosity keeps us alive.

In a way, and without denying the responsibility of the most powerful among nations, the whole world is guilty for the state of the world; for its chaos, for its confusion. Every individual, every nation, as small as it is, could have done more than they did…and they didn't. It's not only the "big guys" that led us to where we stand. This admission of guilt, which does not divide the world between those who are "absolutely evil" and those who are "absolutely good," is, it seems, the starting point. It gives absolutely each and all the right and the duty to express sentiments and opinions about the current state of the world and to do something, according to one's conscience and capabilities, about it.

The innocent victims of the Towers' destruction are talking to us and telling us that we are living in a radical moment of truth: the past is begging to survive through its archæological sites and finds, which belong to the whole world; its monuments, old cities, libraries…The future demands our attention. As for the present, let's listen to the people. To say it in simple terms, whole populations on all of the continents are simply terrified. They are asking not only what happened, but also what's next? Let's be wise. Let's be human. Let's have peace.

Sent by Earth:
A Message
from the Grandmother Spirit
Alice Walker

Delivered to the Midwives Alliance of North America
Albuquerque, New Mexico, September 22, 2001

Love is not concerned
with whom you pray
or where you slept
the night you ran away
from home

Love is concerned
that the beating of your heart
the beating of your heart
should harm
no one

…The great danger in the world today is that the very feeling and conception of
what is a human being might well be lost.

—Richard Wright to Jean-Paul Sartre, in the 1940s
from Constance Webb's biography *Richard Wright*

THIS IS ONE OF THE EPIGRAMS I CHOSE TO PREFACE MY
first novel, *The Third Life of Grange Copeland* (1970), which was
about the challenge of remaining human under the horrific conditions of American Apartheid in the southern United States during my parents' and grandparents' time. They and their children
faced massively destructive psychological and physical violence
from landowners who used every conceivable weapon to keep the
sharecropping/slave labor system intact. It was a system in which
relatively few ruling class white people had the possibility of having as much food, land, space, and cheap energy to run their enter-
prises as they wanted while most people of color and many poor

white people had barely enough of anything to keep themselves alive.

"We own our own souls, don't we?" is that novel's ringing central cry.

In my opinion, this is also the ringing cry of our time.

I have been advised that there are several different groups of people in the audience; not just members of the Midwives Alliance of North America. I have been warned that some of these people are afraid I am just going to talk about birthin' and babies.[1] However, I came to Albuquerque especially because I wish to be with midwives, whose business of birthin' and babies is, I believe, the most honorable on Earth.

A few days ago I was in the presence of Sobonfu Somé, a contemporary carrier of traditional, precolonial, and perhaps prepatriarchal Ancient African life-ways. She taught us that in her culture, among the Dagara people of Burkina Faso, the most important thing that happens in a person's life is that they be welcomed when they are born. If they are not welcomed, all their lives they experience a feeling of not quite having arrived. There is anxiety. There is unease. This made me think of the title I had originally chosen for this talk, which changed after the bombing of the World Trade Center and the Pentagon, "Seeing the Light: The Importance of Being Properly Born."

Some of you who attended my talk last year may recall my story of my own birth: The midwife and my grandmother were present in the room, but alas, they were busy chatting by the fireplace as my mother, overwhelmed with pain, fainted as I was being born. Several minutes passed before they knew what happened. Was the fire going out? I wonder, even today. Were they busy, perhaps,

....

1. From Prissy's response to an abusive Scarlett O'Hara in *Gone with the Wind*: "Lord, Miz Scarlett, I don't know nothing 'bout birthin' no babies!"

restoring it? I realize that even at this late date I wish they'd been beside or on the bed, waiting to receive me, instead of halfway across the room. And that my mother had been conscious.

I wished this even more fervently after being permitted by a midwife friend to attend a home birth and to see for myself what is possible in terms of welcoming the newborn into its mother's arms, into the light of its father's smile, into the world and into its immediate community.

Sobonfu Somé then asked us to stand, as I am now asking you to do, and to turn to the person on either side, take their hands, look them in the eye, and tell them: I welcome you here. Take your time doing this, there is no hurry. If this is a person you've never seen before in your life, so much the better.

The Story of Why I Am Here
OR, A WOMAN CONNECTS OPPRESSIONS:
(Putting My Arms Around Sadie Hussein, Age Three)

An address given at a Peace for Cuba rally, February 1, 1992
from *Anything We Love Can Be Saved: A Writer's Activism*

Last January, when the war against Iraq was started, I was in Mexico writing a novel about a woman who is genitally mutilated in a ritual of female circumcision that her society imposes on all females. Genital mutilation is a mental and physical health hazard that directly affects some one hundred million women and girls worldwide, alive today, to whom it has been done. Because of increased risk of trauma during delivery, it affects the children to whom they give birth. Indirectly, because of its linkage to the spread of AIDS, especially among women and children, it affects the health and well-being of everyone on the planet.

With no television or radio, and no real eagerness to see or hear arrogant Western males discussing their military prowess, their delight in their own "clean-handed" destructiveness, I relied on a friend's phone calls to his son in San Francisco to keep me informed. His son told us about the huge resistance to the war in San Francisco, which made me love the city even more than I did already, and informed us, too, that he had been one of those demonstrators so outraged they'd closed down the Bay Bridge.

What to do? Go home and join the demonstration, or continue to write about the fact that little girls' bodies are daily bombed by dull knives, rusty tin can tops and scissors, shards of unwashed glass—and that this is done to them not by a foreign power but by their own parents and societies? I decided to stay put. To continue this story—which became *Possessing the Secret of Joy*—about female genital mutilation, also known as female circumcision, which I believe is vital for the world to hear. But, of course, I could not forget the war being waged against the earth and the people of Iraq.

Because I was thinking so hard about the suffering of little girls, while grieving over the frightened people trying to flee our government's bombs, my unconscious, in trying to help me balance my thoughts, did a quite wonderful thing. It gave me a substitute for Saddam Hussein, the solitary demon among tens of millions on whom the United States military's bombs were falling. Her name was Sadie Hussein and she was three years old. So, as the bombs fell, I thought about Sadie Hussein, with her bright black eyes and chubby cheeks, her shiny black curls and her dainty pink dress, and I put my arms around her. I could not, however, save her.

As it turned out, this was the truth. Saddam Hussein still reigns, at least as secure in his power over the Iraqis, according to some media sources, as George Bush is over North Americans. It is Sadie Hussein who is being destroyed, and who, along with nine hundred thousand other Iraqi children under the age of five, is dying of cholera, malnutrition, infection, and diarrhea. Since the war, fifty thousand such children have died. It is Sadie Hussein who starves daily on less than half her body's nutritional needs, while Saddam Hussein actually appears to have gained weight.

This is the story of why I am here today. I am here because I pay taxes. More money in taxes in one year than my sharecropping parents, descendents of enslaved Africans and Indians, earned in a lifetime. My taxes helped pay for Sadie Hussein's suffering and death. The grief I feel about this will accompany me to my grave.

I believe war is a weapon of persons without personal power, that is to say, the power to reason, the power to persuade, from a position of morality and integrity; and that to go to war with any enemy who is weaker than you is to admit you possess no resources within yourself to bring to bear on your own fate.

I will think of George Bush vomiting once into the lap of the Japanese prime minister—and all the media considered this major news—and will immediately see hundreds of thousands of Iraqi children, cold, hungry, dying of fever, dysentery, typhoid, and every other sickness, vomiting endlessly into the laps of their mothers—who are also emaciated, starving, terrorized, and so illiterate they are unable to read Saddam Hussein's name, no matter how large he writes it.

THERE IS NOT A MIDWIFE IN THIS ROOM WHO WOULD bomb a baby or a child or a pregnant woman. Perhaps in this particular room there is not one person who would do so. And yet, that is the position we find ourselves in. The war against Iraq continues.

In the ten years since I wrote my lament, millions more have died, the majority of them small children. Unlike most North Americans I did not watch the initial bombings on television; I did see later, however, the footage showing the bombing of a long line of what looked like old men trying to flee. They were running this way and that, their eyes filled with terror. I recognized more than I ever had that it is the very soul of the people of North America that is being lost, and that if this happens, for the rest of our time on the planet we are doomed to run with the dogs of war. The dogs of war. This is the vision that I have of this period. Ravenous, rapacious dogs, mad with greed and lust, red tongues out and salivating, running loose across the planet. They are the dogs that show up in some of the art of our time, in cartoons, or in the movie *Natural Born Killers* by Oliver Stone. It is an ancient image, however, and what astonishes me is how accurately and irresistibly it has risen in the psyche. And the psyche recognizes this image, not because it is only external but because some part of it is internal as well. Which means we must all look inside and get to know our own dogs of war. Some of our war dogs, we have to own, are paying taxes that will be used to destroy people almost identical to us. Many of our war dogs are connected to heating our homes and driving cars.

A Native Looks Up from the Plate
OR, OWNING HOW WE MUST LOOK TO A PERSON WHO HAS BECOME OUR FOOD

They are eating
us.
To step out of our doors
is to feel
their teeth
at our throats.

They are gobbling
up our
lands

our waters
our weavings
&
our artifacts.

They are nibbling
at the noses
of
our canoes
& moccasins.

They drink our oil
like cocktails
& lick down
our jewelry
like icicles.

They are siphoning
our songs.

They are devouring
us.
We brown, black
red and yellow,
unruly white
morsels
creating life
until we die.

Spread out in the chilling sun
that is
their plate.

They are eating
us raw

without sauce.

Everywhere we
have been
we are no more.
Everywhere we are
going
they do not want.

They are eating
us whole.
The glint of their
teeth
the light
that beckons
us to table
where only they
will dine.

They are devouring
us.
Our histories.
Our heroes.
Our ancestors.
And all appetizing
youngsters
to come.

Where they graze
among
the people
who create
who labor
who live

in beauty
and walk
so lightly
on the earth
there is nothing
left.

Not even our roots
reminding us
to bloom.

Now they have wedged
the whole
of the earth
between their
cheeks.

Their
wide bellies
crazily clad
in stolen goods
are near
to bursting
with
the fine meal
gone foul
that is us.

WHERE DO WE START? HOW DO WE RECLAIM A PROPER
relationship to the world?

It is said that in the Babemba tribe of South Africa, when a
person acts irresponsibly or unjustly, he is placed in the center of
the village, alone and unfettered. All work ceases and every man,

woman, and child in the village gathers in a large circle around the accused individual. Then each person in the tribe speaks to the accused, one at a time, about all the good things the person in the center of the circle has done in his lifetime. Every incident, every experience that can be recalled with any detail and accuracy is recounted. All his positive attributes, good deeds, strengths, and kindnesses are recited carefully at length.

The tribal ceremony often lasts several days. At the end, the tribal circle is broken, a joyous celebration takes place, and the person is symbolically and literally welcomed back into the tribe.[2]

This will not be the fate of Osama bin Laden, accused of masterminding the attack on North America. In a war on Afghanistan, he will either be left alive, while thousands of impoverished, frightened people, most of them women and children and the elderly, are bombed into oblivion around him, or he will be killed in a bombing attack for which he seems, in his spirit—from what I have gleaned from news sources—quite prepared. In his mind, he is fighting a holy war against the United States. To die in battle against it would be an honor. He has been quoted as saying he would like to make the United States into a shadow of itself as he helped make the Soviet Union, which lost the war in Afghanistan, become a shadow of itself. In fact, he appears to take credit for helping the Soviet Union disintegrate. I personally would like him to understand that the shadow he wishes upon us, of poverty, fear, an almost constant state of terror, is merely the America too many of us already know. It is certainly the shadow my ancestors lived with for several hundred years.

But what would happen to his cool armor if he could be reminded of all the good, nonviolent things he has done? Further, what would happen to him if he could be brought to understand the

_____

2. This story was passed on to me by the great Buddhist teacher Jack Kornfield.

preciousness of the lives he has destroyed? I firmly believe the only punishment that works is love. Or as the Buddha said: Hatred will never cease by hatred. By love alone is it healed. This is the ancient and the eternal law.

Recommendation

From *Call Me by My True Names*
by Thich Nhat Hanh

Promise me
promise me this day,
promise me now,
while the sun is overhead
exactly at the zenith,
promise me,
even as they
strike you down
with the mountain of hatred and violence;
even as they step on you and crush you
like a worm,
even as they dismember and disembowel you,
remember, brother,
remember:
man is not our enemy.

The only thing worthy of you is compassion —
invincible, limitless, unconditional.
Hatred will never let you face
the beast in man.

One day, when you face this beast alone,
with your courage intact, your eyes kind,

untroubled
(even as no one sees them)
out of your smile
will bloom a flower.
And those who love you
will behold you
across ten thousand worlds of birth and dying.

Thich Nhat Hanh, beloved Buddhist monk and peace practi-
tioner, wrote this poem in 1965 for the young people he worked
with who risked their lives every day during the war in Vietnam.
Remember that war? The napalmed naked children fleeing down
a flaming road? He wrote it to recommend that they prepare to die
without hatred. Some of them had already been killed violently,
and he cautioned the others against hating. He told them: "Our
enemy is our anger, hatred, greed, fanaticism, and discrimination
against [each other]. If you die because of violence, you must medi-
tate on compassion in order to forgive those who kill you. When
you die realizing this state of compassion, you are truly a child of
The Awakened One. Even if you are dying in oppression, shame,
and violence, if you can smile with forgiveness, you have great
power."

Thich Nhat Hanh reminds us, "When there is a mature relationship between people, there is always compassion and forgiveness." This observation is crucial to how we must now, more than
ever, understand our world. Every thought, every act, every gesture, must be in the direction of developing and maintaining a
mature relationship with the peoples of the planet; all thought of
domination, control, force, and violence must be abandoned.

Recommendation

From Horses Make a Landscape Look More Beautiful

I tell you, Chickadee
I am afraid of people
who cannot cry
Tears left unshed
turn to poison
in the ducts
Ask the next soldier you see
enjoying a massacre
if this is not so.

People who do not cry
are victims
of soul mutilation
paid for in Marlboros
and trucks.

Resist.

Violence does not work
except for the man
who pays your salary
Who knows
if you could still weep
you would not take the job.

As Clarissa Pinkola Estés, master *contadora* and *curandera*, points out: while it is true that the soul can never be destroyed, it can certainly leave us and take up residence elsewhere. I was struck by how many people I talked to after the bombing of the World Trade Center and the Pentagon said they were numb. Felt nothing.

Or didn't know what to feel. I myself experienced a sensation of hollowness. Emptiness. Insubstantiality. I felt weak, slightly nauseated, and as if my own body were disintegrating. I knew enough to let myself fully feel my feelings, whatever they were. At one point I remember laughing because one of our leaders, perhaps at a loss for something to say and to put a quick us-versus-them spin on the deeply traumatic events, called the pilots of the planes going into the Trade Towers "cowards." It was not a word that came to my mind at all. In fact, when I watched the suicide glide of the plane into the second tower, what I saw, and instantly recognized, was pain. And desperation. And disconnection. Alienation. And a closed-hearted, despairing courage, too, to sacrifice one's life (along with the lives of thousands of others) to make a point. What is the story whose fiery ending I am witnessing, I wondered. This was an act by a man who did not believe, definitely did not believe, in the possibility of love, or even common sense, to transform the world. I can easily imagine there will be thousands like him born in our time, that from the roots of this one man's story, they will come to birth practically every minute; and our government will not be remotely able to "smoke" all of them "out of their holes." The world being what it is, some of those "holes" are likely to be uncomfortably close to us.

What are we going to feel like if we kill thousands and thousands of people who somewhat resemble this man? I can tell you: We are not going to feel fine. We are not going to feel happy. Some of us, perhaps the very young, will feel triumphant and larger than life for three weeks or so. After that, we will begin to wonder who exactly it was that we killed. And why. And whether a hungry, naked boy herding goats on a land-mine-saturated hill was really the right guy. Murder, after all, is murder, even if it is done in war. It is very intimate. The beings we kill become, somehow, ours for life. Ironically, we become responsible for them in death, as we were not in life. With time, we are going to be reminded of a few facts that speak to this: that, for instance, during the Vietnam War, in which America bombed a country many of us had never heard of, fifty thousand Americans died. But since the end of the war more than sixty thousand who were in the war have died from suicide and drug overdoses and other ailments of the spirit and soul. George Bush *père* counseled us to "put the war (that war) behind us." But as Michael Meade, magical storyteller and warrior, so emphatically reminds us, when speaking of that war, in which he refused to fight: "What is behind us is a long, long row of coffins and we'd better turn around and genuinely grieve and give our dead, both Vietnamese and American, a proper burial. Then we might all be able to talk about going on."

It is not too hard to imagine that those who are now calling for war, so many of them old men, have not engaged their true feelings in so long that they think to bomb country after country is to grieve.

What grieving is not:

Grieving is not the same as massacre.

Grieving is not the same as shopping.

Grieving is not the same as overeating.

Grieving is not the same as worrying about one's weight (or one's color, sex, or age).

Grieving is not the same as trying to stay young.

Grieving is not the same as coloring your hair a new shade each month to forget you've turned over money that will be used to blow off people's heads.

Grieving is not the same as seeing the shadow in everyone but yourself.

To grieve is, above all, to acknowledge loss, to understand there is a natural end to endless gain.

To grieve means to come to an understanding, finally, of inevitable balance; Life will right itself, though how it does this remains, and will doubtless continue to remain, mysterious.

The Taliban in Afghanistan, for instance, who have treated the indigenous women with such brutal contempt (thousands have been driven to suicide) now face a moment in time when theirs is the position of the women they have tortured. It will always be so.

It is this natural balancing of life that we fear. That is why, given the history of our own country, many feel a need to be protected by Star Wars.

AT THIS TIME OF MOURNING, MAY WE BE CONNECTED to each other. May we know the range and depth of feelings in ourselves and in each other. There is vulnerability, fear, love, rage, hatred, compassion, courage, despair, and hope in ourselves, each other, and the world. May we know our most authentic feelings and voice them when we speak. May we tap into soul and spirit when we are silent together. May healing begin in us. May we form and become a circle.

Begin by holding hands in a circle (even two people can be a circle). Be silent and feel the clasp and connection of hands and heart. Then each in turn, speak for yourself and listen to each other. Put judgment aside. Remember that anything voiced that you want to silence may be a silenced part of yourself. Sing what spontaneously wants to be sung and end each circle as it was begun. Hold hands once again.

Hold silence. For meditation, contemplation, prayer.

Invite blessings.

Until we meet again.

I RECEIVED THIS MESSAGE FROM JEAN SHINODA BOLEN, M.D., master healer of the psyche and author of *The Millionth Circle*, among many other books. She writes: "A circle is a healing and connecting prescription accessible to everyone. Every family, any group of people anywhere can form one. In preparation for the fifth U.N. Conference on Women and the United General Assembly Special Session on Children, the Millionth Circle 2005 planning committee wrote this statement of intention:

> Circles encourage connection and cooperation among their members and inspire compassionate solutions to individual, community and world problems. We believe that circles support each member to find her or his voice and to live more courageously. Therefore, we intend to seed and nurture circles wherever possible, in order to cultivate equality, sustainable livelihoods, preservation of the Earth and peace for all. Our aim is to celebrate the millionth circle as the metaphor of an idea whose time has come.

The "millionth circle" metaphor was taken from the title of Jean's book, which in turn was inspired by the story of the "hundredth monkey and morphic field theory" that sustained activists in the 1970s and 80s in the face of conventional wisdom that said ordinary people could not deter the nuclear arms race.

Jean advises: "Wherever you are today, tomorrow, next week— bring people (include the children) together to form circles. If you are in a group, transform it into a circle. If you are already in a circle, get together. In response to the destruction of buildings, families, lives, and everyone's sense of security, this is something you can do to help."

I have been part of a circle for three years. It is one of the most important connections of my life. One reason the circle is so powerful is that it is informed, in fact shaped by, the Grandmother Spirit. The spirit of impartiality, equality, equanimity. Of nurturing but also of fierceness. It has no use for hierarchy. Or patriarchy. Tolerates violence against itself for a while, but will sooner or later rise to defend itself. This is the spirit of the Earth itself.

And so today, I feel sent to you, midwives of North America, by the Earth herself. You are, against the cruelest odds of history and laws, attempting to bring human beings into the world in a way that welcomes them. I have seen your work with my own eyes and

I know it is essential in getting humankind back on the right track. Women must be supported, loved, listened to, cared for, as they are carrying life and attempting to deliver it to our world. To us, Life's community, not to the war machine. The child must be able to feel, emerging from the womb, that we are honored it is here. We are thrilled. We are called upon in this frightful time to labor for the body and the soul.

We must learn nothing less than how to be born again.

Just as the body loves exercise, though it complains, the soul loves awareness. For a long time I've pondered the expression "Never let the right hand know what the left hand is doing." This advice, I believe, is wrong. We must struggle to see both our hands, and their activity, clearly. We must see, for instance, the Palestinians and what has happened to their homes, their fields, and their trees; and we must see what is happening to the Israelis and their homes and their fields and their trees. We must see where our tax dollars flow and try, in awareness, to follow them. We, as Americans, have a hand in each nation's fate, but we tend to look only at the hand the news media shows us, constantly. This situation in the Middle East, a war between brothers and cousins, may mean the end of life as we in North America know it. It may ultimately mean our lives. The soul wants to know the truth: what is really going on. Nor must we fall asleep while Afghanistan, a country with 700,000 disabled orphans, is being bombed. We must struggle to stay awake enough to imagine what it feels like to be small and afraid, not to have parents, to be disabled, to be hungry and lonely, and not be able, either, to get out of the way of America's wrath. The soul wants to know why we have paid taxes to support the Taliban. Why, through that group, we have so heartlessly supported the debasement and assassination of the Feminine.

While we trudge onward, trying to remember what Black Elk observed—that all living beings are essentially alike—I recommend the wearing of two threads of different colors, one of them, representing the feminine, red. The red thread should be worn on the left wrist, closest to the heart, and the brown or white or black thread, representing whatever endangers the feminine, the Grandmother, Earth, on the right. These will remind us to stay awake.

It will also help, I think, to create an altar, especially for our children who make up so much of the military. It should be kept beautiful with flowers and candles and bowed to every day. There is no way most of them will ever understand who they are killing, or why. The souls of many of them will go so far from their bodies during war that they will never return. There should be feathers and stones and other meaningful objects on this altar, but above all, there should be a mirror. And pictures of our loved ones who never knew what struck them on the 11th of September. Together they, our children, and the children our children will kill, will create a circle. Let us acknowledge that.

While thinking of the Grandmother Spirit that I believe should be guiding Earth, and must for humans to survive, I thought of three women, all unmarried as far as I know, two of them childless, all relatively young. Still, they exemplify the spirit of which I speak. They are Julia Butterfly Hill, who sat in a precious, old-growth redwood tree for two years, trying to save it from being cut down; Amy Goodman, of Democracy Now, who has clung to the airwaves to bring us truly informative radio; and Representative Barbara Lee, who alone voted not to give away Congress's (and therefore, the People's) right to declare war. I invoke their names to honor them in this gathering of wise, strong women who will understand exactly how this kind of courage differs from the kind that speaks calmly of "collateral damage," i.e., obliteration of infants, pregnant women and small children, old men running in terror meted out from the sky.

A mudra is a hand gesture used in meditation to evoke a particular state.

A chant is a repetitive vocalization of One's deepest beliefs and hopes in an effort to inscribe those hopes and beliefs in the courageous and compassionate heart of One's self and others.

ON THE DAY OF THE BOMBINGS I REALIZED WHY CHRISTians cross themselves. And why the people of Islam turn toward Mecca. I knew that I also needed a gesture of self-blessing that would, at the same time, symbolize blessing and protection of the world and its varied inhabitants.

I realized we, as humans, need a New World peace mudra and a chant to help us through the days ahead, which will undoubtedly cause unprecedented suffering and pain. Partly because more people than ever before will be conscious of what is happening. And untold thousands will feel completely helpless to do anything about it.

Spirit, the Grandmother Spirit of Earth, sent me this mudra and chant:

The mudra is to hold the thumb and first two fingers together, symbolizing unity, while making a circle around One's heart. A circle that covers as much of the body as possible. Or as large a circle as one has need. This is done three times, while chanting:

One Earth
One People
One Love

One Earth
One People
One Love

One Earth
One People
One Love

Please stand and let us together chant this blessing seven times; seven is the ideal number of people in a circle that is designed to grow the soul and transform the world.

There are only two or three human stories, and they go on repeating themselves as fiercely as if they had never happened before.

WILLA CATHER | *O Pioneers!*

Seeking the Ordinary
Ehud Havazelet

I HAVE TWO SONS. THE OLDER, THIRTEEN, LIVES IN PHILA-
delphia with his mom. We're rarely together anymore for April
Fool's Day, so we have over the years contrived a series of elabo-
rate pranks, him calling to tell me about some miraculous trade the
Yankees just made, me telling him we'd won an all-expenses-paid
trip to the Salt Lake City Olympics. There's a measure of optimism
in these games, the sense that the joke, once revealed, will not
prove too disappointing (I gave him the world's hairiest potato as
an after-school snack one time, but had a bag of M & M s ready), that
what will follow this revelation, quickly, is the welcome solace of
the old order still intact (when he was three he so convincingly

aped hurting himself that I came running up the stairs, to his impish triumphal grin).

My mother has never been a good sleeper. I remember as a boy being fascinated, disturbed, even entertained, by the way she woke, always with a gasp, eyes momentarily wild, a split-second transition from what seemed to be deep, placid rest to panic. The telephone, in particular, would startle her, a frantic looking- around to make sure everything was safe. I had no idea what it was about, then. Having a child grow up a continent away, I have a better idea now.

So when the phone rang a little past eight in the morning I was awake instantly, had answered by the end of the first ring. It was Michael—he was all right. And when he said, "A plane hit the World Trade Center," I found myself groggily trying to remember if it could be April already.

My wife, beside me, was in the immobile, flung-into-sleep posture of a new mother snatching some rest between feedings. Our six-week-old boy was in his crib nearby. When I turned on the television and she woke, she first said, "What city is that?" She later told me she couldn't recognize New York, the landmark she was searching for was the very one missing from the middle of the picture. She also told me she assumed for a minute, seeing the rubble, the smoke, the sight of an urban landscape reduced to wreckage, that it must be Europe somewhere, or the Middle East.

We brought the baby into bed with us. We played with him and he nursed and slept, woke and nursed again. We made our calls. I was able to get through to my parents in Queens, one sister in Manhattan, my family was safe. Everyone we talked to made a reference to where this day fit into a personal hierarchy of disaster— "Not since Pearl Harbor...," "...JFK...," "...Challenger...." My son said to me, "Nothing like this has ever happened before."

Like millions across the world, I watched TV for probably sixteen hours that day, trying to locate, then to determine what to do with my feelings. I remembered the Challenger explosion; that day, too, I was in front of a TV screen for hours. But that day, as shocking and inexplicable as it seemed—we, as the technological superpower, were supposed to be beyond the reach of such catastrophes— that day was containable, if that's the word I'm looking for, assimilable. A terrible, appalling thing—for the families of the astronauts, for the schoolchildren watching it on TV back in Massachusetts, hard news for our Space Program, for our national sense of ourselves and our ambitions.

But it remained outside, not in the room with me. I was a spectator, concerned, horrified, my empathetic sense humming and dismayed. But it hadn't happened to me, except by inference, and while it was on my mind, and everyone's for months to come, there was not a sense that this event would not go away, that it had somehow changed everything.

On September 11, playing with our baby, calling back east, I wondered, absently, what was wrong in me, what was different, and it was precisely this, I realized. The return to normalcy I anticipated wasn't coming. The solace of the old order, once the event itself has been digested—that was gone. I felt, as I assume millions did, isolated, exposed, unsure of what else could possibly happen that day, where and to whom it would happen next. Maybe me. Maybe my family.

The anxious fear at the pit of my stomach was not just for the horror of the event, but for what it meant, for us all. As my thirteen-year-old put it, "Nothing like this has ever happened before." I sensed he was right, and what would that mean?

AND WHAT WERE MY FEELINGS THAT DAY?

Shock. Mesmerized by the images in constant repetition—the second plane hitting, the plume of fire and smoke erupting from the building's side; the south then the north tower collapsing, in an orderly downward motion—a reverse mushroom cloud, someone called it—so cleanly (at least on TV, at least 3,000 miles away) they looked like those planned demolitions of old Sears buildings and Vegas hotels that people gathered to enjoy; then a tourist's home video, catching the first plane as it banked into the south tower. On every network, the same pictures, the same images over and over from every possible angle, until someone realized it couldn't be good for children, or maybe for any of us, these images, already unforgettable, seared like nightmares into our brains by hours of watching. An eerie sense that everyone in the country was seeing what I was seeing, and millions around the world, all staring with rapt and helpless and oddly vacant attention—no new information, but we watched anyway—at the same two planes, the same two buildings falling, the same smoky emptiness left behind, at something we couldn't understand.

Relief. My son in Philadelphia was okay. Our baby slept and nursed, his fist batting my wife's chest, his bright, intent eyes roving the room, as oblivious to everything beyond his senses, as utterly, miraculously local as he had been the night before. My family was safe. My parents, who live on Queens Boulevard, one of New York's busiest and most dangerous streets, saw the ambulances and fire trucks racing west and thought there must have been an unusually bad accident somewhere toward the City. My two sisters in Manhattan were okay, they had to walk miles to get home since the subways were closed, but they were fine. My sister on the Island, and her children, okay. Relief, something like driving by a horrific wreck and your hormones, adrenaline or endorphins, whatever chemicals alert you to danger then send out the all-safe signal, surging. It had been close, but we were spared.

Fear. There was a sense that day, and in the days that followed, that if something this huge and awful could happen once, it might continue happening. There hadn't been one plane, after all, but four, aimed at several targets. There was planning and coordination and intelligence behind this, it didn't feel like the Murrah building or the attack on the *Cole*, the sudden and brief flaring of madness or zealotry, terrifying then done. Nobody I know worried back in 1998 that there might be another Murrah. But here was something new, a new war, the pundits began calling it, meaning, I think, new in the sense of who our enemies were, and their methodologies, new ideas about tactics and fields of battle. But something else was new, as well, the illusion, suddenly shattered, of our invulnerability: this had happened here, in America, and to us, not to some riotous and unstable group of foreigners, who, by their very inability to resolve their problems and prosper, to protect themselves and sustain a peaceful, orderly life, probably somehow—not that you'd say so in polite company—brought their troubles on themselves. There had never been a foreign attack on American soil since 1812. These things just didn't happen—here.

Hate. I could call it something else; I'd prefer to label it an admixture of the feelings above, some biochemical (therefore involuntary) trace of adrenaline overload. But as I watched the buildings fall and fall, watched people fleeing in terror (sometimes clichés actually get it right), people like me, or my family, a rage, murderous and intractable, rose in me. There were people out there who would slaughter us, our children, our innocents, because of an ideology; because of their beliefs, abstractions about god and justice and the holiness of battle, they would see all of us die. I told my wife if I saw bin Laden I'd kill him myself.

But as the day wore on, this seemed too easy. Comforting as it was, this hormone-stoked, manly, kick-ass aggression was too simple a response. Interspersed with the Pentagon's stoved-in side, the Towers' collapse, were tapes of bin Laden himself. As I watched I was disturbed in a way I was unprepared for, in a way I had not registered when he earlier had made the evening news. He did not seem insane. On December 13, when the State Department released tape of his visit to a sheik on which he happily discussed the triumph of the attacks, at one point smiling when saying some of the men boarding the planes did not realize they were on a suicide mission, experts everywhere said this was irrefutable proof of his madness, his cold-blooded psychosis. I didn't see it. I wanted to, but I didn't see it.

We have an image of madness. It comes associated with the pomp, the silly adolescent playacting in Hitler's barks and semaphore gesticulations, in Mussolini's moronic, self-satisfied smirk; it comes with the dress-up, dime-store regality of dictators in gold brocade and epaulets, with Jim Jones in Elvis sunglasses languorous on his makeshift throne. It comes with the petulant desperation to impress of David Koresh, in Tim McVeigh's stony, fuck-you glare. It comes with the otherworldly glint of insanity in Charlie Manson's leering grin.

What it comes with is an unmistakable mark of otherness. You take one look at these people and recognize it, their absolute self-involvement, their creepy need to dominate, insinuate themselves into your head, the stolid, dead-in-the-eyes complacency of someone for whom there is no longer any question about his absolute right. You take one look and you recognize them, on a level close to instinct you see them for what they are, you get away soon as you can. And it is their mark, their separateness, their impossible-to-conceal otherness that is our great consoler. At least you know whom you're dealing with.

This is what the experts were saying about bin Laden in the tapes, and I wanted to see it. But what I saw was a man calmly, pleasantly discussing his work, speaking quietly, no boasting or haranguing. He had limpid, sad eyes that in someone else's face I would have called wise, and long, tapered, delicate fingers that reminded me of an artist's. His voice was modulated and reasonable. If anyone made a disgusting impression it was his fawning host, delighted to have a celebrity in his house.

I do not discount his actions. If I had any possible doubts about his involvement, this tape took care of them. I felt no mitigation in my rage toward the man and what he had done. But when they said, Here is the face of a madman, Here is the face of a mass murderer, I looked for that face, I wanted to see it. If I could cast this man as monster and push him beyond the ken of what was acceptably human, the task would be relatively easy for us. Find the fucker and grease him. Job over.

My son goes to a Quaker school in Philadelphia. In their regular meeting for worship, in which there is no liturgy, no organized prayer, just silent meditation and the opportunity for whoever likes to stand and speak his mind, my son stood and spoke. He said there was no excuse for what the terrorists had done. But we needed to remember these people come from places where there is hunger and war and exile, and often they lead pretty miserable lives. And they hate us. They hate us enough to do this to us. Why? Until we look at the conditions these people live in, and how different their lives are from ours, we will never really learn what had happened that day in New York and in Washington.

My thirteen-year-old helped me see what I was struggling to figure out. What was scariest, most appalling about bin Laden enjoying a friendly chat with his host was his lack of agitation, the absence of the hallmarks of derangement I expected to see. The man believed in what he had done, saw no reason his faith should be shaken. This was the crux of the insanity he did suffer—that he saw no conflict between the political and religious aims he harbored and the murder of thousands of civilians to achieve them. This was what made me queasy as I watched.

And the feeling did not slacken over the next weeks as I listened to our own politicians preen and orate about American values. We were attacked, we were told over and over, because of our democratic way of life. We were attacked because some people hate freedom. We were attacked because America is the beacon of justice and liberty and free trade in this world and this just pisses some people off enough that they want to kill us. When asked if 9/11 would lead to an examination of the policies that might have led to such hate—among them, at various times, our expedient support of brutally repressive regimes; our inability, in our determined support of Israel, to heed the just—no less so because they are complicated, difficult to achieve—calls of the Palestinians for self-determination and an end to Israeli occupation; the devastating suffering, according to the Red Cross and other international aid organizations, of civilians, a great many of them children, due to our sanctions against Saddam—Ari Fleischer, the President's Press Secretary said, unequivocally, absolutely not.

I listened to our leaders, political and cultural, reasonable sounding, calmly speaking men and women who clearly believed, deeply, in what they said. And the queasiness revealed its source: on every side, people so certain, so monolithically and imperviously certain of the absolute justice of their beliefs that the simplest human truths—that people are dying on both sides because of these policies of smug, willful indifference—just disappear behind bluster and rhetoric's intellectual smoke.

I am no politician, certainly no policy maker. But I found myself having a hard time distinguishing between the language of those who say their deity delights in the slaughter of civilians, and those who say whoever attacks us is attacking freedom. It simply isn't that easy.

I asked a friend of mine who lives in downtown Manhattan about her impressions after the attack. The one thing that stood out above all others, she wrote me, was the smell:

More than anything, my nose was the body part that registered what had gone on. As late as two months after, you could be up on Forty-second street and get a sudden whiff of it. In my mind the smell became "it," as in "that's it, isn't it? Do you smell it?" And in the early weeks it pervaded Manhattan and many parts of Brooklyn. It was distinct, acrid, quasi-familiar. The smell was the way the horror became infused into your day; you literally could not escape it.

The smell, she did not need to explain, was the bodies rotting at Ground Zero.

I don't believe the leaders on either side. The people I believe are the ones who live it. Not the Israeli soldiers driving the bulldozers over a Palestinian home, but the mother and children who then have nowhere to go. Not our pilots' gleeful whoops when registering a direct hit in Afghanistan (just as my son does playing on his Nintendo), on a target thousands of feet below, but the people, soldiers or not, at the other end of the video game. Not the smoothly indifferent spokespeople on all sides, Hamas or the Taliban or the Israeli government or our own, who get to speak in abstractions about freedom and oppression and divine provenance, while someone is picking up the pieces of the bodies and preparing to tell the parents. Not the dignitaries who get to dress up as firemen for a day and tour the site, salute the brave—indeed, astonishingly brave men and women working weeks after all hope has vanished to recover every body from the ruins—and then make a speech for the cameras, but the people whose families are shattered, who thought the world had ended one morning, who for weeks after breathed in the atomized remains of their neighbors.

I'VE BEEN HAVING SOME TROUBLE WRITING THIS ESSAY, and some trouble understanding why. It can't be that I have nothing to say about 9/11—when the editors of this volume approached me I thought the problem would be deciding what, among so many ideas and emotions, I would choose to focus on. But it's been difficult. I am not sure what I, 3,000 miles away, can add to what's been said. I'm reluctant to do what writers do, deal in metaphor and analogy and context, all for the sake of making a point. I don't know what I can say that is as true or more worth hearing than what my friend Carol wrote me.

So, as happens when the writing doesn't come easily, I fret. I try on different voices, read for guidance, take walks in my backyard hoping for the spark of an idea. This morning, I got the baby up and dressed, my wife fed him, and the dog and I saw them off to daycare and work. I made myself breakfast and sat down, determined finally to focus my thoughts, organize my ideas, marshal a suitable and comely rhetoric to express them. To write well. The phone rang. I let it. A few minutes later it rang again, and I let it, but when it rang almost immediately a third time I answered. A woman said, "Hello, this is Capitol One?" Thick Hispanic accent, uncomfortable with the words, sounding rushed, maybe anxious. No, I told her, wrong number. Over the next half hour the phone rang almost constantly. I tried ignoring it. Again, the writing wasn't going well and this certainly wasn't helping things. Finally, growing annoyed, I picked the phone up and said, sarcastically, "No, still the wrong number." Next time I lost my patience. This is a private house, I scolded the woman, not Capitol One. You are disturbing people. Someone had given her this number, she said. I understand, I said, but it's the wrong number and it won't become the right one just because you keep dialing it. People here are trying to work, I said, and I didn't say, they're having a hard time of it, as a matter of fact, and there's no way they'll figure out what it is they have to say for this important book of essays if the goddamn phone keeps ringing every minute and a half. She understood me anyway. "Oh," she said, "I sorry." She hung up. I felt sorry, too, immediately. I said "Good luck," but I don't know if she heard me before she put the receiver down.

So the idea I've got isn't a very original one, certainly not the stunning nexus of feeling and intellect I'd hoped for. After I hung up I went and listened to the messages she had left on the machine. Her name was Naomi Perez. Something about a conversation she'd had with a Mr. Wilson at Capitol One. Four messages, a couple of hangups. Could he please call her back. This was the number she had been given. I thank you, she said at the end of each message.

I could have taken a minute to help Naomi Perez. I could have looked up the number in the phone book for her, or asked what number she was given. She deserved better luck than to reach an irascible, badly focused writer on a Tuesday morning, but she'd figure it out without my help—she sounded competent, despite her difficulty with the language—and she'd find Mr. Wilson, the prideful annoyance creeping into her voice in the last message told me that. She'd be all right. So my point isn't about Naomi Perez. It's about me: I could have used that moment to help her. A small thing. But if I had done it, I would have had that today, even if the writing continued to be hard. The point is about me and how often, while seeking so diligently what I think I need, I'm looking in entirely the wrong direction.

WHEN I LEFT NEW YORK IN 1978 IT WAS FOR THREE months only, of this I was certain. I would have bet everything I owned that I would not only return at the end of the summer but that New York would be my home, always.

It had been this way since I am able to remember. After moving from Jerusalem when I was two, my great determinants became the City and the state of being American. I remember, at four, staring in triumph at the clock on the kitchen wall, thinking, impossibly, of course, that I had one Hebrew word left to forget— *ophanaim* (bicycle)—after which I would be a fully American boy. Sports played a big part in my identity seeking; once I was old enough, the Yankees became my religion. I can still summon the absolute devastation I felt on the school bus heading home in October of 1964, when, despite two solo home runs by Clete Boyer and, of all people, Phil Linz, the Yankees came up short and lost to Bob Gibson and the Cardinals in seven games. In my dreams I was Mickey Mantle; in the day's soberer light I was Bobby Richardson, sleek-fielding, clutch-hitting second baseman. One of the great thrills of my life, still, was being there in 1977 when Reggie Jackson hit his three home runs to crush the loathed, smarmy, renegade Dodgers in game six of the Series.

As soon as I was old enough I fled the boroughs for Manhattan, the center, as far as I was concerned, of the world. I went to high school and college in the City, and made it my own. I knew every stop on the subway in Manhattan, Queens, Brooklyn—my knowledge of the Bronx was limited to the two routes to the Stadium. I spent more time than was good for my grades on the streets, in the east side museums, and assumed I'd end up in the Village sooner or later, where the musicians and hippies were, where I'd seen Bill Evans at the Vanguard, Muddy Waters at the Bottom Line, The Band and The Allman Brothers at the Fillmore East.

New Yorkers, politics aside, are, like most people, a conservative lot. When the Verazzano Bridge opened in 1964 there was a celebration, the governor and mayor cutting the ribbon, thousands of people walking across the two spans of what was then the longest suspension bridge in the world. This was a proud moment, the need for a better route from Staten Island to the City had long been clear. And it was acceptable, also, far out as it was on the tip of Brooklyn, far from the City and the Brooklyn Bridge, jewel of bridges, even from its dowdier, respectable neighbors to the north, the Williamsburg, Manhattan, and Queens boroughs. It was an addition, simply, and welcome for that.

Not so the World Trade Center towers. New York had been associated with the Empire State Building for so long, from King Kong forward (I assumed, as a kid, the state had taken its nickname from the building, not vice versa) there was a feeling that the Twin Towers were redundant, tacky, and, even in a town not famous for shying from the hubristic, a bit much. Suddenly mere height seemed a secondary trait (though that, after all, had made the Empire State famous). The beloved landmark had its classical lines, its stately tiers and facing. The towers were monolithic, ungainly, big simply for the sake of being so. They were dubbed "Nelson" and "David" after the Rockefeller brothers, one New York's governor at the time, who rammed the plans through the legislature. When, barely a month after they opened, the Sears Tower in Chicago eclipsed them as the "World's Tallest Building," those of us who preferred the Empire State, the Chrysler, and the Woolworth were quietly pleased. When the Windows on the World restaurant opened to a year-long waiting list and universally terrible reviews, ditto. The Towers showed up immediately on T-shirts, postcards, calendars, but to many of us they never would take; they were for tourists and corporate types, for Rockefeller and Robert Moses and their heirs, Trump and Helmsley.

Another shock then, on 9/11, was how much they had become part of the city, the first thing you saw on the horizon from the west; from the east, driving across the bridges, the guidepost you used to orient yourself to the view, to find the Statue of Liberty or Ellis Island. After the 1993 attack, and the building's survival, emblematic of the city's toughness, the resilience that would be so severely tested eight years later, the Towers seemed to belong after all—ugly, maybe, with all the grace of two steel milk cartons, but tough old buildings, survivors, ours.

But can I say that? I'm an Oregonian now. I've lived here nearly as long as I lived in New York, thirteen years, married and had a child here. My landmarks now are Douglas firs and big-leaf maples;

I see osprey and bats and vultures where I used to see commercial jets and traffic helicopters. I've traded the raspy screech of the etched eastern blue jay, and the sudden flash of a cardinal landing on a bare bush in February, for the hooded Steller's jay who can sound like a distant hawk, and the lovely, painted-looking varied thrushes who pick after grubs in our unraked leaves all winter. While I'm worried my son, when he's able, will walk out into the street, I'm more concerned he'll walk down to the creek.

I've traded buildings for sky, MOMA and the Met for two acres to wander in, and I happily absorb the barbs of my best friends who jealously abuse me about the Yankees' recent successes. My older son loves Oregon, but, a city boy, thinks Corvallis is kind of a joke. For my younger son, this will be home.

Most of my writing life I've brooded about exile. A child transplanted from Israel, I always wanted to be American, never fully felt I could pull it off. I've hardly ever been as hurt as when my first writing teacher, to my tremendous shame, asked if English was my first language—there were traces, apparently, of an accent, of a foreigner's meticulous appropriation in my prose. The son of rabbis, I foreswore religion. A New Yorker to the marrow, I was certain, I've ended up happily in a small town at the continent's far edge. For the book I am writing I've tried to research family roots in Russia, Poland, Moldova, but can find no trace beyond my great-grandfather who kept to his vow the day he arrived in America never to speak about Russia or in the language again. I've long since given up the dream of knowing myself entirely, that hope I had looking at the kitchen clock, and have come to be on better terms with who I am—an amalgam, a work-in-progress constantly being revised, an experiment in loss and reconciliation, ambition and despair, just like most everyone I know and care about.

War endows identity. Where I live the flags still haven't come off the house fronts, cars have American flags out one window, flags for the Beavers or Ducks out the other. Billboards sport company logos over the Stars and Stripes, no further explanation necessary. Soon after 9/11 a newspaper printed fliers of Old Glory with the caption United We Stand, and you can still see these everywhere, in car and shop windows, by cash registers and on restaurant walls. Last week I watched the Super Bowl. During halftime, U2, an Irish band who twenty years ago sang sometimes about revolution, played on a heart-shaped stage surrounded by baton-twirling cheerleaders in a snowstorm of red, white, and blue confetti, while the names of those lost on 9/11 were projected on a huge screen behind them. Sir Paul McCartney assured us the whole world is with the U.S.A. In a Budweiser commercial, the famous Clydesdales trotted through the snow from St. Louis to New York City, where first the lead horse, then the seven remaining, bowed to the knees, if that's what horses have, before Lady Liberty.

We as a nation know who we are again. Even our President, brought to office after the murkiest election in history, is receiving record approval ratings for his leadership in the war against terror.

As someone who cannot claim anything like the shattering experiences of this century's many real exiles, but who nonetheless has inherited something of their psychology, I'm uneasy in the face of such exultation, everyone happily coming together again under a reinvigorated idea of Americanness. Spectacle is what we do best, and spectacle is meant to overwhelm, to sweep you up mindlessly in the joyous moment, and Super Bowl halftime, if this was what it was meant to do, succeeded gloriously, from the evidence of the young faces, proud and shining, on the hundreds of performers that night. Watching, I felt what Edward Said has related about reading Conrad, an "unmistakable…aura of dislocation, instability, and strangeness," and the odd, prickly sensation of fear beginning to gather while watching a mob embrace an idea.

The idea of America represented by two skyscraping towers of commerce and national pride. The World Trade Center, ungainly cousin to the City's more graceful monuments during its nearly thirty years will now, even in its absence, forever symbolize New York to us, America and ourselves to us. And in a sense this is what bin Laden meant to attack, America's idea of itself, though he would have other words to describe the idea than we do. Believing in his idea he was able to do what he did, an enterprise altogether easier to undertake than considering the people inside the two buildings, representing, ironically, the citizens of more than eighty nations.

Watching the halftime extravaganza I thought about this, what a bracing consolation this kind of belief must be, constant, unshakeable, ordained by whatever god you see in the sky above you lit with fireworks.

We Don't Live on Things.
We Live on the Meaning of Things.
Tom Spanbauer

WHEN I FIRST MOVED TO NEW YORK, THE CHRYSLER BUILD-
ing, the Empire State Building, the Woolworth Building, Rockefeller Center, and the Brooklyn Bridge were the edifices that sym-
bolized the spirit of New York. These were the structures I had
read about, seen in movies. Their grace of architecture held a sense
of history.

The World Trade Center, those two monoliths at the bottom
of New York, were garish newcomers. After all, what could be so
important about two big rectangles?

LIKE MOST NEW YORKERS, WHEN MY FEET FIRST HIT THE
pavement, they were running. North is where I ran first, to Colum-

bia University where I'd been accepted into the MFA Fiction program.

I'll never forget the first day I got off the Number One on One Hundred and Sixteenth Street, walked up the stairs, then through the iron gates on Broadway and into the university enclave. I just stood there like a dumb farm animal. I couldn't believe that such a respected institution had accepted the likes of me.

Mid-town is where I ran next, to a theater restaurant where I worked four shifts a week while I went to school.

IT WASN'T UNTIL FRIENDS AND FAMILY BEGAN TO VISIT that I started thinking about the city like a tourist.

Tourist meant Grand Central Station, the Empire State Building, the Chrysler Building, the Brooklyn Bridge, and finally, just for the hell of it, perhaps a trip to the World Trade Center.

Grand Central Station was my first favorite place. If you walked up the side stairs, there was a doorway with a closed door. If you opened the door, you could walk up several flights of steps, which led you to a hallway. But it wasn't a regular hallway. It was a slab of concrete that hangs suspended across the great, grand glass archway of the station's west side.

You could actually sit down on the floor of the hallway and dangle your legs over the side.

I used to sit up there for hours, fifty feet above the main floor, literally watching the world go by.

The Chrysler Building was not open at the top in those days, so just the deco lobby was where I took my visitors.

June 30, 1983, my birthday, I started the tradition of walking across the Brooklyn Bridge. Every year, I'd gather friends and we would walk the bridge before sunset, then we'd end up at the River Café drinking martinis. Each year was different, each year, more friends. One year we didn't walk across, we drove across in a limo, about ten of us. Lots of cocaine. Then, toward the end there, before I left in 1990, there weren't any friends left at all.

The Empire State Building is another story. One time, late at night, a visiting friend and I decided to go to the top of the Empire State Building. We called and found out the elevators ran until midnight, so he and I just put on our ball caps and jackets, hailed a cab, and got in line just in time for the last load of tourists to go up top.

The elevator was full, and my friend and I had to squeeze in. I was standing right next to the elevator operator. He looked up at me as he closed the door.

"Where are you from, young man?" the elevator operator said.

I didn't stop to think. I just blurted out: "Pocatello, Idaho," I said.

I hadn't lived in Pocatello for twenty years, and had lived in Manhattan for three.

There was this great sigh of relief in the elevator. Then laughter.

"My God," a woman said, "I thought I was bad. I'm from Peoria."

"We're from Indianapolis," an older couple said.

"I'm from Billings, Montana," another guy said.

"You're the first one I know of from Pocatello," the elevator operator said.

I MUST HAVE LIVED IN MANHATTAN FOR TWO YEARS before I went to the World Trade Center.

I went with my friend, Mendy. We took the subway. I'd never taken the subway that far south. At the station, the train stopped. There was some garbled message over the intercom that was indecipherable, and we finally realized we had to walk to the back of the train to be able to get off.

Mendy and I walked from car to car, and pretty soon we're running from car to car to car to car, and we're in some kind of Twilight Zone of endless empty subway cars. Finally, we see a guy in a uniform. As we pass him, this guy says, "This is the last car."

Mendy and I jumped onto the platform, kept running through the station, through the check stiles, up the stairs, laughing and running, saying This is the last car! This is the last car! and finally finally, to fresh air, and to the most monumentally huge buildings I have ever seen.

It's hard to describe how big these buildings were.

Totally beyond human scale.

In fact, they were so big that if you squinted your eyes, instead of them being buildings juxtaposed against the skyline, they became the skyline.

Years later, on September 11, 2001, Mendy called as all good friends were calling their friends on that day. She reminded me that one of the things I said that first day when we saw those buildings up close was, "Somebody's going to blow these up."

I think back now on why I would say such a thing.

The answer to that requires that I go back and do some self-investigation.

I was raised a strict Catholic. The Church, my father, and my mother were equally domineering and intractable.

These were the rules and if you didn't follow them, you got a beating or you went to hell. Or both.

In such a world, an independent psyche is a difficult thing to foster. I was slapped around, punished, and made to feel shameful and guilty. I lived in constant fear.

It wasn't until the sixties, when I got into university, that I began to get a sense of autonomy. By 1969, I was deep into the counterculture, smoked pot (and inhaled), railed against the Establishment, and spelled Amerika with a "κ."

And I'm proud of it. I believed then and I believe now that there are forces in America today that, given the chance, would take away my liberty, my freedom of speech, my pursuit of happiness, and by authority vested in them, condemn me to death by public hanging.

Back in 1969, I didn't burn my draft card, but I did enter the Peace Corps, and spent two years in Kenya.

An Idaho boy suddenly dumped in the slums of Mathare Valley in Nairobi was a deep shock to my sense of justice and morality. One day I went to a place called Mji wa Huruma, where they lined up little boys and girls five in a row, set a bowl of milk in front of each child, and that was all the food that child got that day. I remember one boy, when he stepped up he kicked his bowl of milk accidentally and knocked it over. That was it. If I hadn't stepped in, that boy would not have had even his bowl of milk that day.

Returning to the U.S. was quite a shock. I had more culture shock returning to the U.S. than when I left for Kenya. Everything here seemed so materialistic, so affluent, so shallow. Plus the sixties were over.

My fear and hatred of authority, however, had not diminished.

One day, my father asked me to go out into the shed with him. That used to mean that I was going to get a whipping. But I was bigger than him. What followed was my father telling me that I was a hippie communist queer and a disgrace to the family and to America.

America, love it or leave it.

I'd left it. But I'd come back.

Why?

Because it's very American to be un-American. Read Thoreau's *Civil Disobedience*. This is my home.

And because America is one of the few places in the world that I can say what I'm saying right now and not get shot.

IN THE FALL OF 1972, I WAS A DELEGATE FOR SHIRLEY Chisolm to the Idaho State Democratic Convention.

Pinko lefty, my father said.

Chauvinist Pig, I said.

We don't live on things. We live on the meaning of things.

So, twenty years later, that day Mendy and I got off the subway and ascended to the light, when I saw the World Trade Center twin towers up close for the first time, I recognized one of my very familiar archetypes.

The phalli of authority, power, and strength. The Emperor.

New York, the Empire State.

It was their mass, their almost obscene bulk, their Goliath that seemed to beg a David with a sling shot.

Since that day with Mendy, my relationship with the Twin Towers grew more and more intimate. Intimate in the deepest sense. The darkness as well as the light.

For a while there, whenever someone came to visit, that's the first place I would take them. My brothers and my sister all have photos of us standing on top of the World Trade Center.

For me, the unreal size of the towers made them into New York City's big circus ride. The Fat Lady Show at the bottom of the island. Step right up folks, see the largest buildings in the United States of America.

I really became obsessed with them. Sometimes, at night, I'd walk down to Battery Park, find a bench and just stare up at them. Their vastness, their overwhelming proportions, their freakish quality of not relating to anything around them except themselves.

Then, in 1986, there were two big events for me. I graduated from Columbia. And I quit waiting tables. I just couldn't do it anymore. I couldn't iron one more white shirt at three o'clock, I couldn't smile and crumb one more table, I couldn't serve one more *Poulet Roti*.

So there I was with a twenty-five thousand dollar student loan and no job. I had two choices: find a teaching position or write. I chose the latter, which meant I got a job as a super, sweeping and mopping buildings on East Fifth Street, sweeping the sidewalks, taking care of the garbage and picking up dog shit off the sidewalk. I got my apartment and four hundred dollars a month. And I wrote.

I was everybody's janitor. People could call me up at all hours, with any kind of crisis or problem, and I had to fix it. Flooding toilets, broken windows, blown fuses, rat problems, neighbor problems, boiler problems, leaky showers, you name it.

Five days a week, the garbage truck came at 7:30 in the morning and I had to be out there to make sure they took it all. City Inspectors regularly checked the buildings and if there was overflowing garbage or garbage littering the streets, I'd get a pink slip, and the building would be fined.

The owner of the buildings did not like to pay fines.

Often, during the night, homeless people would cut open my black plastic bags, looking for food, for some kind of treasure to sell, sometimes slicing open the bags just out of plain meanness.

How many mornings did I walk out the front door to find my neatly packaged garbage strewn all over the sidewalk and into the curb?

In fact, I was just one step away from being on the street myself. Two, three, sometimes four times a day, I was actually on the street, sweeping and spraying down the sidewalks with a hose.

There was one particular building that was a problem. Actually, it wasn't the building that was the problem; it was the stairwell under the front stairway that was the problem.

It was easy access to under the stairway. At night it was dark. It was the perfect place for homeless people to sleep, shoot up, have sex.

But most of all, the problem was that's where they'd shit.

Many mornings, one of the first jobs that faced me was putting my dust pan down next to a pile of stinking turds, swatting away the flies, then taking the broom and sweeping the mess onto the dust pan.

The dregs of humanity. I was that close.

One time there was a dead man under the stairway.

Then, there was this one time. I was putting in a new toilet and sink in my apartment. I hadn't been able to wash properly for maybe two days. I had no toilet. I went to a restaurant on Second Avenue, ordered a cup of coffee and asked where the bathroom was.

The owners threw me out.

I told them, "Look, I'm Tom Spanbauer and I have a Masters from Columbia."

But to them, I looked like one of the people who lived under my stairway at night.

Plus, there I was with no place to shit.

It was about that time, once or twice a week, I started doing catering work with my friend, Chef Ivan. He needed some help and I needed extra money. I'd go to Ivan's kitchen on Thirteenth Street, clean, wash pans and utensils, cut up vegetables.

I could make fifty dollars a gig. Sometimes more.

Most of Chef Ivan's catering gigs were in the World Trade Center.

We'd load up Ivan's van with braised chicken breasts, rice pilaf, endive with gorgonzola and walnuts, coffee, tea, wine, water, pots and pans, knives, forks, spoons, the whole Magila.

You never know how much shit you need until you have to schlep it across Manhattan on a hot day in the back of a van.

We'd always be running late and the traffic was always bad. Finally we'd get to the World Trade Center, and we'd drive up to a check point where a security guard would check Ivan's ID, then we'd circle down and down and down into the bowels of the Trade Center, six floors down, and park.

Then we'd unload the braised chicken breasts, the rice pilaf, the endive with gorgonzola and walnuts, the entire van-full of hot trays, cold trays, coffee pots, tea bags, forks, knives, spoons, you name it onto little gurneys and we'd push the gurneys to the corner of the parking lot, to the freight elevator.

Then we'd load the freight elevator. It would be so full in the freight elevator, so jammed with catering stuff, there would be hardly a place left to put our bodies, but we'd put our bodies in there, sometimes the elevator doors catching an elbow, an ass cheek. Once the door closed on my nose.

Then began the slow ascent to the trading floor. It seemed like hours sometimes, stuffed inside the hot elevator, waiting for the elevator doors to open.

One time, stuffed in there like that, the lights went off and the elevator stopped.

Thus began my slow flirtation with claustrophobia, until, at the end there, getting on an elevator was out of the question.

Then we'd have to unload the freight elevator. Then it was setting up. Spreading out the linen, lighting the cans of Sterno under the serving trays, icing the white wine and the soda pop, making the iced tea, making the coffee, setting out the creamers, the sugar packets, the substitute sugar packets, the napkins.

At twelve o'clock a bell would ring and two big doors would open. The trading floor—a jived-up, espresso-swilling, smoking, yelling morass of methamphetamined traders—descended like locusts onto our tiny circle of tables, devouring, eating, drinking everything in sight.

In one half of an hour everything was gone.

THERE'S ONE PARTICULAR DAY I REMEMBER. RATHER, there's one particular day I will never forget.

It was in 1988, I think, and Wall Street was closing day after day with its highest points ever in trading history. We had just finished cleaning up and Chef Ivan sent me to another floor with some pots of coffee and a bus tray on a bus cart. For some reason, Ivan told me to take one of the main elevators instead of the service elevator.

The doors opened and I pushed the cart onto the elevator, pushed the number of the floor I was going to. There were several people on the elevator, then, as the floors passed, more and more people got off, and then it was only myself and another man, about my age, in a double-breasted shiny brown Armani suit.

I didn't pay much attention to him. I watched the floors go clicking by.

I suddenly thought that I'd forgotten the pot of decaf and I quickly checked the bus cart, bending down to see if the pot of decaf was on one of the lower shelves.

"Looking for this?" the guy said.

I looked over and his Armani trousers were open and his dick was out.

"While you're down there suck on this," he said.

We don't live on things. We live on the meaning of things.

It solidified. The World Trade Center, from that moment on, became an arrogant greedy white male yuppie with his Armani pants open, expecting me to go down on my knees.

The World Trade Center was the Reagan administration's $750 billion in corporate tax breaks.

The World Trade Center was the Reagan administration's $110 billion cut in social programs.

The World Trade Center was joblessness that rose to over ten percent.

The World Trade Center was calling ten percent of Americans "Welfare Queens in Designer Jeans."

The World Trade Center was this guy with his hubris out in the elevator, his "trickle-down theory" much more than just a metaphor.

And AIDS. Reagan's administration, the following Bush administration, and the anti-gay legislation of the New Right, in Elizabeth Taylor's words: "...(couldn't) even spell AIDS."

For me, every Republican vote was a vote for another death from AIDS.

Those dark nights after a catering gig at the World Trade Center, walking home past the loud bars of suddenly rich young white heterosexual people, the streets lined with BMWs and Mercedes Benzes, my heart was sore and heavy.

Sometime in there, one morning, as I was spraying down the sidewalk with a hose, I looked down the street to where I'd just finished sweeping and hosing down the sidewalk. There was a man just pulling down his pants, leaning his ass into one of my garbage cans. I started yelling and ran to him. By the time I got there it was too late.

The man was old and holding his stomach.

"Why did you shit in the garbage can?" I said.

"I'm sorry, man," he said, "I'm sick and there was no place else."

"Couldn't you just go in the gutter?" I said, "Now I've got to clean the garbage can out."

The old man looked at the gutter.

"A man needs some privacy," he said.

ON AUGUST 8, 1988, THE HUNGRY, THE DISPOSSESSED, the jobless, the homeless gathered in Tompkins Square Park and barricaded themselves in.

I wasn't actually there the night of the riot but I had friends who were there. One friend was sitting in a restaurant, at a table on the sidewalk. She saw the police on horses coming down the street six abreast. The police were wielding clubs and people were running frantically, trying to get away.

There's some guy who got a videotape of the policemen. They all had tape over their badge numbers.

That night, known as the night of the Tompkins Square Park Riot, the battle was fought and won by the police.

I left New York on July 18, 1990. All my friends were dead and I was HIV+. I was queer and I was going to die.

And my country couldn't give a shit.

SEPTEMBER 11, 2001.

We don't live on things. We live on the meaning of things.

Strange how an object can stay the same while the meaning of it changes. All those years I hated those buildings, what they stood for, oversized phalli, my father—who voted for Reagan, who hated Mexicans and hippies and niggers and spics and kikes, who thinks we'll miss them salmon about as much as we miss them buffalo.

I've always been the David to my father's Goliath.

But I always looked to him, down there at the end of Manhattan, to the twin towers sparkling darker than the sunset sky, to find out where I was.

September Eleventh from Abroad
Jennifer Lauck

THERE'S A WONDERFUL RHYTHM TO MY DAYS AT HOME.
They start just before the sun rises, our little boy Spencer coming
into our room to be let under the warm covers, sleepy words of
"good morning" and a little talk about our dreams. Spence, too en-
ergetic to stay for long, usually takes off to play in his room, and
my husband Steve and I talk about the day ahead. By the time the
sun is up, we are into the routine of bed making and breakfast, and
then hugs goodbye. In the afternoon, back together again, Steve
and I watch the kids play on our street and we make plans for dinner. At night, the sun long gone, the day ends with a story and good-
night kisses for Spencer, then an hour when my husband and I

just hang out and talk or watch TV.

It might sound boring, but to me it's everything. I haven't always had these comforts. My mother died when I was seven, my father when I was nine. My brother and I were separated after our parents' deaths, and then he committed suicide when I was twenty. My own home and family have helped heal the deep hurts of my past.

In the fall of 2001, five months pregnant with our second child, it seemed more important than ever to nest in this safety, but long before becoming pregnant I had committed to do a two-week book tour of Holland, Sweden, Denmark, and Finland. When September came, I knew I had to go. I told myself the two weeks away would go by quickly and when I got back, everything would be just the same.

In Holland, I was greeted by Hanca, my publisher, whom I had met a year earlier in Frankfurt, Germany. Hanca was one of the people I liked right away. She laughed the way people who are really happy laugh, with her hands clapping together and her head tilted back. Her happiness stayed in her blue eyes even when she wasn't laughing.

On our way into Amsterdam, Hanca and I talked like old friends. I showed off photos of Steve and Spencer, even the ultrasound print out of the new baby, and she gave me a tour of the downtown area, showing me the canals and cobbled roads and arched bridges.

While Hanca and I were together, and later, when I was on my own, I stuffed down my homesickness by comparing home to this new place. It was fall and gray and rainy, just like home, but past the weather and season, so many things were different. Hanca told me about how the Dutch have a nationalized health care system, as well as public education through college. They live in small homes, drive tiny cars down narrow roads and even choose not to have cars, opting to ride bicycles instead. I saw many cyclists with two child seats rigged up, not the big plastic Toys "ʀ" Us models with their endless safety precautions and warnings, but simple seats, covered with black vinyl, that held the children quite safely as the parents pedaled over the wet, cobbled roads.

It was such a revelation of economy I was a little embarrassed by my own excesses. I wouldn't dream of relying on a bike, let alone riding it in the rain. I rarely use public transportation, and worse, I'm one of those people who drive an sᴜᴠ.

As time passed, I became more and more critical of my lifestyle, and the American lifestyle that included overconsumption, expensive health care insurance, and the ever-growing costs of college education.

On September 11, late in the afternoon, I was in search of a bouquet for Hanca and stopped in a tiny shop just around the corner from my hotel. Flowers were packed into dozens of white buckets that crowded both the front of the store and its narrow aisle within. At the rear of the shop, a man in a denim apron stood with his wrists cocked back on his hips, his attention on the radio from which voices spoke in Dutch. His face was lined and long, and as I stood in the aisle, he fixed a look on me.

"Are you an American?"

Its funny how he knew I was American, even before I spoke. I wondered what it was that gave me away.

I nodded yes, and he came to where I stood.

"Your country has been attacked," he said, tilting his head back toward the radio and then telling an impossible story of hijackers taking over commercial jets and flying them into the World Trade Center.

Although JFK was assassinated a month before I was born and the Vietnam War was fought when I was a toddler, I grew up in a period of relative peace. I never gave much thought to international events or the possibility of war. The larger world felt safe. My battles were the very personal.

As this man spoke of something so big and so unimaginable happening to my country, I simply could not take it in. I thought of that stupid movie *Independence Day* where aliens blow up the White House and figured: It's a hoax. At least that's what I kept telling myself until I could buy my flowers and make it back to my hotel room, where I immediately turned on CNN.

For the decade after college, I was a television reporter. Every day in the news room was crazy: police scanners blaring, assignment editors yelling at reporters and photographers, typewriter keys beating out words, teletype machines buzzing off national wire reports of this bombing or that fire or the latest government scandal.

I covered murders and abductions and every kind of terrible human tragedy at a pace that made me numb to any real feeling. I went on a kind of autopilot of fact gathering: who, what, where, when, why. Ask the questions, write the story, get it all on the news before the five o'clock deadline. I told myself that I was being objective but as I look back at my twenties, I know that the chaos of the news business was a mirror of the chaos in my own past. Instead of writing the story of my own terrible tragedy, I wrote the story of other people's suffering, doing so in a way that required no real feeling.

I hadn't been a reporter for years, but on September 11 I slipped back into that mode again. I watched the news, turned off my feelings, and pulled in the facts. My old cynical self was sure that some idiot with a computer and a handheld camera had manufactured the whole thing and sent the tapes to CNN. I waited for one of the talking heads to come on and explain it away. Instead, there were more and more of the impossible images.

I called home, hoping that Steve could explain more than I

could get on the news. It was 8 a.m. in Oregon, and, of course, Steve was busy with the morning routine of getting Spencer off to school and himself ready for work. He had no idea of the attack and immediately turned on the news.

"What the hell?" he said, unable to finish his sentence.

In the background I heard our son, "Daddy, an airplane just flew into that building."

Steve, who sounded like the wind was knocked out of him completely, turned down the television, and I asked to talk to Spencer.

"Hey Mom," Spence said, "there's a fire on TV."

"I know," I said.

"Someone should call Tonka Joe," he said.

Tonka Joe is the world's greatest mechanic, firefighter, and construction worker. He's a likable, all-American type with clean good looks, created by Hasbro to market a line of construction games, action adventure videos, and mega-awesome rescue vehicles. There are even books. Spencer loves to hear the stories of how Tonka Joe beats off a blizzard or tames an erupting volcano.

Part of me feels bad pawning this kind of thing off on my kid, letting him think you can beat a blizzard with a souped-up monster truck or stop an overflowing volcano with a grappling hook. But another part of me really likes Tonka Joe. He's big and strong and optimistic, in a lot of ways the American image of being an American.

My son's wonderful, naïve assumption that his world was safe, that Tonka Joe could take care of this, that I could explain it away, caught on an edge of my heart. What wise thing could I say? What would make a difference? I wished that we did live in a world where a mega-awesome hero could solve all our problems. As the World Trade Towers imploded faster than a poorly built stand of Legos, I turned away from the television.

"You know what?" I said. "Someone has called for help and a lot of firefighters are there right now."

"And Tonka Joe?" he said.

"Sure," I said, "maybe Tonka Joe, too."

"Well, that's good," Spencer said, as if it all made sense, and was gone to put on his shoes and coat for school.

When Steve got back on the line we spoke a little more, but we were scared. We were grown up enough to know this was the real thing.

Were more jets being hijacked right now?

Could I make it home?

What kind of home would be there when I did get back?

Separated by miles and time and this new unknown, all that mattered to us was each other. We tried to say words that, in the end, couldn't really be said, about how much we loved and needed each other.

"Be careful," Steve said.

"You too," I said.

What a feeling of helplessness. I couldn't go home if I wanted to. Flights into the U.S. were grounded. I couldn't get a telephone call through to New York. The telephone lines were jammed. All I could do was send a few e-mail messages to people I knew in New York, asking if everyone was safe.

I had another appointment to keep, so I pulled myself together, reluctantly turned off the TV, and left.

In the elevator going down to the lobby, I looked at myself in the mirror and buttoned my coat over my big stomach. The idea of traveling to Sweden, Denmark, and Finland to talk about my book, about my past, seemed silly now. I didn't have the heart for it at all. I was just scared for myself, for the baby growing inside of me, and for all the people back home.

At lobby level, the elevator door opened to a small group of people headed by an older woman, clearly an American, wearing a black fur coat and bright red lipstick. "We are going to bomb the hell out of someone," she said to no one in particular, and the rest of her entourage nodded in agreement.

She charged into the elevator, shoving into me as I tried to get out, and began pounding her floor number, still talking as the door closed. "We are going to bomb those bastards. They'll be sorry."

I just stood there as the door closed and took them away. Was that how people were thinking back home? Was that what the president was thinking? Were we about to go to war?

It felt as if the whole world was shifting under my feet and there was nothing I could do.

Not knowing what to do with my fear, I made myself go through the motions of the evening ahead. In the rain, I walked over the uneven bricks of the cobbled road to the publishing house, where Hanca offered to cancel the event if I wasn't up to it. I said no, I was fine, and carried on with the work of talking and shaking hands and signing books.

At dinner, the attack was all anyone could talk about. I was still afraid but acting like I wasn't. I kept thinking like the old reporter. I didn't know much about Afghanistan or the Taliban or Osama bin Laden, but I did know that the U.S. wasn't that innocent. Our government has supported corrupt regimes all over the world, we've looked the other way as our corporations exploited third world countries for cheap labor, and we were the ones who dropped the atomic bombs.

I was under a landslide of American guilt, heaping up all of our shortfalls as if they were a justification for what was happening.

A woman with deep brown eyes and short brown hair shook her head, waving a hand for me to stop. "Don't burst my bubble," she said, "I love Americans."

The others at the table nodded in agreement.

Hanca looked at me, her blue eyes holding my own.

"It seems we are more upset about this than you are," she said.

Hanca hadn't known me as the cynical reporter. She knew me as the author who had written about the loss of family. In our time together, she had listened to me talk about my son and husband and the baby I couldn't wait to meet.

In the same way Spencer had caught one edge of my heart, Hanca's words caught another.

I sat back in my chair, silenced, and listened to the stories of how these people truly loved the U.S. One woman told about her first trip to New York and the electric energy of Manhattan. A man described how he drove from the East Coast to the Midwest, and how free and open the land felt to him. Hanca talked about how she went to New York every year, how she had good friends there, how shocking and sad it was that the city was attacked.

I had friends in New York, too. I loved that city. I even loved being an American, for all our faults. What was wrong with me?

Later that night, back in my hotel room, I still couldn't feel what had happened. There was just shock that moved around my fear.

It was only the next morning, Hanca's words still in my head, that I could finally watch the news again, not as a reporter, not as a cynic, but as an American, a mother, and someone who was more frightened than she'd been since she was a child. Those poor people in the World Trade Center buildings, falling, jumping, holding hands. All those people like me, who had children and homes and dreams. The people on the airplanes, calling the people they loved on their cell phones just to say they loved them. God, my whole heart hurt watching it happen again and again. I sat alone in my hotel room and cried and cried.

It's such a simple thing, the act of crying. But after those tears fell and were wiped away, everything felt different. The cynicism and numbness were washed away. My fear had stepped back a little bit, too. I stood at the windows of my room, the sun lifting in the sky, its light sparkling on the canals, and that song that begins

"Morning has broken, like the first morning…" came into my head. Just as cutting facets in a diamond allows the whole spectrum of color to shine through, life felt as if it had been given new dimension.

The simple act of crying shifted the rest of my journey. The world was still changing, the future was unknown, but I felt strangely calm and connected to the people around me.

I hated to leave my new friends in Holland who had helped me toward my new awareness, but those waiting in Sweden were just as kind and supportive and genuinely upset about what had happened in the U.S. In fact, it felt as if the whole world was connecting over the tragedy when, in the midst of a busy book fair in Gothenburg, I stood with one hundred thousand people who went completely silent for three minutes. Conversation, the ringing of cell phones, the opening and closing of cash register drawers, everything stopped as all of Europe held still in honor of the U.S.

Amidst so much destruction and death, everyone seemed to know that living needed to be done completely, without wasting time, and without being separate.

The calm and connection stayed with me for the rest of my journey to Denmark and Finland. On September 21, waiting to board one of the first international flights allowed back into the U.S., I stood in the long lines, went through the security checks, and was even patted down by an apologetic policeman. I felt patient and even thankful for the extra security. Standing behind a couple who was talking about going home to Portland, the two-hour wait passed as if it were ten minutes.

On the flight I thought about everything that had happened, about how the world felt different, how I had been changed, and how it would probably be years before I could fully understand all the layers.

I watched out the window as we crossed the Atlantic and flew over the upper tip of the East Coast, and I wondered how long I could stay open and connected. Was it inevitable that I would slip back into being my old cynical self, numbing myself to things that I was afraid to let in? Was that cynicism and numbness important to survive the impact of the deepest tragedies, as protection until it was really safe to open my heart?

Over Canada, still hours from home, I put my hands over my stomach. The baby, kicking around inside of me at take off, now felt peaceful. I wondered what she was going to be like. Would she have blue eyes like Steve, or brown ones like me? I fell asleep then, not thinking about anything anymore, except how nice it was to be going home.

9/11 Blues
Wanda Coleman

for Peter Reese of Youngstown, Ohio

Into the Valley of the Shadow of Death
Strode the Three Hundred…

GETTING MY TONGUE AROUND THE EVENTS OF SEPTEM-
ber 11, 2001, is still more than I can presently handle six months
after. Events of such magnitude deserve more than the Robocop
rhetoric and knee-jerk sappiness that have dominated whatever
dialogues, beyond jingoistic amens, that have taken place in public thus far. America is a nation at war. And while I am as patriotic
as the next soldier over, I take critical issue with many of the decisions my country, with its predominantly white male leadership,
has made in its manic effort to address what it calls terrorism, its
reluctance to acknowledge that the ideological horse has been for
a long time out of the sociological barn.

Complex emotions have governed my response to 9/11…

I am against your arrogant, bigoted, self-righteous, imperialistic posturing, which you sanctify by evoking God and Jesus Christ. I am against your hypocritical foreign and immigration policies, which you have used to marginalize my people, your African American constituency. Now Osama bin Laden knows what it's like to be a Nigger in America, where a campaign of economic terrorism has been waged against citizens of color since Plymouth Rock. I am amazed at the resources galvanized against the Islamic world by Americans reluctant to eradicate the evils of racism and anti-intellectualism, and whose combat against the scourge of AIDS has been lackluster. I am amazed at the willingness of my fellow Americans to reach deep down into their pockets to financially compensate the victims of 9/11 and the city of New York but who won't spend a penny in reparations to compensate the victims of American Slavery. Many of those same Americans have tolerated the thirty-year destruction and decline of urban centers nationwide, fleeing Blacks by moving to the suburbs, yet they were subdued and welcoming and hopeful investing their trust in a Colin Powell as U.S. Secretary of State and in a Condoleezza Rice as National Security Advisor to President Bush, individuals who are exceptional products of the very same racism that fosters nationwide urban blight.

…I'm not above my own rhetoric.

As a public person, an artist, more definitely, as a Southwesterner, as an African American woman, as a Black writer, as a working-class poor mother, as a poet sickened by the demographics that govern my participation in whatever cultural dialogue must take place, I have chosen to remain silent, absorbing the images of the days following the collapse of the World Trade Center and the assault on the Pentagon. If I am certain of anything, I am certain that my true feelings would not be universally appreciated.

With the exception of my husband and my children, I keep my truest opinions and observations to myself…beyond those revealed here. Also, I am reluctant to cheapen or to capitalize on the horrific experiences and losses of those at the epicenter of the collapse, those who died on United flight 93, and those who died in the Pentagon crash. (Not to mention the innocents who have died in those anonymous anthrax killings; as the pathological rises to compete for headlines with the sociopolitical.) I know that many of their stories are yet to come, that theirs are the most poignant, except for those dozen or so individuals in the West (most notably in Arizona and California) who lost their lives to RACIST vigilantes who rightly read in President Bush's clumsy Texas-cowboy rhetoric a declaration of war against Americans with dark skins.

One specific incident of violence comes to mind.

The victim did not die.

It prompted me to call my daughter and warn her to stay close to home, to not leave the house unless she had an emergency. (Status post 9/11: I tease the Mexican American driver who regularly delivers my UPS packages, cautioning him to beware of being mistaken for "an A-rab." He laughs, and then says his wife tells him the same thing.) My daughter, trying to raise her three children, is left virtually alone in their Lancaster, California, home because, in order to make a living, her trucker husband is on the road, crisscrossing the nation twelve days out of fifteen. My daughter, her husband, and their children compose a mixed-race family. My daughter, a complex mixture of Caucasian, African American, and Native American, has almond-colored skin. Her husband, a Nicaraguan and Puerto Rican mix, is often mistaken for Mexican American. Their children, my grandchildren, are olive-skinned variations on those ethnic themes.

The Lancaster-Palmdale area in which they live is a former lily-White enclave whose promising future collapsed in the 1980s when the aerospace industry failed to flourish in the High Desert and government contracts were awarded elsewhere. With that decline, homes intended for young White families were sold off to minorities. A hundred miles north of L.A., surrounded by mountains, the community became a magnet for those trying to raise families in South Central Los Angeles, where Blacks are discouraged from buying real estate. As a result, constant disharmony and racial incidents characterize the High Desert.

My daughter and her family live two doors down from a family in which one grandson was assaulted by a skinhead with a hatchet or machete. I remind my daughter of this, that certain ignorant folk might not see a black person when they look at her, like that unfortunate man who was chased from his car by two young White males. They were going to make him pay for the destruction of the WTC, and all those lives lost, most likely ignorant of the fact that most of those who died were foreign nationals. They chased the screaming man into his home and through it, until they discovered their victim was not an Arab, but a Mexican American.

See?

I have so much to say, and yet I feel unable to be completely clear and cogent about it. Organizing it into a simple essay is more than I can handle right now. A riot of images plays across my eyes as I write. I've never felt so unable to do a subject the justice I feel it deserves. I sense that I have not said all I need to say. But this must suffice for now. Until the events move through me and, like the stuff of my poems, express themselves "organically" on some other page.

But of all the events that have moved me most recently, including the death of journalist Danny Pearl, with his courageous pregnant bride of mixed racial parentage, there is one that stands out above them all.

My heart was pierced by that tiny little single-engine Cessna that crashed into the forty-two-story Bank of America office building in Tampa, Florida, on Saturday, January 5, 2002. My heart was rent and collapsed by the solo flight of Charles Bishop, young, gifted, and White.

That little American boy, and the statement he made with his life...

On a Clear Day...
Lawrence Grobel

IT WAS JUST PAST SIX IN THE MORNING WHEN THE PHONE
rang, waking me. My sister's voice on the other end was high-
pitched and emotional: "Turn on the TV, a plane has crashed into
one of the Twin Towers. Oh God." It was after nine where she was
calling from, in Brooklyn, and I knew one of her concerns was
about Zachary, her son, who attended NYU Law School and lived
downtown. I stumbled out of bed and went downstairs to turn on
CNN. I saw the fire, I listened to the commentary, I heard my sister's
voice. "This is terrible. Remember when they tried to blow up the
World Trade Center? Now this."

"But this looks like an accident," I said. What else could it be?

It was an American plane. It went off course. Those buildings are so tall. In a fog...

But there was no fog that morning. It was a beautiful blue-sky day in Manhattan. I stayed on the phone with my sister, the die-hard New Yorker. While I had left the family to go to college in California, then to West Africa for three years in the Peace Corps, then after a brief interlude in New York, back to California to live, my sister had never left Brooklyn. She and her husband just couldn't imagine living anywhere else. He did the *New York Times* crossword puzzle every morning, she took photographs of every festival in all five boroughs and showed them at the New York Historical Society. Their son went to Stuyvesant High School. I visited them whenever I returned to New York, but my life was 3,000 miles away. The last time I visited, my sister wanted me to see the view from the restaurant at the top of the World Trade Center, so we went to Windows on the World for a drink. I was wearing jeans, sufficient California attire, but was turned away. I never got to see the view.

"OH NO! OH NO! THERE'S ANOTHER PLANE!" From behind the smoke of the first tower, a more distant camera angle captured the second plane, framed across that heavenly cloudless sky that made what was happening that much more surreal. "GOD, MY GOD, NO, IT'S CRASHING INTO THE OTHER TOWER!" My sister was now hysterical. I didn't need her commentary; I was watching the same horrible event that she was. But she was living just across the bridge from where it was happening. And from the screaming I was hearing, it could just as easily have been happening to her own house. "WE'RE BEING ATTACKED! NEW YORK IS BEING ATTACKED!" And then, after I spent minutes trying to calm her down, trying to be rational about something completely irrational, the first building started to crumble. "IT'S GOING DOWN! THE BUILDING'S COLLAPSING! ARE YOU SEEING THIS? THIS CAN'T BE!

IT CAN'T BE HAPPENING." And when the second building began to disintegrate, my sister was so out of control I thought that she might have a heart attack. I, too, was in shock, but I was so worried about her that my attentions were divided.

"The world has changed," I remember saying to her. It was the second time in my life that I truly felt this. The first was November 22, 1963. I was sixteen and in a bus with other students on a trip to Washington, D.C. When we arrived, we were told to stay on the bus. One student, Daniel, got off and got right back on. "President Kennedy has been shot," he announced.

"Not funny, Daniel," I said. "You don't joke about something like that."

But Daniel wasn't joking and within ten minutes, when we were told that an NBC reporter was going to come and talk to us, I felt as if there had been a death in my family. Kennedy's murder was the death of a loved one. I had followed Kennedy from the time he announced his candidacy. I read everything about him. I listened to records of his speeches. I never missed a televised press conference. When he asked us to think of what we could do for our country, I vowed to join the Peace Corps when I was old enough. He was young, virile, handsome, witty, and the leader of the free world. He made me want to go into politics. It was impossible to believe that one lone gunman hiding out in the Texas Book Depository could take out the President of the United States. Kennedy wanted to do too many things, he wanted to go after organized crime, he wanted to get out of Vietnam, he wanted to get black people to vote, he had a liberal agenda, there were too many southern conservatives, too many generals, too many racists who considered him a threat. It couldn't have been one lone nut. And in the end, it didn't matter. Kennedy was dead, my idealism was shattered, Johnson became president, the war in Vietnam escalated, and I no longer wanted to be a politician. I became a conscientious objector. I joined the Peace Corps when I could, not out of idealism, but to escape the draft for as long as I could. The sense that "They" could get you if "They" wanted to became palpable. The world, my world, had changed on November 22, 1963.

It changed, again, on September 11, 2001.

As I watched the towers collapse, as I watched those planes slicing into them over and over, I thought of my children, both in college, one on the west coast, at Berkeley, the other on the east coast, at Amherst. The older one, when we spoke, asked me what was happening, and what was going to happen. Then she and her roommate made a videotape of their feelings, knowing that this was a new day in their lives, a day of tragedy and of dread, a day of historic importance. The younger one, a freshman, just two weeks into this new experience called college, wanted to come home and be hugged. Instead, she joined a campus candlelight vigil at Amherst and sent me an e-mail:

"Everyone keeps saying to go on with our lives and I will, but not today or probably tomorrow. It is scary to think this is not the end, that the world is not safe right now. I am afraid to go to New York and not see the towers; I am afraid to step on a plane wondering if I will make it home for Hanukkah."

I understood her fears, of course, but I wasn't worried about her getting on a plane. The awful thing had happened. Terrorism was in our midst. But the terrorists had played the plane card. As a result, flying would probably be among the safest ways to travel. I was far more concerned about what other methods they would use to rupture our collective psyche.

What my daughter remembered about her planned trip to New York during her spring break was that her aunt had promised to take her to the same restaurant she tried to take me to, at the top of the World Trade Center. My sister never gave up. She could sell New York like few others, and she never tired of showing off the city to out-of-towners. That view, she knew, was special. It was like no other. I had told Hana to remember not to wear jeans when she went and regretted the night that I did. Now I realized I would never get the chance to see that view, from that height, on a clear or even an overcast day. And the thought of not having that made me both sad and angry. What right did anyone have taking something so magnificent and grand away from us?

For most of my life I've kept a journal. But on this day, when my sister became hysterical, when my daughters lost their innocence, when the greatest city in the world came under attack, I had no answers, and had very little to say.

What do you say to your children when terrorists turn airplanes into missiles and crash them into buildings, killing thousands of people? That their world is no longer safe? That they have to look not only both ways before they cross, but also up in the air, and below their feet? That stepping out into the world might be dangerous? This crazy act, these incredible images…you look deep into your heart and wonder whether you want to cry out for revenge knowing more innocent people will be killed or just pray for a stop to the madness. But you know that the madness will not stop because the people who do these things believe they are righteous and sane, believe they will die a martyr's death and go to a heaven where dancing virgins and an infinity of cheers surround them for all eternity.

9/11 was our children's 11/22. It was a more explosive wake-up call than the crash of the dot-coms that turned young paper millionaires into cynical disbelievers. This wasn't about money, about personal wealth, about expensive toys that had to be sold—this was about a way of life taken for granted; this was about complacency, invincibility, new realities. This was about being shaken to our very core. What happened on September 11 was taken very personally by New Yorkers, who felt not only violated but suddenly extremely vulnerable. But it affected us all, from coast to coast.

I tried calling my best friend's son for days after the chaos of that day until I finally reached him. I wanted to know how he reacted to what happened. He told me that from his balcony on the nineteenth floor of his East Village apartment building he could see the Twin Towers, and he and his roommate stood there as they came down.

"And how did you feel?" I asked. "Were you devastated?"

"We were jumping up and down," he said. "It was like it wasn't real. We were going, 'Holy shit!' and watching like it was a movie. We thought it was funny."

My friend's son is a sensitive, smart kid. He was a political science major at Columbia before entering graduate school. I enjoy talking to him because he has an opinion about everything, and often makes me rethink my own. When he told me he thought what had happened right before his eyes was funny I felt ashamed. But then I realized that it was his way of dealing with it. When those two towers went down, it was just too big an event to comprehend. These are kids who have grown up watching *Die Hard* and *Independence Day* and dozens of other movies where subways are hijacked, buildings blown up, the Statue of Liberty reduced to rubble. They've played video games all their lives where when crazy things happen they press the Reset button. My sister didn't think it was funny. I didn't think it was funny. And neither did my friend's son, who broke down in tears on the subway the next day. But when it happened, it was like being on the set of a movie. It was not real. It couldn't be real. The World Trade Center doesn't just collapse, not even after a plane crashes into it. It goes against our faith in architecture, our trust in the safety of buildings, our very freedom to walk the streets of New York without feeling danger from above.

I spoke to a friend who lives in the shadow of Wall Street. He had been out late the night before and didn't awake until after noon on that Tuesday. He told me that when he got up he looked outside and saw that it was a beautiful day. He decided to walk up Second Avenue to Central Park. It was one of the most remarkable days he had ever experienced in New York: the sky was *Simpsons* blue, the weather was warm, there were no people on the street, no cars, it was like a dream. He had no idea what had happened just hours before. He thought it was just a great, great day.

It wasn't.

The Sky Had Fallen
Jessica Maxwell

EACH MORNING I OPEN MY DOOR TO A SWEEP OF VALLEY
and hills, even the Coast Range on clear days forty miles due west.
My house rides the upper backside of College Hill, a nice old neighborhood filled with English professors and physicians. To say that
College Hill is peaceful is redundant: there's the collegiate hush
of endless reading and thinking, and there's the hill, high above
the traffic. The most common disturbance here is NPR's endless
reports from the Gaza Strip.

Mostly when I step outside I read the weather. Sometimes you
can watch it roll in from the Pacific. Great pewter Portuguese man-
of-war clouds moving steadily east until they've got their tenta-

cles wrapped around every western window. Usually, though, it's just there, the weather, passive, not active, laid down across the sky like an old wet quilt, leaking cotton. This is what we live with on the saturated edge of Oregon. This is our nine-month vigil, our Celtic cross to bear—a climactic shroud in which those of fainter heart and thinner blood find little solace or liturgy (and often end up heading south to the golf-lands of Phoenix, the beach life of L.A.). During our better months the western vista is blue. Easter-egg blue. Delphinium blue. Dutch Swedish Prussian Provençal Sistine Chapel blue. The upper atmosphere smiling down on itself blue, grand, shimmering, still, lovely, happy. On September 11 all I read from my picture window was one more precious polished morning, a rhapsody in blue that arced over America from the West Coast to the East. But when I stepped outside I knew the sky had fallen.

READING ENERGY IS A PRIVATE PASSION OF MINE. EVERY-one does it, really. When you walk into a room and get a bad feeling. When you take an instant liking to someone the first time you lay eyes on them. When you turn to your husband and say, "What's wrong, honey?" and he wonders how you knew. I try to use my nonverbal radar just to see if I can, but on the morning of September 11 the signals weren't delicate emanations, they were anvils flying through the air. Except there was no air. It felt as though the entire community was holding its breath. No, as if no one could breathe. Something was wrong. Did the Ducks lose last night? I skimmed the newspaper at my feet. No, the sports guys were still writing about their win three nights ago. The rest of the news was unexceptional, too. I looked out over the treetops again. But there were no sirens, no traces of smoke, no signs of local distress, so I shrugged and went back inside to make tea and read my e-mail.

Pop. "Incredible morning, huh?"

It's an Instant Message from Chris Messina, my Portland sports radio buddy. I think he's talking about the weather.

"Is it pretty up there, too?"

Long pause.

"You don't know what's happened, do you?"

No, I don't.

Then he tells me some outrageous tale of terrorism and destruction and I laugh. I actually laugh. And write back: "Right."

"I'm serious," he replies. "Turn on CNN."

Quickly, I look again at the little photograph of smoke blooming out of a building that, like millions of other AOL users, I'd unconsciously dismissed as an action movie ad.

My God. It's true. It's happening.

Pop. "I've been watching it from my rooftop."

It's Rona Cherry. One of my closest New York editor pals. Ha ha. She says she's all right, being a couple of miles away, but the whole thing is just unbelievable. So many lives. So unexpected.

Pop. Pop. It's Bruce Stutz. My best editor/writer friend, watching it from his home in Brooklyn.

"Fucking Islamic militant extremists." He rants. "Fucking extremists!"

Are you sure?

Of course he is. He is the one who taught me how to say "schlemiel." He's the one who reads Walt Whitman poems to his family every Passover. He's the one who wants to write a book on the Jordan River, predicting that water rights would be the real undoing of Israel and Palestine. He is the most brilliant Jewish literary mind I know, so Bruce knows if nobody does. Nobody else seems to. No one knows what's happened or what's happening or what will happen next or why. No one knows what it means. New York. The Pentagon. An attempt on the White House. This thing is organized. A primitive, limbic terror sears my psyche. This does not compute, not to me, not to any now shell-shocked American. We have no tools whatsoever to cope with this. None.

Now the second tower has collapsed. The American Express building is gone, too. I try to call my editors at the AmEx editorial offices many blocks away. Nothing. I call Mary-Powel Thomas at *Audubon*. "We're okay here. We're pretty far away." So good to hear a familiar New York voice. I call my editor at *Forbes*. Busy. I e-mail him, receive a quick response: "We're all fine here. My wife and I are about to flee the city. Friends are putting us up." Flee? This sounds like war. Could it be? Then the worst thought. Is it over for us? Is it?

"US" IS THE OPERATIVE WORD. WHEN YOU'RE ATTACKED by "them" you become an instantly fortified "us." But New York under siege has far deeper implications to West Coast writers than to those who both live and work Out West, as New Yorkers like to say. New York is the heart of the publishing world. The center of a writer's work life, a glowing cresset lighting the way for every literary dream you ever had. In the crazy, solo work environment of the professional writer, editors are your only workmates…and they all live in New York. A West Coast writer, really, is just a New Yorker on a long leash. For writers working way over here, September 11 was far too up close and personal.

"Today the machine that is New York became something organic." That was the first media sentence I heard that day, the panting voice of a Colorado-based NPR commentator who just happened to be in downtown Manhattan at the time. NPR had him on live. "People on the street are desperate for eye contact now, something, anything to help them make sense of what's happening here." It was the debut of what would become a sluiceway of on-air attempts to cognize these cold-hearted events, designed, really, to talk ourselves down. Maybe the revolution won't be televised, but a terrorist attack sure will.

Just as the rest of the world didn't know how much it loves America until September 11, neither did the rest of America know how much it loves New York until then. All the Big Apple's archetypes emerged center stage right away: the Italian mayor, the Bronx firefighter, the Irish Catholic priest, killed, for God's sake, by a falling body while he was ministering last rites. These are *our* New Yorkers, the stars of the play we all call "New York" that runs in perpetuity inside every non–New Yorker's head. If writers add their own roster of New York editors and agents to the cast, they end up with a tragedy of weirdly personal proportions. You find yourself wandering around like Guinevere, wondering what happened to your own mythical version of Camelot.

For me, small signs of deepwater disturbance surfaced soon after, fissures in the daily order of things that continually took me by surprise. I beat an egg. Then wept when the soft yellow and white tissues broke. I washed my hair. In the mirror I saw head bandages, not a towel. I baked a pie. When flour dust clung to my hands I panicked. The softening effect of those horrifying days was absolute. No one I knew could work. Calls came in from all points east and west, especially former boyfriends, I noted. Everyone wanted to meet for tea or lunch. Some of my more politically minded friends called for a State of the World Dinner; one of them was about to receive the baby he and his wife were adopting from Outer Mongolia—we ate hummus and talked more about that than the Taliban or their über-leader with the tongue-twister name a comedian called "Osama bin Hidin'," and wondered aloud how many Afghan orphans would be left in the wake of our President's War on Terrorism. Meanwhile, political analysis flew around the Internet. We needed to rethink Israel. We needed to study Islam. We needed to recognize the results of our longtime attitude of global entitlement. "Why?" a shaken David Letterman asked a shattered Dan Rather. "Jealousy," Dan replied, then he cried like a baby.

Families, of course, needed to be together, a tall order in America-the-Free-and-Mobile. My eight-year-old niece wanted to leave her California home to visit me, but she also never wanted to fly on a plane again as long as she lived. It didn't occur to me then but her proclamation was the battle cry that brought the travel industry to its knees, and very nearly my own career. Magazines had been having a rough time of it since advertisers launched a mass mutiny earlier in the year, when American Express, for instance, suffered a seventy percent profit loss in one quarter. Publications were folding left and right. The survivors were cutting back so severely some barely had the minimum page count needed for perfect binding. Even famous nonstaff writers were not getting work. No one had ever seen anything like it. Ever.

Travel writers like myself swiftly were reduced to *pâté de foie gras*. Assignments virtually stopped. Meanwhile, I was supposed to be writing a travel book, the research for which I'd completed only weeks before September 11. The travel book was not the book I wanted to write, anyway. I'd spent two years trying to convince the editors at my New York publishing house to let me write a spiritual adventure, but publishing houses are run by marketers these days, not visionaries, which, I suppose, is why the first *Harry Potter* book was turned down nine times by nine different houses. Visionaries and artists get their information from a different source, and we can only hope that the publishing industry will celebrate true inspiration again one fine day. Magazine readers sure do, since *Oprah*, with its emphasis on spiritual growth, is enjoying 100 percent advertising increases even in these most inauspicious times.

The irony is that it also bodes well for spiritual books, because ever since crazy people flew airplanes across that perfect blue sky into the twin towers, that's all New York publishers want. And while there was a bit of uncomfortable grinding as the publishing engines shifted gears, editors and writers like me are, once again, in the same movie. This all seems somehow inevitable. Because, I think, when the walls of the World Trade Center came tumbling down, we grew up. In those few terrible moments, our adolescent emphasis on self shifted to the more mature matrix of relationships while our previous obsession with surfaces contracted into a time of genuine and much-needed interior examination.

As a matter of fact, the great Plot Writer in the Sky actually telegraphed this bittersweet ending when I was walking my dog that fateful morning. It was more of a going-through-the-motions than anything else. I was numb and scared like the rest of us, clinging to the most elementary of routines just to feel that something is still familiar and good. We had climbed the hill we usually sprint up with me breathing in the hollowness of the time as if there were no oxygen in it at all. Panting, we headed back to the house. And just before we got there, I heard it. The beautiful clear notes of Mozart's Piano Sonata no. 11, falling like petals or feathers or office memos from the third-story window of my piano-teacher neighbor's home against the watchful turquoise eye of the western sky.

The dead do not hear the bells tolling.

DENIS DIDEROT | *Le Neveu de Rameau*

Empty Cup
Genny Lim

I AM SILENCED BY A PAIN SO POWERFUL THAT JUST THINK-
ing of the day ahead wearies me. Mornings are hardest, when
perception's most clear. It's all too clear. She's gone. Gone forever.
I face reality for the twenty-seventh day since her death. I will never wake up to her smiling face or hear her voice calling to me from
down the hall. I anticipate her bare feet padding down the carpet-
ed corridor. The squeak of the door as she heads to the bathroom.

   Little things are the hardest to let go. The tangle of black hair
still clinging to the bristles of her hairbrush. The clipped discount
coupons and her older sister's ID card tucked inside her wallet, waiting for a night on the town. Even her soiled clothing is precious

now. I am loath to wash them for the last time. The socks and panties look so forlorn. So, too, her overnight toothbrush abandoned inside a plastic sandwich baggie. Thank god she had the good sense to take photographs at camp the night before. I love the one with her arm tucked around her sister's elbow. Both of them are beaming.

The plans we make are as ephemeral as sand castles. My dreams have dissolved like dandelion puffs in the wind. As a mother you never imagine that such a vibrant, joyful life bursting with potential can come to an abrupt halt. There are no reasons. "Why" is a sad mute. I'm half a mother only. One half continues to live and breathe, while the other half dies with my daughter. One half yearns to hold her. The other half dies each day I awaken without her.

San Francisco never had any real seasons. But now winter has put down roots and is staying for good. My mind refuses to accept the logic of sudden circumstance. The "why" multiplies. Silence festers. Seven years on empty cushions and I never suspected that the death, which I was told to prepare so carefully for, would trick me by taking my innocent young daughter instead. She gave birth to my dreams and I ravishly consumed her triumphs as if they were my own. Her popularity, her academic prowess, her easy laughter, her fast tongue, her confidence, her attitude composed a dance. This perfect vision of youth and vitality, whom I nurtured and who nurtured me from birth is suddenly gone.

The scent of a rose is never compromised by its thorns. Danielle's memory endures the tumult of a war instigated by complacent delusion. A bereft mother. A nation cut off at its prime. We have stealth bombs, cluster bombs, smart bombs, scuds, you name it, but where is our enemy? It is the third day of bombing and I sigh at our lost youth.

Danielle drowned two days before the terrorist attacks. A row of shoes leans innocently with their heels flush against the wall.

Where is the pair of feet to fill them? There is much work to be done before the forty-ninth day.

The Afghans have fled on foot with only a handful of possessions and the clothes on their backs. They are running to hide from bombs. Cache Creek is hidden far from view. The river is deceptively narrow and calm, sliding over rocks like a snake. How did a nineteen-year-old young woman, who swam like a fish one moment, become inanimate as a stone the next? How did 3,100 people burn to ash in the time it takes a commuter to gulp down a cup of coffee? With heavy heart I prepare the *Sur* Offerings for beings in the *Bardo*. It must be performed three times a day. The monks at Sera Jey will perform the *Bardo Thödol*, Liberation Sutra, one hundred times before the forty-ninth day, the completion of the Bardo cycle. In this way her consciousness will break the chains of *Samsara*.

We all are our history. We are living one dream. Endowed with collective memory, our American dream, which grew out of wild, unimaginable industrial growth and profit, has finally spun out of orbit, leaving the global degradation of nature and human poverty in its wake. Our ancient karma is exploding out of deficit. We are consuming ourselves like the ouroboros. We are orphans of our own tragic want. Our children are the sacrifice. If the Native Americans and Africans believe that the decisions we make now will affect the seventh generation, then surely our continuing acts of violent global aggression and exploitation of the earth's resources will bequeath a denuded planet. No wonder so many youth are resorting to drugs, sex, and booze to numb their rage. They see all too well the hypocrisy of their parents' and past generations with sobriety. And so they cry out, "*Shame, shame!*"

Danielle wanted to be a low-income lawyer. She said she wanted to represent poor people who couldn't afford to defend themselves, while the rich squirmed out of their crimes because of money. She saw all too well the hypocrisy of a system predicated on an unequal playing field. Junk bond swindlers doing next to no time, while some innocent people languish on death row. No one loss outweighs the other, no one child is more precious than the other, and no one pain more profound than the last.

Every morning I search for Danielle. I walk into her room and search for her in the framed photos, among the stuffed animals, desk drawers, and wall posters for a trace of her. There is a dearth of material from which to resurrect her. And yet I never give up the ghost. Today I received a book of poems from another mother who lost her eleven-year-old daughter, Liana, in a similar rafting accident. She says, *"Don't ask me unless you want to hear how I'm coping with the death of my daughter."*

I used to shake my head with pity at mothers who had lost their children, now I have become one of them. Afghanistan is only a news frame away. When the Taliban destroyed the ancient Buddhas carved in rock, little did they know, or care, how useless it was to cut off the finger that points at the moon. The moon shines regardless.

In the faces of others we glimpse the moment of our own demise. Terror cries out from our ancient cells. Can we ever reach our loved ones through the genealogy of flesh or through a litany of conquest? Bombs destroy life. They will never bring about peace. One can never hope to resolve death with more death. Death is nonnegotiable, nonrefundable. Death is clean. But life? Life is messy. We scratch our heads, puzzled by the shape and form of our suffering. Violence lies at the root of the struggle. What is lost is lost. Yet we are blinded by our insatiable fear. There is no raising the dead. A prayer cannot breathe life into our lost ones. It cannot replace the empty cup from which a mother who's lost her child must drink. If Danielle's death was a harbinger of the apocalypse to come, then the prophets of doom were correct.

The Indians call this the *Kali Yuga*, the age of darkness and destruction, when civilization is depicted as a cow teetering on one leg. The Buddhists call this the age of degeneration, when human morals are at their lowest ebb. The Hopi prophecy recorded in petroglyphs on a slab of rock warn of a worldwide conflagration if we do not take the spiritual path. I don't believe that the innocent lives lost served no purpose. The Hopis believe that the departed's duty is to be the messenger, link, or bridge between the realm of the living and the land of the spirit. If that is so, then it would have been so like Danielle to have gone on ahead to hold the gate open with a welcome smile for those who followed soon after. She would tell her sister Colette to walk tall and be strong. She would ask me to take care of her sister and her ninety-five-year-old grandmother. She would tell her friends to live their lives well and without regret.

Danielle, I am preparing a burnt offering to stave your hunger and that of the children who must feed on this terrible war. The pain and suffering etched on the silent faces of the mothers mirror my own. The distance between life and death is much closer than I once thought. And the proximity between the Taliban women, covered head to toe like fleeing apparitions, and the shadow of myself lying awake with dread at what awaits our world is stunning. We are fleeing the same enemy. We are tasting bitterness from the same cup. But I am offering holy water to quench your thirst, my daughter. May you share amrita with our teachers whom we will soon follow. My well's run dry, but I know that yours remains ever sweet, ever full.

Just Now

Just now you are waking in the Bardo
Wandering the empty streets of the mind

Do not be afraid of the spirits who greet you
The Wrathful Herukas and Guaris who arise
They are the terrifying messengers of the Five Buddhas
Who open the gates for you

I will make burnt offerings for your safe journey
Fragrant incense smoke from Bhutan
Carefully gathered in the gentle breeze of
alpine meadows under the full moon
Plants and herbs containing the precious essences of heaven
and mountain earth baked in sunlight to guide your way
Saffron water will quench your thirst and roasted
    tsampa with
The three white and three sweet ingredients will fill
    your senses
With the lost pleasures of the body

No tears! warns Garchin Rinpoche
Or you might cling to *Samsara*
Better to chant the *Mani* and let you go your way
The amrita of pure awareness awaits you and the
Honored guests at your table are anxious to meet you
But I will not be there to greet you, my sweetheart
To nag you to take along a sweater or extra cash
No I will not be there to ask you who's driving and
What time will you be home?

How difficult it is to let go of what we hold most dear
How difficult it is to shed your smile for all of time
More precious than life itself was the gift of your love to me
More precious than breath itself was the miracle of your life
So boundless with compassion yet so limited in span
Yes I was attached to you

That was my downfall
So now the cord is cut
You often asked me why I stared?
I was drawn like a moth to the warmth of your smile
Your self-assurance came freely
So young, so beautiful, so natural
You knew the shortcut to Nirvana
Without arduous retreats
Your yearbook quote,
Once you're capable of taking in the water,
You don't mind the coming and going of the waves...[1]

They said you floated
Arms raised above your head, perfectly serene
Your face shrouded in the halo of afternoon light
Down, down stream you floated on your back
Arms high above your head
Eyes shut
Dreaming

....

1. Thich Nhat Hanh

Mariposas and *Colibríes*
Alejandro Morales

IT ALL STARTED WITH ME WANTING TO WATCH THE MOR-
ning news. At times I think that if I hadn't turned on the television
at that instant it would have never happened. I wouldn't have
seen the catastrophic aftermath of the first plane crash into the
first tower and about eighteen minutes later the second plane
wouldn't have exploded through the second tower.

As I watched the smoke rise high above the New York City skyline, for some strange reason what came to mind were the *Mariposas*, butterflies, and the *Colibríes*, hummingbirds, at Central Park
and enjoying a hot dog at the entrance to the World Trade Center.
I thought of the hard-working hot dog vendor, who was probably

starting his day, as I watched the towers—steel, wood, plaster, and glass mixed with the blood, flesh, and bones of the country—one by one collapse, brought down in an innocent flight toward immortality. I stood in the middle of the family room, helpless! How could I reach them? Go to them?

I imagined then the island of Manhattan. The towers built on a solid base, on a consecrated place, roamed by Native American spirits and accompanied by European ghosts. They were still there, I prayed. The television was off, hours had passed, and I felt that the blood, flesh, and bones of the loved ones had fallen into the warm and loving arms of the spirits of the island's past.

The towers are symbolic. It's the people, their blood, flesh, bones, and hearts that make the country. The solid base of the island, Manhattan, still stands rooted deep into the core of the earth and the nation. The land is still there and the people are still there.

They have moved from a peaceful place through a moment of great fear, terror, and violence to a heavy loving memory, but they are not gone. They remain working and constructing for the future of the living. Blood, flesh, bones, and hearts are standing on the solid ground of the nation, reminding us that we, the living, are anchored to the sweet memory of their lives. Their blood sustains us; their flesh warms us; their bones make us stand proud; their brave hearts make us move forward. They are the nation's revenants, spirits of loved ones who have died a violent death and are in search of eternal peace. They are always present, seeking us out, constantly invoking us not to forget. Their spirits never completely leave us and that is why we can pray to them and speak with them. They are the country's *animas en pena*, souls residing between life and death, desiring contact once more with the living, to say the final good-bye before they move on to eternal peace. They are the sentinels, formidable and magnificent *Mariposas* and *Colibríes*, at the gate defending against erasure, protecting a way of life, an army of angels who stand against those forces that would bring harm to the country. Their memory is resistance engraved in our daily life; their memory lies just under the surface of our daily activity; their memory has become the base, the deep solid base of the island, Manhattan.

Their memory reminds us of what they did—they were working that day! The receptionists, the security guards, the maintenance workers, and the waiters were starting the day that morning. Their memory, their work, spurs us on to reshape our lives.

They are the intra-history of the nation, ordinary, everyday hard-working anonymous men and women, the heart of the nation, who came from all over the world to work at the World Trade Center in Manhattan. Janitors, accountants, police officers, restaurant workers, doctors, firemen, CEOs, stock brokers, shop owners, their work is a diversity of labor individually contributing to and laying claim, and ownership, to the nation's dreams. Like me, they are dreamers. They are my brothers and sisters, my nation, my family, but I don't think of them as gone. They survive in a memory independent of the living. They have come through the center of an apocalyptic experience, through the forces of destruction and now cling to the energies of creation and cry out that they should not have died in vain. They beseech the living to work toward a new birth of freedom, an inclusion of all those involved, and toward an understanding of the catastrophe. They ask us to recognize the hidden lesson revealed in the calamities of history. No one is blameless. There is not just one provocateur. Perhaps we are part of the cause, along with those we call our friends and those we call our enemies. The *Mariposas* and *Colibríes* are present, asking the living to consecrate that ground again.

THE SHOCK SUBSIDES. THE ANGER RISES AND LINGERS.
Prayer booms. If you break down my door, invade my home, *mi*

pequeña nación, harm my family, *mi querida familia,* I will respond with as much force as I can bring forth. You can't invade my turf and not expect consequences.

When I go to New York, I always go to the Metropolitan Museum of Art to visit an old friend, Vincent Van Gogh. I visit him in his self-portrait that stands alone. There I speak with him. Now when I go to New York I go to Ground Zero, a sacred place, and stare into the emptiness where I wait to feel the embrace of *los miles amados de las torres,* of the thousands of loved ones, the *Mariposas* and the *Colibríes* of the towers. I wait to hear their voices, to hear them speak to me like family and remind me that I am anchored to them for eternity.

Memorial
Maxine Hong Kingston

ON SEPTEMBER 17, 2001, 12,000 MEMBERS OF THE U.C. Berkeley community gathered in Memorial Glade. This was the largest crowd on campus since the 1960s. People lay flowers around the Memorial Pool, a gift of the War Classes honoring Cal students who died in World War II. Chancellor Robert Berdahl and ASUC President Wally Adeyemo ended their jointly written speeches saying, "Let us continue as we have begun, with compassion, understanding, and peaceful discourse. Let us each bear ourselves in a manner of which we will always remain proud. Let us remember that peace and justice can come only from a determination to seek peace and to act justly. Let us exemplify our motto: *Fiat lux!*"

I led the following ceremony:

I'd like to teach you a breathing meditation, which I learned
from Alice Walker, who learned it from a Tibetan nun.

At the sound of the Bell of Mindfulness, breathe in and
breathe out.

Breathing in, breathe in sorrow, suffering, anger, fear.

Breathing out, breathe out healing, relief, joy, love.

Let's breathe together for three silent minutes.

(*Bell*)

Breathing in, I breathe in the world's pain.

Breathing out, I send it healing love.

(*Three minutes of silent breathing*)

May all beings be happy.
May all beings be peaceful.
May all beings be kind.
May all beings be free.

(*Repeat three times*)

(*Eleven bells ring*)

"May all beings be happy" is *metta*, the oldest prayer on Earth. I
learned it from a Vietnam veteran.

I hope that as you breathed with the Cal community around
you, you felt our connection one to another. And the wider connection to the people in the rest of the country, and the rest of the
world. That feeling of connection with all of humankind is an in-
timation of the collective consciousness, the universal soul.

We have just sustained an attack on America, and also on the
collective consciousness. America is badly wounded. The collective consciousness is badly wounded.

America is a historically special country. We are a nation made up of people from every nation on earth. Americans are people from every continent and island. People from all nations become one people—Americans.

In war, we suffer a special American pain. Whomever we shoot, whomever we bomb, we are shooting and bombing relatives, brothers, sisters, cousins. All our wars are civil wars. We go through again the horrors of our own War Between the States, when blood relatives fought blood relatives. The consequences of that war continue to affect us to this day.

It is possible to heal the wounds. We heal our wounds with every act of compassion, with every loving, kind action. It is a law of human nature, as sure as a law of physics or a law of chemistry: Compassion, love, and kindness end suffering.

For the sake of those we mourn today, for our own sakes, for the sake of the children, the generations that come after us, be compassionate. Be loving. Be kind.

The Pilots
Tom Clark

Ziad Jarrah danced at his female cousin's
Wedding. Slender with glasses, intelligent
Looking, a seemingly happy young man,
Smiling pleasantly, his arms waving in the festive air.

Having lost his son, Mohammed Atta's
Father rages against the Americans. Mohammed's
Boyhood friend weeps to recall the "delicate,
Innocent, virgin" youth of their childhood hours.

Marwan Al-Shehhi lived behind that gate
Between the two buildings, see that obscured
Backyard, where the street starts to get real
Ramshackle—dedicated, serious, committed to the cause.

The standing pool of language, thickened then with
The algæ and flotsam of guilt and time
And fear, coagulating to clog
The throat; the conscience anyway never clear…

How to build sentences of such transparency
The strange accidence of those pictures of the dead
Peels away to reveal a grammar of humanness
Life our school, knowledge of suffering our teacher.

Contributors

DIANA ABU-JABER has a Ph.D. from SUNY-Binghamton and is currently a Writer in Residence at Portland State University. She does food writing for *The Oregonian* and has been published in *Good Housekeeping, Ms., Salon, Gourmet, The Washington Post,* and *The Chicago Tribune.* Her first novel, *Arabian Jazz,* was published by Harcourt Brace and won the Oregon Book award. She has also received an NEA grant and a Fulbright scholarship. Her new novel, *Crescent,* will be published by W.W. Norton in 2003.

ETEL ADNAN is a Lebanese-American poet, painter, and essayist living in Sausalito, California, and Paris. Her novel *Sitt Marie Rose* has been published in seven languages worldwide and is considered a classic of Middle Eastern literature. Her latest books are *Paris When It's Naked, Of Cities and Women,* and *There* (all three from Post-Apollo Press).

T. CORAGHESSAN BOYLE is the author of fifteen works of fiction, including *Water Music, World's End, The Tortilla Curtain,* and *Riven Rock.* His most recent novel is *A Friend of the Earth* (2000) and his latest collection is *After the Plague* (2001). A new novel, *Drop City,* will be released next year. He earned his MFA and Ph.D. degrees from the University of Iowa and has been a member of the English Department at the University of Southern California since 1978. He lives with his wife and three children in Santa Barbara.

SUSIE BRIGHT is a best-selling author and editor of twenty-one books on sexual politics and erotica. She lives in Northern California, and can be found at *www.susiebright.com.*

MICHAEL BYERS is the author of *The Coast of Good Intentions,* which was nominated for the 1999 Pen/Hemingway Award and received the Sue Kaufman Prize from the American Academy of Arts and Letters. His work has appeared in *Best American Short Stories* 1997 and 2000 and in the O. Henry collections in 1995 and 2000. He lives in Seattle.

TOM CLARK was born in 1941 in Oak Park, Illinois. He is the author of numerous volumes of poetry, including, among others, *Stones* (Harper & Row, 1969), *Air* (Harper & Row, 1970), *Neil Young* (Coach House, 1971), *At Malibu* (Kulchur, 1975), *When Things Get Tough on Easy Street* (Black Sparrow, 1978), *Paradise Resisted* (Black Sparrow, 1984), *Disordered Ideas* (Black Sparrow, 1987), *Fractured Karma* (Black Sparrow, 1990), *Sleepwalker's Fate* (Black Sparrow, 1992), *Like Real People* (Black Sparrow, 1995), *Empire of Skin* (Black Sparrow, 1997), *White Thought* (Hard Press/The Figures, 1997), and *Cold Spring: A Diary* (Skanky Possum, 2000). He has also written novels, including *The Exile of Céline* (Random House, 1987) and *The Spell: A Romance* (Black Sparrow, 2000), as well as literary biographies, including *Jack Kerouac* (Harcourt Brace Jovanovich, 1984), *Charles Olson: The Allegory of a Poet's Life* (Norton, 1991), *Robert Creeley: The Genius of the American Common Place* (New Directions, 1993), and *Edward Dorn: A World of Difference* (North Atlantic, 2002). Since 1987 Clark has been a member of the core faculty in Poetics at the New College of California, San Francisco.

JOSHUA CLOVER is the author of *Madonna anno domini* (Louisiana State University, 1997), a collection of poems; he is a film, book, and music critic for the *Village Voice*. He is currently the Roberta Holloway Lecturer in Poetry at the University of California, Berkeley, and curator of the 21st Century Poetics series.

WANDA COLEMAN is a former columnist for the *Los Angeles Times* magazine. Coleman's fiction appears in *High Plains Literary Review*, *Obsidian III*, *Other Voices*, and *Zyzzyva*. Her recent books from Black Sparrow Press are *Bathwater Wine* (winner of the 1999 Lenore Marshall Poetry Prize), *Mambo Hips & Make Believe*, and *Mercurochrome: New Poems* (bronze-medal finalist in the National Book Awards, 2001). *Love-Ins with Nietzsche: A Memoir* (Wake Up Heavy Press, 2000) was nominated for the Pushcart Prize. She is also featured in *African American Writers: Portraits and Visions* by Lynda Koolish (University Press of Mississippi, 2001).

PETER COYOTE is an accomplished actor who has appeared in more than seventy films and is the Emmy Award–winning narrator of more than eighty documentaries and fourteen audio-books. His work has appeared in such publications as *Zyzzyva*, *Tricycle*, *The Sun*, and *San Francisco Magazine*. His memoir *Sleeping Where I Fall* was published in 1998 by Counterpoint Press. In 1993 his *Carla's Story* won the Pushcart Prize for Literature.

JOHN DANIEL lives in the Coast Range foothills north of Noti, Oregon. A poet, essayist, and writer of memoirs, he is the author of six books, including *Looking After: A Son's Memoir* and *The Trail Home*, a collection of nature essays. He has been a Wallace Stegner Fellow at Stanford University, a two-time winner of the Oregon Book Award for Literary Nonfiction, and the recipient of a creative writing fellowship from the National Endowment for the Arts. His newest book, *Winter Creek: One Writer's Natural History*, has just been published by Milkweed Editions.

HARLAN ELLISON has been called "One of the great living American short story writers" by the *Washington Post Book World*. He has written or edited 75 books; more than 1700 stories, essays, articles, and newspaper columns; two dozen teleplays, for which he received the Writers' Guild of America's most outstanding teleplay award for solo work an unprecedented four times; and a dozen movies. He has won the Edgar Allan Poe award twice, the Bram Stoker award six times (including the Lifetime Achievement award in 1996), the Nebula award three times, the Hugo award 8½ times, and received the Silver Pen for Journalism from PEN, not to mention the World Fantasy Award, the British Fantasy Award, the American Mystery Award, two Audie Awards, the Ray Bradbury Award, and a Grammy nomination for spoken word recordings. His 1992 novelette *The Man Who Rowed Christopher Columbus Ashore* was included in the 1993 edition of *The Best American Short Stories*.

LAWRENCE FERLINGHETTI is the founder of City Lights Bookstore and Publishing. His book *A Coney Island of the Mind* has been translated into nine languages, and there are nearly one million copies in print. His most recent books are *A Far Rockaway of the Heart* (1997) and *How to Paint Sunlight* (2001), published by New Directions. He has been the recipient of numerous awards, including the *Los Angeles Times* Festival Award, the National Book Critics

Circle Ivan Sandrof Award for Contribution to American Arts and Letters, and the ACLU's Earl Warren Civil Liberties Award. He was named San Francisco's Poet Laureate in August 1998. His column "Poetry as News" has run regularly in the *San Francisco Chronicle*.

AMY GERSTLER is a writer who lives in Los Angeles. *Medicine*, her most recent book of poems, was published by Penguin Putnam in 2000. Her previous books include *Crown of Weeds, Nerve Storm*, and *Bitter Angel*. Her work has appeared in a variety of magazines and anthologies, including *The New Yorker, Paris Review, American Poetry Review*, several volumes of *Best American Poetry*, and *The Norton Anthology of Postmodern American Poetry*. She does a variety of kinds of journalism, and teaches in the Bennington Writing Seminars Program in Bennington, Vermont, and at the Art Center College of Design in Pasadena, California.

LAWRENCE GROBEL is a freelance writer living in Los Angeles. His work has appeared in the *New York Times, Newsday, Playboy, Rolling Stone, Reader's Digest, Details, Modern Maturity, Movieline, Architectural Digest, Writer's Digest*, and numerous other publications. He is the author of *Conversations with Capote, Conversations with Brando, The Hustons, Talking with Michener, Above the Line: Conversations About the Movies*, and *Endangered Species: Writers Talk About Their Craft, Their Visions, Their Lives*. He is the recipient of an NEA Fellowship for Fiction and a PEN Special Achievement Award for his book on Truman Capote. He currently teaches a course on the Art of the Interview in the English Department at UCLA.

EHUD HAVAZELET's most recent book, *Like Never Before*, won the Oregon Book Award. He lives in Corvallis and is at work on a novel.

MAXINE HONG KINGSTON is a native of Stockton, California, and the first of six children born in America to Chinese immigrant parents. She has been a professor at the University of California at

Berkeley since 1990 and is the author of four books: *The Woman Warrior: Memoirs of a Girlhood Among Ghosts, China Men, Hawai'i One Summer*, and her most recent work, *Tripmaster Monkey: His Fake Book*. She has received numerous awards and honors, including a National Book Critics Circle Award in 1976 for *The Woman Warrior*, which is now a staple of many high school reading lists.

MICHAEL HOOD is the lead restaurant critic and a food columnist for the *Seattle Post-Intelligencer* and a political analyst and reporter. He's a commentator for NPR's *All Things Considered* and has written for Garrison Keillor's *A Prairie Home Companion*. His work was included in the anthology *Best Food Writing 2000*, edited by Holly Hughes. He also writes hard news for Agence France-Presse, an international news wire service. Before beginning a writing career, he traveled the world as a chef and owned a successful fine-dining restaurant in a quaint Northwest small-town destination. His writing has appeared in *The New York Post, Seattle Times, Seattle Magazine, Seattle Weekly, The Stranger, Washington Law & Politics, Tucson Weekly, Spokane Inlander*, and *Libido*.

KEN KESEY is best known as the author of the novel *One Flew Over the Cuckoo's Nest*. He is also well known as the hero of Tom Wolfe's nonfiction book about psychedelic drugs, *The Electric Kool-Aid Acid Test* (1968), and became an icon of the counterculture movement with his Merry Pranksters. Other novels include *Sometimes a Great Notion* (1964), *Sailor Song* (1992), and *Last Go Round: A Dime Western* (1994). He also has published three nonfiction works, *Kesey's Garage Sale* (1973), *Demon Box* (1986), and *The Further Inquiry* (1990), as well as two children's books, *Little Tricker the Squirrel Meets Big Double the Bear* (1990) and *The Sea Lion: A Story of the Sea Cliff People* (1991).

JENNIFER LAUCK is the author of two memoirs, *Blackbird* and *Still Waters* (PocketBooks). She studied journalism at Montana

State University and was a television reporter/producer for six years. The mother of two, Lauck lives in Portland, Oregon, and is currently working on a novel.

STACEY LEVINE is the author of *My Horse and Other Stories* (winner of the 1994 PEN/West Fiction Award) and *Dra-*, a novel. She lives in Seattle and has written for the *American Book Review*, The *Seattle Times, The Stranger, Seattle Weekly Nest*, Fodor's Guides, and other venues.

GENNY LIM is a native San Franciscan poet, performer, playwright, and educator. She has been featured on the PBS series *The United States of Poetry*, KQED-TV's *San Francisco Chinatown*, and in *Genny Lim: The Voice*, a feature documentary that premiered at the San Francisco International Asian American Film Festival in March 2002. Her literary works include *Paper Angels*, which aired on PBS's *American Playhouse* in 1995; a book of poems, *Winter Place*; and *Island: Poetry and History of Chinese Immigrants on Angel Island* (1989). Lim teaches at the New College of California in San Francisco and at Naropa West in Oakland, California.

BETH LISICK is a writer and performer. She is the author of *Monkey Girl and This Too Can Be Yours* (Manic D Press), and has released a CD, *Pass* (Du Nord Recording), with her band *The Beth Lisick Ordeal*. In addition to performing around the U.S. and Western Europe in dive bars, nightclubs, museums, and elementary schools, Lisick also has played at soul-wrenching corporate affairs like Lollapalooza, the South by Southwest Music Conference, and the Lilith Fair. She has been published in *Best American Poetry* (Scribner) among other publications, and writes a weekly column for SFGate.com.

JESSICA MAXWELL is a former California beach girl who discovered Oregon's "malachite beauty" on a childhood camping trip and vowed to live there someday. A graduate of the University of Oregon, she has lived in the Pacific Northwest for two decades and has been a regular contributor to *Esquire*, *Audubon*, *Forbes*, and the *Los Angeles Times Magazine*. An NEA Creative Writing fellow and PEN Syndicated Fiction winner, she prefers nonfiction and is the author of three books: *I Don't Know Why I Swallowed the Fly: My Fly Fishing Rookie Season* (Sasquatch Books, 1997), *Femme d'Adventure: Travel Tales from Inner Montana to Outer Mongolia* (Seal Press, 1997), and *Driving Myself Crazy: Misadventures of a Novice Golfer* (Bantam, 2000). Her work has appeared in numerous anthologies, including *Best American Travel Writing* 2000. She is the West Coast Editor of the *Love* magazine newsletter, and lives in Eugene, Oregon, with two benign predators—her trial attorney husband and her part-bobcat kitty—where she is at work on her beloved spiritual adventure book, *Roll Around Heaven*.

COLLEEN MCELROY has had work published in numerous magazines and journals, including: *Massachusetts Review*, *The Big Muddy*, *New Bones: Contemporary Black Writers in America*, and *Best American Poetry* 2001. Her collection *Over the Lip of the World: Among the Storytellers of Madagascar* was noted in *The New Yorker*.

JEFF MEYERS is a poet, playwright, screenwriter, and theatrical director. His collection of poetry *Hereafter* (Quiet Lion Press, 1999) was a finalist for the Oregon Book Award. His work has appeared in *Exquisite Corpse*, *Paramour*, *Rain City Review*, *Nexus*, *Playboy*, and numerous other publications. He is currently working on a book entitled *Liar*. He lives in Seattle.

ALEJANDRO MORALES was born in Montebello, California. He is a professor in the Chicano/Latino Studies Program and the Department of Spanish and Portuguese at the University of California, Irvine. He resides in Santa Ana, California, and is currently writing his next novel. His works include *Barrio on the Edge / Caras viejas y vino nuevo*, *Reto en el paraíso*, *The Brick People*, and his most recent novel *Waiting to Happen*, volume one of *The Heterotopia Trilogy*.

JESS MOWRY was born in Mississippi in 1960 and raised in Oakland, California. In 1988, he began writing stories for and about the kids in his West Oakland neighborhood. Since then, his stories have appeared in numerous magazines and anthologies, including *Zyzzyva*, *Obsidian II*, *The Los Angeles Times Magazine*, *Brotherman*, *In the Tradition*, and *Children of the Night*. His essays have appeared in *The Nation* and *The San Francisco Chronicle*. He has written seven books, which have been published in eight languages, and he wrote the screenplay for a feature-length film based on his best-selling novel *Way Past Cool*. He helped found a children's refuge in Haiti, works with disadvantaged kids in Oakland, and mentors young writers.

ISHMAEL REED teaches at the University of California at Berkeley. His first novel, *The Free-Lance Pallbearers*, was published in 1967. Other publications include the highly acclaimed novels *Yellow Back Radio Broke Down* (1969), *Mumbo Jumbo* (1972), *The Last Days of Louisiana Red* (1974), *Flight to Canada* (1976), *The Terrible Twos* (1982), *Reckless Eyeballing* (1986), and *Japanese By Spring* (1993); *New and Collected Poems* (1989), *Conjure* (1972), *Chattanooga* (1973), *Catechism of D Neoamerican HooDoo Church* (1970), and *A Secretary to the Spirits* (1978); and the plays *The Ace Boons* (1980) and *Hell Hath No Fury*, as well as the collections of essays *Shrovetide In Old New Orleans* (1978) and *Airing Dirty Laundry* (1993). He has been nominated twice for the National Book Award, once in poetry (*Conjure*) and once in fiction (*Mumbo Jumbo*), and received a T. MacArthur Foundation Fellowship and the Lila Wallace *Reader's Digest* Award. *The Reed Reader* (2000) includes two of his plays, *Hubba City* (1989, 1994) and *The Preacher and the Rapper* (1995).

VERN RUTSALA's two most recent books are *Selected Poems* (1991) and *Little-Known Sports* (1994). Among his awards are a Guggenheim Fellowship and two NEA grants.

FLOYD SALAS is the critically acclaimed author of four novels, a memoir, and a volume of poetry. His publications include *Tattoo the Wicked Cross* (1967), winner of the Joseph Henry Jackson Award and a Eugene F. Saxton Fellowship; *What Now My Love* (1970); *Lay My Body on the Line* (1978); *Buffalo Nickel* (1992); *State of Emergency* (1996), awarded the 1997 PEN Oakland Literary Censorship Award; and *Color of My Living Heart* (1996). He is editor of *Stories and Poems from Close to Home* (1986) and other anthologies of San Francisco Bay Area life. His other awards and honors include a Rockefeller Foundation Fiction Scholarship and two outstanding teaching awards from the University of California, Berkeley. All his work and biographical information are archived in the Floyd Salas Collection in the Bancroft Library, University of California, Berkeley. He is a founder and president of the multicultural writing group PEN Oakland and a former boxing coach for U.C. Berkeley.

TOM SPANBAUER was born in Pocatello, Idaho, on June 30, 1946. He has published three novels: *Faraway Places*, *The Man Who Fell in Love with the Moon*, and *In the City of Shy Hunters*, and three short stories: *Sea Animals*, *Mr. Energy*, and *Breakfast, Dinner, and Supper*. He received his MFA in Fiction from Columbia University. He now lives in Portland, Oregon, and is at work on his fourth novel, whose working title is *All the Beginnings*.

PRIMUS ST. JOHN is a professor of literature and creative writing at Portland State University. He has co-edited the award-winning anthologies *Zero Makes Me Hungry* and *From Here We Speak*. St. John is the author of four collections of poetry, was nominated for an American Book Award, has been a finalist for a PEN USA West

Award, and has received a Discovery Award, NEA fellowships, an Oregon Book Award, and a Western States Book Award. His latest collection, *Communion,* is published by Copper Canyon Press.

BARBARA EARL THOMAS is a painter and a writer. She has artwork in collections throughout the U.S. In 1998-2000 she received the Seattle Arts Commission award for new creative nonfiction. Her essays have appeared in numerous publications and anthologies. *Storm Watch: The Art of Barbara Earl Thomas* was published in spring 1998 by the University of Washington Press.

SALLIE TISDALE is the author of *Sorcerer's Apprentice, Harvest Moon, Lot's Wife, Stepping Westward, The Best Thing I Ever Tasted: The Secret of Food,* and *Talk Dirty to Me.* She has contributed to numerous publications, including *Vogue, The New York Times, Harper's, The New Republic,* and *The New Yorker.* Tisdale received the Pope Foundation Fellowship in 1998. Her latest work-in-progress is titled *The Swing of Light.*

ALICE WALKER, winner of the Pulitzer Prize and the American Book Award for *The Color Purple,* is internationally honored as an essential writer of our time. She is the author of six novels, including *The Third Life of Grange Copeland, Meridian, The Temple of My Familiar, Possessing the Secret of Joy,* and *By the Light of My Father's Smile*; three collections of short stories: *In Love & Trouble, You Can't Keep a Good Woman Down,* and *The Way Forward is with a Broken Heart*; three collections of essays: *In Search of Our Mothers' Gardens, Living by the Word,* and *Anything We Love Can Be Saved*; and five volumes of poetry: *Once, Revolutionary Petunias and Other Poems, Good Night, Willie Lee I'll See You in the Morning, Horses Make a Landscape Look More Beautiful,* and *Her Blue Body Everything We Know.* Her many honors and awards include a Guggenheim Fellowship, the Rosenthal Award for Fiction from the National Institute of Arts and Letters, the Lillian Smith Award, and the Radcliffe Medal.

EDITORIAL SERVICES: Michelle Piranio, Portland, Oregon.

FORM: Adam McIsaac, Designer & Typographer, Portland, Oregon.

Set in FF Clifford.

Printed in Hong Kong through Print Vision, Inc.